Intellectual Character

Ron Ritchhart

Foreword by David Perkins

—⁓— **Intellectual Character**

What It Is, Why It Matters, and How to Get It

JOSSEY-BASS
A Wiley Company
San Francisco

Published by

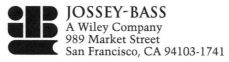

JOSSEY-BASS
A Wiley Company
989 Market Street
San Francisco, CA 94103-1741

www.josseybass.com

Jossey-Bass books and products are available through most bookstores.
To contact Jossey-Bass directly, call (888) 378-2537, fax to (800) 605-2665,
or visit our website at www.josseybass.com.

Substantial discounts on bulk quantities of Jossey-Bass books are available
to corporations, professional associations, and other organizations. For details
and discount information, contact the special sales department at Jossey-Bass.

We at Jossey-Bass strive to use the most environmentally sensitive paper stocks available to us.
Our publications are printed on acid-free recycled stock whenever possible, and our paper
always meets or exceeds minimum GPO and EPA requirements.

Library of Congress Cataloging-in-Publication Data
Ritchhart, Ron.
  Intellectual character : what it is, why it matters, and how to
get it / Ron Ritchhart ; foreword by David Perkins.—1st ed.
    p. cm. — (The Jossey-Bass education series)
Includes bibliographical references (p.   ) and index.
  ISBN 0-7879-5683-X (alk. paper)
  1. Effective teaching. 2. Learning, Psychology of. 3.
Cognitive styles. I. Title. II. Series.
  LB1025.3 .R58 2002
  371.102—dc21   2002001268

FIRST EDITION
HB Printing 10 9 8 7 6 5 4 3 2 1

The Jossey-Bass Education Series

～～ Contents

⚊ᴧᴧ⚊ List of Tables, Figures, and Exhibits

Tables

Figures

Exhibits

⟿ Foreword

Six Intellectual Characters
in Search of an Author

Intellectual character is a very natural idea. Look at who you know, directly or through the media, and you will find plenty of vivid intellectual characters. It is these characters, their presence, their vitality, their commitment, that suggest the general concept of intellectual character and make it persuasive at the same time.

One of my favorite intellectual characters, one I knew well before I ever thought to make a particular study of the nature of thinking, is Sherlock Holmes. Fictional, to be sure, but he walks through a foggy London with more presence than Mick Jagger, who is certainly not an intellectual character. Sherlock Holmes is an embodiment of the observant and analytical mind directed to a particular end. In one of Arthur Conan Doyle's stories, Holmes shocks Watson by confessing that he does not know whether the moon rotates around Earth or vice versa. How can a man with such a mind as Holmes lack such a trivial piece of information? Because, Holmes explains to Watson, he has turned his mind in a particular direction, with ample room in it for esoteric data about types of soil and cigarette ash.

Perhaps it is not fair to turn to fictional characters, authorial constructions that they are, but a look at the real world reveals plenty to choose from as well. Another favorite of mine is Marie Curie, discoverer of the elements polonium and radium. Curie brought not only a powerful intellect to her inquiries but also an almost frightening dedication. The isolation of radium required endless days of backbreaking toil with pots of pitchblende, the mineral that contained traces of the evasive element, and Marie Curie and her husband toiled like stevedores to isolate radium and prove their case.

If we are turning to scientists, many others suggest themselves. Surely one of the most vivid exemplars of world-class intellectual character in recent times was Richard Feynman, with his obsessive curiosity about almost everything. Physics was his center of gravity but hardly his only interest, as evidenced by the well-known episode toward the end of his life when he pursued a correspondence about and planned an expedition to explore Tuva and Tuvan throat singers in Central Asia.

Science is hardly the only place to look for people who embody intellectual character. In the arts, the most obvious choice is Leonardo da Vinci. But perhaps this is too easy an election. Indeed, he could count nicely for both science and the arts. Wandering a little further, let me confess to a particular affinity for the U.S. poet Emily Dickinson. No doubt it seems odd to think of Dickinson, as represented through her works, in terms of intellectual character. Most people do not think of poetry as an intellectual pursuit, although certainly it is an intellectually demanding one. Besides its passion, Dickinson's poetry reveals a strong intellectual character in two ways. First, it routinely deals with very general and fundamental things: the nature of faith, of life and death, of fear and hope. It is, that is to say, philosophical. Second, her poetry quite deals with how we know things through perception and logic and other means; it is epistemological. Consider this witty pair of lines:

> Tell all the Truth but tell it slant—
> Success in Circuit lies

As for a sixth intellectual character, again from the arts, who better than Luigi Pirandello, author of the play *Six Characters in Search of an Author*. In a 1925 essay on the composition of *Six Characters,* Pirandello (1952) reveals something of his own intellectual character. He confesses that the characters around which he built the play presented themselves to him and would not go away, although he could not, indeed did not care to, make something of a more conventional play out of them. He relates how the shape of the play grew in his mind over time, reminding me of what many artists in many media have said about the dialogue between themselves and the work under way, which often seems to have a mind of its own. He confesses to being a philosophical writer, trying to express a complex idea discovered along the way rather than formed in advance, "the deceit of mutual understanding irremediably founded on the empty abstraction of the words, the multiple personality of everyone corresponding to the possibilities of being to be found in each of us, and finally the inherent tragic conflict between life (which is always moving and changing) and form (which fixes it, immutable)" (p. 367).

To illustrate intellectual characters, I've brought on stage figures with a public presence for my six, figures from Sherlock Holmes to Pirandello, and would have no trouble introducing private figures, people whom I know and have known for a long time, except that I would not want to embarrass anyone either by selection or neglect. However, look about you. I'm sure you will find, as I easily do, that you know a number of individuals with strong and distinctive intellectual characters.

People with intellectual character we have in plenty, but so what? What does it matter? It matters as a lesson about our views of the nature of intelligence and good thinking. Looking across a vast literature, one finds that science, philosophy, and education have proved considerably more adroit at recommending how to think well than at explaining why people so often don't do so. Science, philosophy, and education all recommend, and for good reason, practices like breaking set, seeking evidence on the other side of the case, avoiding hasty decisions, and on and on, an extended litany of good cognitive counsel directed to conspicuous shortfalls in everyday thinking. The advice would not be so vehement were the lapses not so common. Yet how are we to understand these lapses? Most accounts of thinking and intelligence are abilities-centric. The usual way of understanding shortfalls turns to lack of ability, either raw mental capacity or appropriate skills and strategies, and the usual remedy looks to training the mind with appropriate skills and strategies. And a certain amount of this is all right. Skills and strategies can make your tennis game better, why not your thinking game?

However, a good deal of evidence shows that the abilities-centric explanation for shortfalls does not tell the whole story, nowhere near. A number of studies, some of them undertaken as part of a research program I've conducted for years, joined by Ron Ritchhart and other colleagues, show that people are quite able to think considerably better than they do. They just don't get around to it. If it's not lack of ability, how can we understand this sort of lapse?

We could view it as a problem of lack of character—intellectual character. After all, character in general concerns not what people are able to do as such but how they invest their efforts within the scope of what they are able to do, whether they keep their word, persist in challenging endeavors, and so on. Roughly, character is not a matter of ability but commitment. So with intellectual character: it basically has to do not with how smart people are but how they invest their intelligence, with what commitment to imagination, evidence, inquiry, fairness, and the like. Another way to make the same point is to speak of thinking dispositions, which refer to how people are disposed to invest the intellectual resources that they have. In summary, intellectual character offers a kind of explanatory missing link, a way of understanding widespread bias and lack of imagination in thinking and learning that cannot be understood sufficiently in terms of ability.

The world of fiction is populated by good and bad characters. The good characters, like Sherlock Holmes, give us someone to root for, and the bad characters, like Professor Moriarty, make things interesting. And of course, there are the vexed characters, perhaps the most interesting of all, with their sweet strengths and pungent weaknesses. Indeed, Holmes himself had conspicuous weaknesses, such as his penchant to relax with drugs. What we generally do not encounter in fiction is the lack of character, the emphatically nondescript.

Yet with the challenge of intellectual character in mind, this is just what we do find in the real world, in many casual conversations, working relationships, newscasts, political speeches, newspaper editorials, and more. The problem is not so much bad intellectual character as simple lack of intellectual character. It's not so much that the world is full of dedicated anti-intellectuals out to ignore evidence, think along narrow tracks, sustain prejudices, promulgate falsehood, and so on— for this is what would count as starkly bad intellectual character—as it is that the common lot is to be neither here nor there, neither high nor low, neither strong nor weak, in fact mediocre in the Latin root sense of *medius,* middle, without much distinctive intellectual character at all. In a way, that's unfortunate. More intellectual villainy would at least give those of us concerned with education more drama and comedy to energize our efforts.

So we have six intellectual characters in search of an author. And on top of that, because intellectual character, even bad intellectual character, seems to be widely lacking, we have intellectual character itself in search of an author. That would be Ron Ritchhart, author of this volume, longtime friend, colleague, and fellow researcher into the mysteries of mind and education, who will engage and regale you with a very different way of looking at good thinking and flexible intelligence—what they are, where they come from, and how perhaps learning and education could help people to get more of them.

Harvard Graduate School of Education   DAVID PERKINS
Cambridge, Massachusetts
August 2001

For my mother

Preface

I learned early in my school career that thinking could get you into trouble. From missing my turn in round-robin reading because I became preoccupied with the story to puzzling over the workings of an algebra equation while the rest of the class moved on, I quickly discerned that school was more about style than substance, breadth than depth, and speed above all else. And like most of my peers, I learned that being smart meant having the answers readily at one's disposal, not having to work too hard to solve problems, and finishing your work before the rest of the class.

No doubt many students today continue to experience school in much the way I did: as an encounter that often denies one's natural intelligence and curiosity, as an act that serves to bind rather than free the mind, and as an institution that treats "creative intellect as mysterious, devious, and irritating" (Henry, 1963, p. 287). It is even possible that today's students feel more of a burden than I did growing up. In households where what-every-child-needs-to-know books fill the shelf, some students today may find that the pressure to acquire discrete bits of knowledge extends beyond the school door into the home, squeezing out opportunities to develop original questions and to cultivate their more diverse patterns of thinking.

But this is neither a book about the pathology of schools and the intellectual sparseness of classrooms nor a treatise on the costs of society's preoccupation with the acquisition of skills and knowledge. As important and engaging as these issues are, this is well-worn terrain, traveled by educational philosophers, theorists, and reformers who have gone before me.[1] Rather than chronicling the generally low level of expectations for thinking in classrooms, this book explores a new and more hopeful vision of education as the development of students' intellectual character. What if education were less about acquiring skills and knowledge and more about cultivating the dispositions and habits of mind that students will need for a lifetime of learning, problem solving, and decision making? What if education were less concerned with the end-of-year exam and more concerned with who students become as a result of their schooling? What if we viewed smartness as a goal that students can work toward rather than as something they either have or don't? Reenvisioning education in this way implies that we will need to rethink many of our well-accepted methods of instruction. We will need to look beyond schools as training grounds for the memory and focus more on schooling as an enculturative process that cultivates dispositions of thinking.

In conducting the research for this book, that is precisely what I set out to do: to look beyond the norm of schooling and to explore classrooms where promoting rigorous, high-end thinking is an ongoing priority. By spending a year with a group of teachers adept at creating thoughtful classroom environments—that is, classrooms that are literally full of thought and actively cultivate students' thinking—I sought to learn from examples of best practice. My goal was not to evaluate these classrooms or to understand a particular program of instruction but to uncover the ways in which these skilled teachers enculturated students into patterns of thinking and, in the process, nurtured what I call students' intellectual character. *Intellectual character*, a term I appropriated from my colleague Shari Tishman and others, refers to the overarching conglomeration of habits of mind, patterns of thought, and general dispositions toward thinking that not only direct but also motivate one's thinking-oriented pursuits.[2]

Educational reform efforts—and today's standards movement is no exception—always place great emphasis on the written curriculum appearing in teachers' guides, frameworks, and scope and sequence charts. But thinking dispositions and intellectual character develop largely through the implicit curriculum (Eisner, 1994). Through the daily routines, expectations, encouragement, and relationships of the classroom, students develop ideas about what is expected of them, the nature of knowledge, and what it means to think and to be smart. Through observations and interviews in classrooms, I set out to uncover the hidden or implicit curriculum being conveyed by the teachers I studied. By observing in each classroom from the first days of school, I strove to understand how teachers went about sending messages to students about what types of thinking they valued and expected. I wanted to understand how teachers established a classroom culture that actively promotes not just students' ability to think but their disposition to think. My interviews with the teachers sought to uncover the teachers' own thinking about thinking: What, for them, does it mean to think? Of what does thinking consist? What makes a good thinker? Through teachers' answers to these and other questions, I learned what types of thinking each teacher valued and sought to nurture in his or her students.

Although the basic goals of my research were to better understand how teachers cultivate students' disposition to think and what makes them effective teachers of thinking, my hope is that the stories of these teachers, their practice, and their beliefs will do more than that. In this age of standards, high-stakes exams, curricular frameworks, and accountability, I hope that the discussion of intellectual character and the vivid examples of students' learning and thinking presented here will raise questions about what it means to be educated. I hope that the stories of teachers told in this book will help us as educators rethink what it means to be a good or effective teacher and question some of our cherished and ingrained teaching habits. I hope that these pictures of practice will cause us to examine the hidden or implicit curriculum that we are teaching through our daily routines and interactions. Finally, I hope that the work of these six wonderful teachers will serve to inspire parents, teachers, and other educators as we go about the task of nurturing intellectual character both in ourselves and in others.

To achieve these many goals and honor the fact that this is a report of research, I have chosen to write this book in a format that departs somewhat from the dominant scholarly tradition while still trying to maintain its integrity. First, my interpretive voice as a researcher is clearly present throughout the work. Rather than hide my perspective and passions in an effort at objectivity, I am fully present in the writing, sharing my experiences as a teacher and my impressions as a researcher. I have sought to balance my interpretive voice with lengthy accounts of teachers' instruction, which provide opportunities for readers to make their own interpretations about what is going on in these classrooms. Consequently, it is important for you as a reader to play an active role in making sense of and generalizing from the examples of practice provided. Only you can decide what evidence rings true for you in your teaching situation and which practices seem transportable and adaptable to your setting. Finally, I include the voices of the teachers themselves, when appropriate, as yet another interpretive voice.

Keeping with the scholarly tradition, Part One of the book begins with some theoretical grounding. In Chapter One, I explore the question and role of ideals in education. What are we teaching for? When we reframe the goals of education, how does that change the way we look at the process of schooling and methods of instruction? In Chapter Two, I introduce the concept of intellectual character and explore how a dispositional view of intelligence departs from standard abilities-based views of what it means to be smart. I then examine the specific dispositions that seem most important and worthy of consideration in guiding our thinking about intellectual character. Chapter Three looks at how it is that dispositions operate in the world. The model of dispositions presented here provides a theoretical grounding for understanding how teachers' indirect instruction actually supports dispositional development.

In Part Two of the book, I focus on the findings from my research into teachers and their practice. Each chapter focuses on an important element of teaching related to the development of intellectual character. Chapter Four examines how teachers go about establishing a classroom culture that promotes the thinking dispositions they value. This chapter portrays examples from individual classrooms to describe how teachers establish norms and create a foundation for thinking early in the school year. For those thinking about beginning new schools or new school years, these pictures of students' first days in the classroom will be very instructive. Chapter Five focuses on the role of routines in the enculturative process. Specifically, I introduce the idea of thinking routines. Throughout this chapter, teachers will find many specific practices and techniques that they can readily apply. Chapter Six looks at how teachers use language to prompt, prime, and pattern the thinking of students. I explore the actual language of thinking itself and the uses of language as a tool for thinking. Chapter Seven returns to the idea of a culture of thinking and looks at what it takes to sustain such a culture. I present eight cultural forces as the foundational elements that work together to establish the culture of any classroom. These cultural forces can be valuable tools for anyone trying to understand classrooms as learning environments.

Part Three of the book moves the discussion from the research to an exploration of ways that educators can make the development of students' intellectual character a reality in the settings in which they work. Chapter Eight examines the foundations of teaching for intellectual character by looking at how teachers' goals, values, beliefs, and knowledge about thinking affect their teaching. Chapter Nine presents three big lessons from my research about teaching for intellectual character. I examine the implications of these lessons for individual teachers as well as the education community. Chapter Ten is a very practical guide for those interested in exploring more about what it means to teach for intellectual character. I include specific exercises, questions, strategies, and advice.

For those interested in the research process itself, I have provided a methodological appendix. The Appendix provides information about how I selected the teachers for the study and went about collecting and analyzing data. The Appendix also addresses the issue of validity in my findings, providing information about how I checked my assumptions and worked to get the story of these teachers right. I hope the Appendix will be useful to my research colleagues as they think of ways to extend and improve on my research and carry the exploration and examination of intellectual character further.

Cambridge, Massachusetts   RON RITCHHART
October 2001

—᷈— **Acknowledgments**

This work would not have been possible without all the assistance, guidance, and encouragement I received along the way. My colleagues at Harvard Project Zero did much to shape my thinking about these ideas. David Perkins and Shari Tishman in particular stand out in this regard. Dennie Palmer Wolf and Martha Stone Wiske were helpful in guiding the research that forms the foundation of this book. The research itself was made possible in part through the generosity of the Spencer Foundation. Much needed encouragement, support, and advice came from the many wonderful educators who read chapters in progress and assured me I had something that would benefit education, among them Eileen Anderson, Laura Benson, Betsy Berry, Mark Church, Randy Comfort, Jim Reese, Connie Weber, and Leslie Yenkin. Seana Moran's editorial assistance helped to make the expression of my ideas clearer, and Karen Uminski worked diligently to pull the loose ends of the manuscript together. Throughout the process, my partner, Kevon, gave me the time, space, and support I needed to make this book a reality. I can't thank him enough for his ongoing generosity and love.

Finally, this work would not have been possible without the six extraordinary teachers who let me into their classrooms and gave so generously of their time. In many ways, teaching is a private performance seen only by the teacher and his or her students. I appreciate the willingness of these six teachers to make their practice public by exposing themselves and their teaching to me as an outsider. Each shares a commitment to teaching and to students that makes me proud to call them colleagues.

R.R.

───── The Author

RON RITCHHART is a research associate at Project Zero, Harvard Graduate School of Education. Ritchhart earned his Ed.D. degree (2000) in human development and psychology from Harvard University. Prior to attending Harvard, he earned an M.A. degree (1990) in curriculum and instruction from the University of Colorado at Denver and a B.S. degree (1982) in education from Indiana University.

Before joining the Project Zero research group, Ritchhart taught for fourteen years in Colorado, Indiana, and New Zealand. He has taught middle school mathematics and elementary school, and he has served as a mathematics coordinator. In 1993, he received the Presidential Award for Excellence in Secondary Mathematics Teaching. Ritchhart also helped initiate the Math Project at the Public Education Business Coalition in Denver and taught math and science methods in the Initial Teacher Certification Program at the University of Denver.

Ritchhart is a 1999–2000 recipient of the Spencer Dissertation Fellowship for his work on thinking dispositions, mindfulness, and thoughtful learning environments. He has written numerous articles about this work and other work concerning issues of understanding and effective teaching that have appeared in publications such as *Educational Psychology Review,* the *Journal of Social Issues,* the *Roeper Review, Teaching Children Mathematics,* and *Think.* Ritchhart is the author of several books on teaching mathematics, including *Pythagoras's Bow Tie* and *Through Mathematical Eyes.*

Currently, Ritchhart is principal investigator for the Creative Classroom Project and coprincipal investigator, with David Perkins and

Shari Tishman, for the Innovating with Intelligence Project. The Creative Classroom Project investigates innovative practices that teachers use to develop learning environments that support students' creativity, understanding, and high-end thinking. Each year, the project produces a video and study guide highlighting these teaching practices. The Innovating with Intelligence Project develops materials that help teachers foster students' thinking dispositions through the exploration of six thinking ideals: truth, beauty, imagination, understanding, fairness, and self-direction.

When not working as a researcher, Ritchhart draws inspiration from working with teachers and spending time in classrooms around the world.

Intellectual Character

PART ONE

The Case for Intellectual Character

CHAPTER ONE

Failing at Smart
Or What's an Education For?

A few years ago, I attended a conference entitled "Teaching for Intelligence." The conference had been an annual event for several years, bringing together leading educators interested in promoting and realizing a vision of education designed to bring out the best in all students' thinking. This particular year, the school superintendent from the host city addressed the conference. Unfortunately, as he spoke, it became clear that he was unfamiliar with his audience and hadn't given his opening comments much advance thought. He casually remarked that "Teaching for Intelligence" seemed like a rather vague title for a conference. "After all," he remarked, "what else would we be teaching for?" His remaining comments were unremarkable, but this question, and the rhetorical way it was framed, has stuck with me.

What else would we be teaching for if not intelligence? It is a question I find worthy of considerable attention. Is teaching for intelligence, that is, teaching with the goal of making students smarter, such a cornerstone of our educational systems that we can take it for granted? Is it a goal that parents, students, teachers, and the rest of the community readily recognize and embrace? Is making students smarter a mission that directs our work in schools in a substantive way? Or is there more fuzziness around our goals for education? Do we, as educators and citizens concerned with education, even know what we are teaching for? What other competing goals are capturing our attention?

In this chapter, I take up these questions to lay a foundation for what is to come in the rest of this book. Before we can examine the idea of intellectual character and what it might mean for teachers and learners to embrace it, we first need clarity on where we currently are with regard to our educational goals. What is it that most schools and teachers are, in fact, teaching for? Why? To what effect? By understanding where we stand now and how we got there, we can then take up the issue of what it is we should be teaching for. What kinds of goals and ideals do we need to shape education and the future of our children? Only once we identify them will we be in a position to explore how we can go about making those goals a reality in our schools.

WHERE ARE WE?
A Look at the Current State of Teaching

Karen White (a pseudonym) begins the year with textbook perfection.[1] She is a model of organization and classroom management, conveying a strong sense of authority and confidence as she guides students through the rules and procedures of the classroom. Posters on the wall proclaim the expectations of the classroom—be polite, be prompt, be prepared, and be productive—and Karen enforces these rules immediately, dealing with interruptions and recording tardiness in her grade book as needed. With a minute-by-minute schedule on the board, Karen carefully walks the class through her rules and expectations.

This focus on rules, expectations, and procedures dominates the first week of class, and Karen lets students know that there is no ambiguity or wiggle room within the parameters she has set. In these first days, Karen wants students to know that it is their efforts that shape their success in her class, what she calls earned success. To get this message across, Karen provides constant feedback on students' work performance, posting students' percentage grades beside the front door of the classroom on a weekly basis. For one student, the importance of work is driven home on the fourth day of school when Karen informs him that she is missing two of his assignments and that he has a zero in her grade book. When the student protests that he just joined the class and that this is only his second day, Karen cheerfully replies that she knows and that she just wanted to let him know so that he could complete the work and turn it in. The student seems unclear about why this missed work is significant or why he should have to make it up.

Throughout her instruction during these first days, Karen continually and quite effectively communicates the importance of students doing their work. Although this is a worthwhile message, at times it seems to eclipse any effort students might make to develop understanding. The result is a classroom in which students complete work rather than learn. Although Karen mentions understanding, thinking, reflection, and metacognition (thinking about thinking) as important, students never engage in these practices in a way that imbues them with any meaning. When Karen asks students to write reflections, the focus is on reviewing the day's activities or recording one's feelings about those activities. Reading students' journals, Karen has the opportunity to challenge students' thinking and gently nudge it in a more substantive direction. However, Karen tends to be drawn more to the affective issues that students write about than to the content of their thinking. It is also difficult for Karen to substantively comment on the journals given the time she allots: she reads thirty-five journals in just ten minutes. As a result, her comments mostly take the form of acknowledgments or encouragement: "Great," "Interesting," "Nice." Thus, she acknowledges the effort but only superficially addresses the substance of students' reflection.

Although her teaching may seem extreme, even a stereotype, Karen is a real teacher with real students. Her teaching represents a picture of teaching practice that many will recognize and already embrace. I daresay that the superintendent who addressed attendees of the conference entitled "Teaching for Intelligence" probably would be content to populate his schools with teachers like Karen, as would many administrators and parents. In fact, Karen's methods are deemed so worthy of emulation by her colleagues and supervisors that she leads her district's program for new teachers and is sought after by teachers in training as a student teacher supervisor. Karen may not be your typical teacher; however, she represents what for many is the ideal. Although her teaching is neither state of the art nor status quo, it is considered the standard that many would have us achieve.

If you're not convinced that Karen's practice represents a model to which most teaching is pushed, take a look at Doug Tucker's situation. Doug is a new teacher, full of enthusiasm and dedication. Like Karen, he's interested in promoting students' thinking, but he's also trying to learn and follow the norms of teaching that Karen has already mastered. Consequently, Doug feels pressure to spend a lot of his first days reviewing school rules and going over class expectations. This takes the form of reading to students directly from the school handbook. This early emphasis on rules and discipline is a major focus for all teachers in the school, because the principal expects this consistency. In one class, a student even comments, "We've been doing this all day. We get it already." At times, the days spent going over these rules feel oppressive to me as an observer. What do students make of this preoccupation with discipline? Does this emphasis make them feel that they cannot be trusted? That they are among classmates who can't be trusted? That obeying the rules is the major thrust of school and more important than learning?

WHAT ARE WE TEACHING FOR?

Given that this is the vision many policymakers, parents, and teachers have of good teaching, what does such a model say about what we are teaching for? If Karen represents some kind of prototype of instructional efficiency, what is the aim of that efficiency? To be sure, Karen's and Doug's instruction provides their students with a lot. Their caring, cheerfulness, and good humor provide students with an approachable teacher who will support and nurture them in any adversity. Their consistency provides a smooth-running classroom in which students who want to participate can. And their textbook instruction provides students with the basic skills, a foundation, and often the confidence to continue in their studies. However, when we look behind this instruction to the messages it conveys to students about learning, another picture emerges. These types of teaching actions tell students that school and learning are basically dreary tasks that they must approach in a workmanlike manner. The overriding message is this: do the work, get the grade, and move on. Furthermore, students are told that teachers do not trust them to engage in the work of learning on their own, so they will carefully monitor the students' actions. This is teaching for complacency, for orderliness, for dependence, and for superficiality.

None of the classroom practices of teachers like Doug or Karen precludes the development of students' intelligence. Indeed, Doug does much to engage students in thinking, as we will see later. However, like the superintendent at the beginning of this chapter, these teachers might well assume that schooling naturally develops students' intelligence, that it makes them smarter. But does it? If we take what we might call smartness to be more than knowledge acquisition, to be about who we are as problem solvers and decision makers responding to novel situations, then the outlook for students getting smarter doesn't look good. These kinds of beginning-of-the-year teaching practices and the ones that follow from them do not contribute in any significant way to making students smarter. The emphasis these practices place on work, rather than developing understanding and engaging in thinking, makes it difficult for students to develop their intellectual skills, let alone any sense of inclination and motivation toward thinking and learning. Furthermore, teachers' spoon-feeding of discrete bits of knowledge impedes the development of students' awareness of opportunities for thinking. Without rich opportunities to develop one's ability, to sharpen awareness, and to enhance an inclination and motivation for thinking, it is difficult to get smarter.

The fact is that most schools today do not try to teach for intelligence. Rather than working to change who students are as thinkers and learners, schools for the most part work merely to fill them up with knowledge. Although some may see intelligence as a natural by-product of schooling, in reality the curriculum, instruction, and structure of schools do little to promote intelligence and may even impede it in some cases. When one considers the current emphasis on high-stakes testing and accountability, a more apt description of the mission of schools might be this: to promote the short-term retention of discrete and arcane bits of knowledge and skills. If you think this is too pessimistic a view, take a look at a current high school history, geography, science, or math exam. Chances are that most adults couldn't pass these tests without a refresher course. Those of us with a fair amount of education may recognize the questions as covering familiar terrain but still not know many of the answers offhand—can you still do a geometric proof? And yet, passing these kinds of exams within a few months of being presented with the material is taken as an indicator of mastery of the material, of meeting the standards. However, the only standards being met concern one's ability to do the memory work of school. These standards do not begin to capture who students are becoming as thinkers and learners as a result of their schooling.

WHAT SHOULD WE BE TEACHING FOR?

If we were to ask Karen and Doug, or any teacher for that matter, what it is they are teaching for, we might very well be greeted by a puzzled expression and a response like this one: "What do you mean what am I teaching for? I'm teaching so that my students will do well on the state test in the spring. I'm teaching to my district's proficiencies and standards. I'm trying to make sure kids are prepared for next year. I'm also working to get through the textbook. Is that what you mean by what I'm teaching for?"

Well, no. That's not what I mean, and this confusion around the question of what "teaching for" means is part of the problem. In educational circles, we've come to mistake curriculums, textbooks, standards, objectives, and tests as ends in themselves rather than as means to an end. Where are these standards and objectives taking us? What is the vision they are pointing toward? What purpose do they serve?

By way of analogy, consider what is involved in taking a long car trip. We know that to get to our destination we have to drive a certain number of miles. Furthermore, we know that our driving has to meet certain standards of speed and safety as we progress on our way. However, when we get in the car, our excitement isn't for the road or the driving regulations, it is for our destination. In fact, it is usually only by keeping our sights on our destination that we stay motivated to drive the many miles and maintain the imposed standards. If truth be told, in our excitement to reach our destination, we may even flaunt the standards a bit from time to time, taking some liberty with the speed limit perhaps. Saying that standards, textbooks, and tests are what we are teaching for is like saying the point of our driving is to cover miles of road safely within the posted speed limit. It is a trip without a destination; it is teaching without a reason. Both are ultimately empty and unsatisfying for the driver and the passengers alike.

When I ask, What is it that we are teaching for?, I'm trying to uncover the destination we are aiming toward and the goals we are striving for. What ideals guide us as we teach? This notion of ideals is at the very crux of the matter. Without ideals, we have nothing to aim for as teachers. We have no destination. Donald Arnstine (1995, pp. 22–23) captures well the importance of ideals to education: "Ideals keep us going when the world seems oppressive and unrewarding. They embody our values, our hopes, our deepest beliefs. Specific enough to aim at, ideals are broad enough to allow some freedom of action. While often personal, ideals can be shared with others because their breadth has room for disagreement about the actions they imply. In this way ideals unite people in common efforts without dictating what their behavior must be. The openendedness of ideals makes it possible to share them, and thus makes possible distinctively human communities."

Unlike standards, ideals can't be tested. We can't check them off or set a threshold of performance that must be met. However, ideals can do something that standards cannot: they can motivate, inspire, and direct our work. It is the difference between watching the road beneath our feet and keeping our sights on the mountain growing ever closer before us.

So what ideals are worth setting our sights on when it comes to education? What kinds of strivings are deserving of our time and energy? To answer that, we need to look at what an education can reasonably accomplish. When all is said and done, when the last test is taken, what will stay with a student from his or her education? Memories, certainly. Treasured experiences, positive relationships, meaningful interactions, yes. But what about the knowledge and skills teachers have worked so hard to impart? Surprisingly, we don't have much evidence that these have a very long shelf life (Arnstine, 1995; Semb & Ellis, 1994). So what sticks? What kind of learning lasts beyond a given year that we can grab hold of to guide our vision? I contend that what stays with us from our education are patterns: patterns of behavior, patterns of thinking, patterns of interaction. These patterns make up our character, specifically our intellectual character. Through our patterns of behavior, thinking, and interaction, we show what we are made of as thinkers and learners. Schools can do much to shape and influence these patterns. This is the kind of long-term vision we need for education: to be shapers of students' intellectual character.

MOVING FORWARD

So why are we failing at smart? Why aren't schools doing a better job not of imparting knowledge and helping students attain the standards but of helping students become better thinkers? First, we need to recognize that it isn't merely a problem of not having the right materials or methods in place. We aren't just doing things the wrong way, which is not to say that new methods aren't needed. Indeed, much of this book is about exploring the successful methods and practices that teachers can use to nurture students' intellectual character. But new methods alone won't suffice. The root of the problem is that we are teaching the wrong thing. We don't have our sights set on providing students with an education that develops their intelligence. We've misplaced precisely the kind of ideal that can lead and motivate us. This book is about that ideal: the ideal of intellectual character.

What does it mean to teach for intellectual character? What does it look like in practice? How can we get started on the process, particularly given all the other demands placed on educators? These are the questions that have been at the heart of my work for the past seven years. They are also at the heart of this book. I've struggled with these questions as conceptual and theoretical issues, looking at them from psychological, sociological, and philosophical perspectives. I share this theoretical grounding in the first part of this book by way of defining just what I mean by intellectual character, what I think it includes, and how I think it develops. I've also explored these questions from a practical perspective by spending time in classrooms where teachers are, in fact, teaching for intellectual character. This research forms the bulk of this book, and for most readers, I suspect these pictures of actual classroom practice will be among the most engaging and useful aspects of this work.

There are somewhere in the neighborhood of 3.5 million teachers in the United States, most of whom teach multiple classes of students, creating well over 10 million classrooms for possible study.[2] I chose to focus the research for this book on just six. Why? What can an examination of only six classrooms hope to tell us about the development of intellectual character? Although large-scale educational surveys can be useful in spotting broad trends and identifying variables that appear to affect educational outcomes, more in-depth, close-to-the-classroom investigations serve to illuminate the specifics of teaching and learning. Rather than identifying a set of practices associated with a specific outcome, an inquiry based on the close study and description of a few specific cases helps us to better understand the nature of a particular phenomenon. As Eudora Welty (1979, p. 129) has said and other authors have echoed, "One place comprehended can make us understand other places better."

That is precisely the kind of understanding that I am after in this book: an understanding that can be useful in informing the practice of individual teachers, in helping policymakers consider the importance of intellectual character as an ideal, and in guiding future inquiry by other researchers. Unlike large-scale surveys or experimental research, case studies do not identify causal links or provide convincing evidence for choosing one approach, method, or program over another. Those readers interested in such hard numbers will have to look elsewhere. Case studies in general, and the particular research I present here, might be better compared to a geographic expedition. Such expeditions begin to map the terrain, pointing out both the obstacles and the wonders to help us better apprehend the landscape. The end result is not a set of directions that take you from point A to point B. The outcome is more akin to a topological map that identifies the most salient features of the terrain and highlights the routes others have taken. Consequently, the journeys undertaken using such a map will each be unique, reflecting as much the traveler's interests and desires as the landscape's features. As you begin your personal exploration of what it means to teach for intellectual character, I wish you an engaging and fruitful journey.

CHAPTER TWO

Rethinking Smart
The Idea of Intellectual Character

W alk into virtually any classroom and ask the students there who the smartest kid in the class is, and within seconds you are likely to get a set of convergent answers. So ingrained and universal are Western culture's notions of what constitutes "smart" that it makes little difference whether you enter a history class or a math class, an elementary school or a high school; any member of the class can quickly apply what we might call the smartness sieve to identify a particular member as being smart. Although who is considered smart may vary across contexts, the qualities being assessed tend to remain remarkably consistent.

Such consensus of assessment is due largely to the fact that the smartness sieve reflects a dominant cultural mind-set about the set of attributes and qualities that make up intelligence. Chief among these qualities tends to be one's knowledge and skill level. Within a school context, grades are used as a proxy for these qualities. Second, the ease with which one acquires new skills and knowledge, what Aristotle (1990, p. 122) termed a "quick wit," is considered a factor. We can boil this down to say that the smartness sieve entails an on-the-spot assessment and ranking of each individual's abilities, some general and some

12

specific, and of his or her speed of learning. We might call this the Jeopardy or game-show view of intelligence, in which the winners of the intelligence game are always fast with the facts.

These two qualities, ability and speed, reflect not only our everyday implicit theories of intelligence but the prevailing paradigm within the field of intelligence as well.[1] Throughout the ages, ability and speed have been recurring and dominant themes in Western notions of smartness, intelligence, and giftedness (Sternberg, 1990). Most modern theories of intelligence reflect this focus and tend to be centered around the identification of abilities. For instance, various theories of intelligence have emphasized the presence of general mental abilities, neural efficiency, cognitive processes, and specific skills for thinking and learning.[2] Even the most avant-garde theories of intelligence, such as Howard Gardner's theory of multiple intelligences (1983) or Daniel Goleman's notion of emotional intelligence (1995), are revolutionary chiefly in terms of which abilities they recognize as important. This focus on abilities has come to dominate the way we see the domain of intelligence: shaping the types of questions we ask about smartness, influencing how we seek to measure it, and determining how we try to develop it.[3] We are so steeped in the paradigm of an abilities view of intelligence that we hardly notice it.

But this dominant notion of abilities is easily challenged if we allow ourselves to step out of the schoolhouse environment and leave behind the plethora of testing instruments, grades, and evaluations we have become so accustomed to accepting as evidence of intelligence. We can gain a new perspective and rethink what it means to be smart by simply asking ourselves a few focused questions: What does intelligence look like in action? What are the qualities of thought and characteristics of mind we expect to see when someone is acting intelligently? What are the patterns of behavior and attitudes that we associate with someone who acts smart?

These questions shift our attention from being smart to acting smart. They move us from accepting intelligence as a state of possession to considering intelligence in terms of various states of performance. Because these new questions are aimed at identifying what intelligence looks like in the world, rather than in the artificial world of school and testing, you are just as well equipped to ponder them and pose possible answers as I am. In fact, my experience in talking with parents, teachers, and students all over the world about what intelligence really looks like tells me that our respective answers to these questions are likely to be quite similar. In this chapter, I invite you to ponder the above set of questions about intelligence and to rethink "smart" with me. In doing so, we'll see how our answers can shape a new view of intelligence. In the remainder of the chapter, I'll refine and sharpen this new vision of what it means to be smart, drawing on the work of a variety of critical thinkers, philosophers, and psychologists to identify some core attributes of intelligence in action. But first let's take a brief look at why traditional notions of intelligence are insufficient for capturing what it means to be smart.

MISSING THE MARK WITH IQ

Our view of intelligence has been shaped largely by the use of testing instruments, such as IQ, used to sort and classify students. Because these tests do their job of identifying the haves and have-nots so well, we've come to believe that intelligence really is a bounded entity, measurable through a relatively small set of carefully identified questions. After all, scoring well on these tests certainly seems to indicate that one has the goods to do well in school. In fact, IQ scores have proven to be rather good predictors of one's future success both in and out of school, an indication that the tests do in fact work. So where's the problem?

What Does IQ Predict?

Generally speaking, IQ is an excellent predictor of performance on other similar measures of intelligence.[4] IQ scores can predict scores on vocabulary tests, on the Scholastic Aptitude Test, and even on many of the nonstandardized tests students are likely to take on a regular basis in schools. Furthermore, these measures tend to be good predictors of overall occupational achievement, particularly when such achievement is tied to school performance. The problem with IQ tests as predictors begins to emerge when we look at performance outside of school. When we look at real-life day-to-day settings and contexts, is IQ still a good predictor of behavior? Does smart on the test mirror smart in the world? And what about the performance of the individual versus the group? Studies of IQ's predictive ability consider group aggregates rather than individuals. When we look outside the schoolhouse window to track the behavior of individuals in the world, we can begin to see that the picture of intelligence painted by IQ is a distorted one.[5]

In his book, *The Millionaire Mind,* Thomas Stanley (2000) attempted to understand what set the highly financially successful apart as a group. In the course of his interviews with these entrepreneurs and businesspeople, he discovered something interesting. A common trait among those he interviewed turned out to be their history of mediocre school and test performance. Rather than having a superior IQ, most interviewees reported being clearly middle range in their abilities. Furthermore, many of these individuals were told as children that they were not smart. Stanley reports, "During their formative years, some authority figure such as a teacher, parent, guidance counselor, employer, or aptitude-testing organization told them: *You are not intellectually gifted*" (p. 88).

We see this same thing all the time, not just in business but in many other arenas as well. Although some degree of IQ or school success seems important in the political arena, such early measures do not overly influence later career success. In fact, the populace is often wary of politicians who appear to be too bookish or school smart. Voters tend to have more confidence in what is often called street smarts and the ability to communicate effectively with a wide range of people. Artists, actors, and performers are another group in which success seems poorly predicted by IQ and school performance. Gary Sinise, known as a talented and versatile actor capable of totally embodying a role, as he did when portraying the sergeant in the movie *Forrest Gump,* made it out of high school only after attending an additional semester and being granted a D by a sympathetic history teacher.

Even Richard Herrnstein and Charles Murray (1994), staunch defenders of IQ as a predictor, present several examples of the failure of IQ to predict on-the-job performance in their controversial book, *The Bell Curve,* though they tend to downplay these instances. One such case is of marines in technical jobs, such as radio repairmen, automotive mechanics, and riflemen. Although the low-IQ workers scored lower than their high-IQ counterparts on tests of job knowledge, their performance on actual work samples was indistinguishable. To use Herrnstein and Murray's words, this represents a case of "complete convergence" (p. 80), meaning that over time the cumulative effects of experience and the initial advantages afforded by a high IQ converge. SAT scores represent another such case of convergence. These scores tend to be good predictors of performance in the first year of college, but their predictive power decreases as students' experience of being in college increases.

It is not that any of these individuals—entrepreneurs, political candidates, actors, artists, students, or marine technicians—aren't intelligent, only that abilities-based IQ measures fail to capture their intelligence adequately or predict their performance in the world. Being smart, the kind of inert intelligence measured by IQ and other kinds of aptitude tests, simply is not the same thing as acting smart.

Static Intelligence Versus Intelligence in Action

Looking at the questions or tasks on a typical measure of intelligence, we can begin to see why such measures fail to predict real-world performance. Most test items lack what Robert Sternberg (1985) calls "ecological validity" or real-world authenticity. There is a gap between the kinds of mental moves called for in the context of our everyday functioning and the thinking processes required for performance on the carefully circumscribed tasks of an intelligence test. The test items call for an extremely stripped-down version of mental functioning, often necessitating the exercise of discrete skills in a decontextualized setting. This gap between the demands of tests and the demands of the real world is a standard criticism of most intelligence tests and has led some critics to contend that test scores are highly influenced by one's test-taking competence and familiarity.[6]

The testing situation itself produces a similar kind of gap. Typically, in testing situations, people are relatively free from distractions; there is little else competing for their attention. In general, though certainly not always, test takers tend to be motivated to try their best, and performance requires isolated concentration in solving fairly well-defined and clearly articulated tasks. When these conditions are met, it is not unreasonable to assume that differences in test performance do in fact reflect differences in abilities being measured. Whether or not these abilities capture intelligence is debatable.[7]

In contrast to the content and context of abilities-based intelligence tests, our intelligent functioning in the world tends to be much messier. We routinely are required to screen out distractions, create our own motivation, frame problems for ourselves, and marshal the requisite abilities needed to tackle, if not solve, the identified problem. The daily demands of intelligent behavior call for much more than a simple application of requested abilities, skills, and knowledge. It is little wonder then that performance under the artificial and controlled circumstances of a test would fail to predict our intellectual performance in the wild.

It might be argued quite reasonably that the problem lies not with the abilities-centered theories of intelligence themselves but with the decontextualization of those abilities so endemic to the measures designed to test intelligence. One could argue that what we really need are better tests, not a new way of looking at intelligence. What would the development of such a test require?

Problems that are more contextualized would certainly be in order, problems that require the pooling of abilities perhaps. But is this enough? In the world, we do not so much encounter problems directly as we encounter problematic situations. For instance, a test might require you to read a passage of text and ask you what evidence the author provides in support of her position. In this situation, the problem task is clearly defined. However, in the real world, the situation is not always so well delineated in terms of what action we must take. As we go about our daily lives, we are more likely to encounter the more open-ended and amorphous task of trying to understand a situation, such as what is really happening in Afghanistan, and must make a whole series of decisions about what specific aspects of the situation to focus on, which sources to consult, and how to balance perspectives, in addition to examining the supporting evidence in people's arguments. Within such situations, the actual problem or problems must be detected, framed, and understood. We might try to capture that in a test, but in doing so, it seems we have begun to transcend typical notions of ability. The kind of detection we are talking about here is more than recognition and identification; it involves spotting opportunities. We might call it an attitude of awareness or a sensitivity to occasions.

In the world, we also have to deal with motivational issues. Unfortunately, our abilities do not always automatically activate themselves when we face problem situations. For instance, when confronted with an anomaly or mysterious situation, we sometimes completely pass it over without giving it a second thought. It's not that we don't know how to ask questions, probe the situation, or carry out some form of inquiry; it's just that for some reason or another, we aren't motivated to do so. However, in our most intellectually active moments, we engage our abilities fully and eagerly. Can we capture this motivational dimension of intelligent performance in a test? This becomes more difficult because it requires disentangling extrinsic, performance-oriented motivation (the desire to do well on the test to get a high score) from a more intrinsic, personally oriented form of motivation. But more to the point, this type of inclination is clearly a departure from what we normally think of as ability.

As this brief examination of real-world problem situations demonstrates, intelligent performance is not just an exercise of ability. It is more dispositional in nature in that we must activate our abilities and set them into motion. Dispositions concern not only what we can do, our abilities, but what we are actually likely to do, addressing the gap we often notice between our abilities and our actions. As John Dewey noted in his observations of the poor thinking of well-educated persons, "Knowledge of methods alone will not suffice; there must be the desire, the will to employ them. This desire is an affair of personal disposition" (1933, p. 30). This theme was picked up a half-century later in Steven Covey's popular book, *The Seven Habits of Highly Effective People* (1989). Covey talks about the inadequacy of training people in techniques while neglecting the development of the accompanying character traits.

BEYOND ABILITY
The Idea of Intellectual Character

The concept of intellectual character is an attempt to move out of the prevailing paradigm of abilities-based conceptions of intelligence. I use the term *intellectual character,* borrowed from my colleague Shari Tishman,[8] as an umbrella term to cover those dispositions associated with good and productive thinking. In contrast to viewing intelligence as a set of capacities or even skills, the concept of intellectual character recognizes the role of attitude and affect in our everyday cognition and the importance of developed patterns of behavior. Intellectual character describes a set of dispositions that not only shape but also motivate intellectual behavior. We'll look more closely at just which dispositions seem most related to good thinking and intelligence a bit later in this chapter.

Intelligence as Characterological

This attitudinal and characterological dimension of thinking, although not captured in traditional theories of intelligence, is well represented in our everyday vocabulary of thinking. We regularly use words such as *curious, open-minded, decisive, systematic, skeptical, judicious, inquisitive, strategic, diligent, fair-minded, reflective,* and *deliberative* to describe intelligent individuals. In doing so, we seek to acknowledge not just an ability but the consistent deployment of that ability. In our vernacular, we recognize "the body of habits, of active dispositions which makes a man do what he does" (Dewey, 1933, p. 44).

We readily recognize the multidimensional nature of character, which includes attitudes, beliefs, habits, sensitivities, inclinations, and dispositions. Character also implies depth and permanence rather than fleeting states. Most importantly, we have a natural sense of character as an animator of actions.

Dispositions and Character

As an overarching construct, the notion of intellectual character can be understood only in terms of the thinking dispositions that give it shape and meaning. But before we turn our attention to trying to identify these specific dispositions, let me clarify my use of the term *disposition.* Nearly a century ago, Dewey struggled with this same task of finding a word to best express the underlying motivator and organizer of intelligent behavior: "But we need a word to express the kind of human activity which is influenced by prior activity and in that sense acquired; which contains within itself a certain ordering or systematization of minor elements of action; which is projective, dynamic in quality, ready for overt manifestation; and which is operative in some subdued subordinate form even when not obviously dominating activity. Habit even in its ordinary usage comes nearer to denoting these facts than any other word. If the facts are recognized we may also use the words attitude and disposition" (Dewey, 1922, p. 41).

As Dewey indicated, it is not immediately evident what word we should use to describe this internal motivator of a set of actions and responses to the world. Various alternatives come to mind: habits, dispositions, temperaments, passions, drives, desires, inclinations, and so on. No matter which word one chooses, there are bound to be difficulties with regards to the word's usage and its various connotations.

The only thing to do is to acknowledge these potential tensions, stipulate our definition of a chosen term so as to delineate a construct, and move on. I do that now, providing references and notes for those interested in delving more deeply into this terrain.[9]

Like Dewey, I wish to invoke by the chosen term the volitional, acquired, and overarching nature of patterns of behavior. I feel the term *disposition* does this better than *habit* because we tend to understand a disposition as a tendency toward a general type of action. When we talk about someone having a friendly disposition, we understand that to mean that the person tends to approach situations in a certain way and to display a general set of actions we associate with friendliness. No one action is specified, but rather a whole range of related actions and responses may be evident. Dispositional behavior isn't automatic, though it does provide a gentle nudging that helps to bring out the behavior.

In contrast, the term *habit* often denotes a mindless and automatic response that is not readily controllable. Unlike *disposition, habit* tends to describe specific actions or behaviors, quite often those with a negative bent, and is thus less broad and descriptive of general behavioral trends. For instance, an individual might have the habit, or custom, of shaking hands when being introduced to someone. Because this gesture is rather ingrained and reflexive in nature, we tend not to infer from it too much about the person's general behavior or way of acting. On the positive side, the phrase *habits of mind* seems to have entered the vernacular of most educators and is widely recognized. Still, this phrase can mean a variety of things to those using it, ranging from ways of working and processing information to the set of values under which one operates.[10]

Of course, the term *disposition* is not without its own baggage. For example, philosophers drawing on the writings of Gilbert Ryle (1949) consider dispositions to be inherent capacities or properties of an object or person that must be brought forth by an external agent. The example they often use is that glass is brittle, but that brittleness is latent and only evident when the glass is struck by another object. Harvey Siegel (1997) expands on this notion of latent potential by arguing that dispositions are "counter-factual properties," which can exist as tendencies that need never be realized. This nonvolitional, nonacquired quality is clearly not what I wish to convey. In contrast, from the psychological perspective, dispositions tend to be seen as voluntary elicitors rather than automatic emitters of behavior (English & English, 1958). Thus, although the environment may prompt dispositions, dispositions represent a consciously controllable response rather than a completely unconscious or automatic response. However, some branches of psychology, such as personality or social psychology, tend to view dispositions as underlying traits, attitudes, or temperaments.[11] From these perspectives, the acquired nature we are after is not well represented.

Acknowledging the inherent tensions and confusions associated with our choice of an appropriate word, I offer the following stipulated definition of the construct of thinking dispositions to move us forward in our discussion: thinking dispositions represent characteristics that animate, motivate, and direct our abilities toward good and productive thinking and are recognized in the patterns of our frequently exhibited, voluntary behavior.[12] Dispositions not only direct our strategic abilities but they help activate relevant content knowledge as well, bringing that knowledge to the forefront to better illuminate the situation at hand. Unlike desire, dispositions are accompanied by behavior and thus assume the requisite ability to carry out that behavior. In contrast to habitual routines, dispositions invoke a general class of responses rather than specific actions. Collectively, the presence and force of these dispositions make up our intellectual character. As Dewey noted, "[Common sense] understands the body of habits, of active dispositions which makes a man do what he does" (1933, p. 44).

WHICH DISPOSITIONS?

If one's intellectual character is shaped by the thinking dispositions one possesses, which dispositions are most important to cultivate and nurture? If the goal is intelligent behavior in the world, which dispositions can best motivate thinking that is reasonably flexible, reflective, and productive in achieving its ends or goals with regard to making decisions, solving problems, or developing understanding?[13] Before we examine lists that the various perspectives of philosophy, educational psychology, and practice propose, take a minute to consider your own feelings about the dispositions that support good and effective thinking. Jot down your own ideas of the characteristics, dispositions, or general attitudes that you feel a good thinker possesses.

Once you've brainstormed a list of candidate dispositions, select the ones you believe are the top four or five supporting thinking that is productive and effective in achieving its desired ends.

If you are like most people, you may have initially included some dispositions not directly related to intelligent behavior but well prized and encouraged within school settings or the broader culture. For example, perseverance is often one of the primary characteristics that teachers and parents want children to develop. It is a highly valued trait, but is it a characteristic directly related to thinking? Perseverance is a trait valued in all kinds of contexts, such as completing a job, dealing with adversity, or achieving one's goals. It can be useful in problem-solving situations as well, but does it always constitute an approach to good thinking? We all know that there are times when it is more fruitful to abandon ideas or approaches rather than stick doggedly by them. For instance, I often try to solve formatting problems when using word processing or layout programs even though experience has taught me that I can better spend my time leaving that task alone for the moment. These kinds of issues regarding thinking and action make it challenging to arrive at a list of true dispositions for thinking, but the issues are important to consider nonetheless.

Strictly speaking, a thinking disposition, at least the positive ones we are trying to cultivate, should always lead toward better and more powerful thinking. If the candidate disposition is something whose value can only be determined situationally, it becomes more of a heuristic or useful back-pocket strategy than a thinking disposition. An example might be planning backward from an identified end goal or brainstorming possibilities or options. These are potentially useful types of thinking but only in specific situations. By contrast, something like open-mindedness is more broadly applicable. Of course, one still must employ some judgment in its application; you don't want students to be so open that they can never make a decision! The important point here is that dispositions generally have broad applicability rather than being confined to a narrow set of situations. At the same time, the application shouldn't be too diffuse. If the proposed disposition has broad application outside the range of thinking, it may be an attribute of general rather than intellectual character. Attributes such as honesty, integrity, civility, and cooperativeness would be some examples.

Our task then is to identify candidate dispositions of the correct grain size, that is, large enough that they specify a range of behavior and small enough that they fit within the general domain of thinking. With our criteria of what we are looking for in a thinking disposition in place, let us examine what others have put forth as key thinking dispositions.

Dispositions from a Philosophical Perspective

Within the critical-thinking domain of philosophy, Peter and Noreen Facione and Robert Ennis have all formulated lists of thinking dispositions, and Richard Paul has developed a list of intellectual virtues and passions (see Table 2.1).[14] The Faciones (Facione, Facione, & Sanchez, 1991), working with a cross-disciplinary panel of scholars, propose an overall disposition toward critical thinking that consists of seven subdispositions (listed in column one of Table 2.1). Not all of the terms are immediately understandable, and some—such as maturity and critical-thinking self-confidence—don't implicate any specific thinking-related actions. Ennis's list for the ideal critical thinker (1991) totals twelve dispositions.[15] However, in seeking to address shortcomings and criticism of critical-thinking programs, Ennis winds up including several nonthinking dispositions, such as "to take a position." We also find maxims, "to try to be well informed," and outright directives, "to use one's critical thinking abilities," which tend to make his list a set of useful rules of thumb rather than true thinking dispositions. Likewise, Paul (1991, 1993), in seeking to reflect both the affective and moral dimension of critical thinking, proposes traits—such as intellectual empathy or sense of justice—that might not strictly be concerned with facilitating productive thinking.

Dispositions from the Perspective of Education

Of course, lists of thinking habits or dispositions are not solely the jurisdiction of philosophers. Several groups of educators have developed such lists as well. These individuals tend to draw on philosophical theory, psychological research, and educational practice. Table 2.2 presents three such lists. In developing their list, Perkins, Jay, and Tishman (1993) set themselves four criteria for a thinking disposition; it must be individually necessary to a conception of good thinking, collectively comprehensive, normatively appropriate in that it fits with cultural intuitions about good thinking, and functionally

Faciones and Sanchez: Seven Subdispositions of a Critical Thinker	Ennis: Twelve Dispositions of the Ideal Critical Thinker	Paul: Thirteen Virtues and Passions
1. Inquisitiveness 2. Open-mindedness 3. Systematicity 4. Analyticity 5. Truth seeking 6. Critical-thinking self-confidence 7. Maturity	1. To be clear about intended meanings 2. To determine and maintain focus 3. To take the total situation into account 4. To seek and offer reasons 5. To try to be well informed 6. To look for alternatives 7. To seek precision as required 8. To be aware of one's own beliefs 9. To be open-minded 10. To withhold judgment when evidence is insufficient 11. To take a position 12. To use one's critical-thinking abilities	1. Passion for clarity, accuracy, fair-mindedness 2. Fervor for getting to the bottom of things 3. Sympathetic listening to opposing views 4. Drive to seek out evidence 5. Aversion to contradiction, sloppy thinking, inconsistent use of standards 6. Devotion to truth 7. Intellectual courage 8. Intellectual humility 9. Intellectual empathy 10. Intellectual integrity 11. Intellectual perseverance 12. Faith in reason 13. Intellectual sense of justice

Table 2.1. **Dispositional Lists from the Philosophical Perspective.**
Sources: Facione, Facione, and Sanchez (1991); Ennis (1991); Paul (1991, 1993).

balanced so as to create a supportive network. Although not all of the meanings for the list's terms are self-evident, the list does capture much of the breadth of thinking while maintaining focus on the big picture. Drawing on the work of psychologists and philosophers, Robert Marzano (1992) identifies four habits supporting creative thinking, five additional mental habits related to self-regulated thinking and learning, and six critical-thinking habits.[16] Art Costa and Bena Kallick (2000), whose work has done much to popularize this field, have assembled a whopping list of sixteen habits of mind, while stressing that even a list of this length is not complete. In their writings, they indicate that the items on the list "begin with the individual and move out to the entire community" (p. xiii). In doing so, they include some traits that aren't necessarily focused on thinking, such as finding humor or responding with wonderment and awe.

Perkins, Jay, and Tishman: Seven Thinking Dispositions	Marzano: Fifteen Habits of Creative, Self-Regulated, and Critical Learning and Thinking	Costa and Kallick: Sixteen Habits of Mind
1. To be broad and adventurous 2. Toward sustained intellectual curiosity 3. To clarify and seek understanding 4. To plan and be strategic 5. To be intellectually careful 6. To seek and evaluate reasons 7. To be metacognitive	1. Engaging intensely in tasks even when answers or solutions aren't immediately apparent 2. Pushing the limits of your knowledge and abilities 3. Generating, trusting, and maintaining your own standards of evaluation 4. Generating new ways of viewing a situation outside the boundaries of standard conventions 5. Being aware of your own thinking 6. Planning 7. Being aware of necessary resources 8. Being sensitive to feedback 9. Evaluating the effectiveness of your actions 10. Being accurate and seeking accuracy 11. Being clear and seeking clarity 12. Being open-minded 13. Restraining impulsivity 14. Taking a position when the situation warrants it 15. Being sensitive to others' feelings and level of knowledge	1. Persisting 2. Managing impulsivity 3. Listening with understanding and empathy 4. Thinking flexibly 5. Thinking about thinking (metacognition) 6. Striving for accuracy 7. Questioning and posing problems 8. Applying past knowledge to new situations 9. Thinking and communicating with clarity and precision 10. Gathering data through all senses 11. Creating, imagining, innovating 12. Responding with wonderment and awe 13. Taking responsible risks 14. Finding humor 15. Thinking interdependently 16. Remaining open to continuous learning

Table 2.2. Dispositional Lists from the Perspective of Educational Practice.

Sources: Perkins, Jay, and Tishman (1993); Marzano (1992); Costa and Kallick (2000).

Central Park East Secondary School (CPESS) and Project 2061 (see Table 2.3) have also developed habits-of-mind lists to inform curriculum and instruction. Without making any claims about the list's comprehensiveness, CPESS's list of five habits of mind certainly have worked well to guide instruction and have withstood the test of time at that school.[17] As a policy document, *Project 2061: Science for All Americans* (AAAS, 1989) seeks to provide a national direction for science curricula. It identifies seven scientific habits of mind that the project authors feel reflect a systematic application of highly regarded everyday values.

As our cursory examination of these lists of thinking dispositions indicates, developing an ideal list is no easy task. It is often difficult to keep the list focused solely on thinking and not to veer off into other values.[18] Likewise, it can be challenging to identify dispositions that are of an appropriate grain size to be useful without being too limiting. Finally, there is the thorny task of coming up with language that is expressive, evocative, and understandable. I've tried to point out a few of the preceding lists' troubling features without being overly critical. My intent in presenting the lists is not to present a critique but to map the terrain of the field, examine some of the challenges, and then look for the broad areas of agreement that seem to emerge in these lists. Let us now turn our attention to identifying those commonalities.

An Integrated Perspective

In comparing these eight lists, I am struck most by the large degree of overlap. All the lists show a general concern with promoting creativ-

CPESS Five Habits of Mind	Project 2061: Seven Habits of Mind
1. Evidence: How do we know?	1. Integrity
2. Viewpoint: Who's speaking?	2. Diligence
3. Connections: What causes what?	3. Fairness
4. Supposition: How might things be difference?	4. Curiosity
5. Meaningfullness: What's the point; why does it matter?	5. Openness to new ideas
	6. Skepticism
	7. Imagination

Table 2.3. Dispositional Lists from the Curricular Perspective.
Sources: Meier (1995); American Association for the Advancement of Science (1989).

ity, encouraging curiosity, and developing deep understanding. In seeking to synthesize these eight lists, six broad categories of dispositions emerge for me. We might further group these dispositions into three overarching categories. The following list displays each of the categories:

1. *Creative thinking: looking out, up, around, and about*
   Open-minded
   Curious
2. *Reflective thinking: looking within*
   Metacognitive
3. *Critical thinking: looking at, through, and in between*
   Seeking truth and understanding
   Strategic
   Skeptical

The six dispositions in this list capture the breadth of thinking by incorporating dimensions of creative, reflective, and critical thinking. At the same time, they don't go too far afield in their scope. In choosing the terms themselves, I've tried to stick with the simplest and most accessible language. However, this certainly doesn't mean that some of the terms themselves aren't open to interpretation. Finally, I've tried to select terms that are broad enough so that a variety of subordinate behaviors might be implicated. What I haven't tried to do in this list is to create a perfect or master list of dispositions. Rather, my intent was to create a useful and tractable list to guide us in thinking about intellectual character. In the remainder of this chapter, I'll elaborate a bit more about what each of the six dispositions contributes to smart behavior and good thinking, and then I'll examine how dispositions affect our performance in the world in Chapter Three.

THE DISPOSITION TO BE OPEN-MINDED. Open-mindedness works against narrowness and rigidity, two common pitfalls in thinking. We tend to accept things as they come to us, allowing our minds to stay in a comfortable groove rather than challenging the way things are. For example, if you had asked someone a few years ago what a computer looked like, that person would most likely have described a box-like contraption similar to a TV set. Then, along came the iMac with its sleek curvature and transparent colored shell. Someone was able to open up his or her, and consequently our, view of things. As this example suggests, being open-minded is not about mere acceptance of new ideas or others' positions; it implies being flexible, willing to consider and try out new ideas, generating alternative options and explanations, and looking beyond the given and expected. The openness implicit in the term suggests an active rather than a passive process. A subordinate disposition that fits here would be what is known as perspective taking: looking at things from different perspectives, attitudinally as well as physically, is a tool for opening up one's mind.

THE DISPOSITION TO BE CURIOUS. Curiosity propels us to explore our world, to ask questions about it, and to wonder at it. The curiosity of young children is renowned, as they set out to find their way in their new surroundings. Intellectual curiosity builds on this innate curiosity but goes beyond mere wonder and delight in the new and exciting. Intellectual curiosity involves finding the interesting and puzzling in the everyday, the mundane, and the ordinary, as well as in the unexpected. It acts as an engine for thinking. It fuels our interest and helps us to generate questions and pose problems. Most importantly, it gives us something to think about. Curiosity isn't an end in itself but the beginning of a process of discovery or problem solving. We value curiosity for where it can take us. One of my favorite traveling companions is extremely curious. I value her company on a trip because of what she finds to show me, despite the fact that she has never visited our destination before. Her curiosity is infectious. It stems from being able to look for the unexpected, to actively compare and contrast situations, and to probe the anomalies that emerge. In contrast, the uncurious mind passively accepts all the input it receives rather than experiencing it with the freshness of an unseasoned traveler.

THE DISPOSITION TO BE METACOGNITIVE. Metacognition, or thinking about one's thinking, is a field unto itself, rich in its own body of literature. Research on the thinking of experts and effective learners has shown that these individuals tend to actively monitor, regulate, evaluate, and direct their thinking. Anyone who has ever taught reading to young children has seen the metacognitive process at work in good readers and dormant in poor readers. Good readers monitor their understanding as they go along and redirect their actions accordingly, whereas poor readers don't. They may read the words on the page without evaluating their understanding of the words as they go along. As a math teacher, I once had a student who struggled in algebra, and her parents expressed their concern. I told the parents I wasn't very worried about the girl because she was so good at monitoring her understanding and then acting accordingly. That is, when she didn't understand, she thought about what was tripping her up and then asked directed questions to clear up her confusion. It was true that math wasn't very intuitive for her, but she went on to do very well in high school and college math classes because she had the tools she needed to develop her understanding.

THE DISPOSITION TO BE SEEKING TRUTH AND UNDERSTANDING. We all are interested in truth and understanding, but truth and understanding can't be handed to someone—though at times we educators may act as if they were ours to deliver. Truth and understanding must be developed actively through certain mental moves, one of which is reasoning based on the evidence we are able to uncover. In part, this reasoning involves weighing the evidence, considering its validity, looking for links between bits of evidence to build up a theory, and then testing the theory by looking at counterevidence and alternative explanations. This kind of thinking takes a person deeper into the topic at hand. In many schools and classrooms, it has become fashionable to solicit students' opinions, beliefs, and ideas on various topics as a way of engaging them with the topic. Unfortunately, this practice doesn't really engage them in thinking. However, by asking students why they think what they do or what is behind their beliefs or opinions, we can begin to engage them in a search for truth and understanding.

As with truth, our understanding is facilitated by examining things more closely. Helpful mental moves include looking for connections, exploring applications and consequences, pushing ideas to the limits, pulling ideas apart, contrasting one idea with another, and building explanations. It is through these and other processes that we build up our understanding and arrive at closer approximations of the truth. No single process or set of processes is a guarantor of our success, however.

THE DISPOSITION TO BE STRATEGIC. At the heart of being strategic is the notion that we are planful, anticipatory, methodical, and careful in our thinking. Rather than merely letting situations, our thinking, or our problem solving unfold, we organize and direct those endeavors. We devise plans of attack and set goals for ourselves. We consider our options and choose tactics to best meet our goals, without losing sight of the fact that we will have to monitor and reassess all strategies from time to time. Being strategic is basically a move toward efficiency. We know that many, though not all, situations can benefit from assessment and planning from the beginning. Our task and our thinking become clearer when we clarify our goals and consider ways to reach them. Of course, this planning can take very different forms. For example, author John Irving (1998) has said that he spends a year just thinking and developing a story before he sits down to write. When he does start writing, he has a clear vision of the entire book before him. Of course, not everyone writes this way, but most authors report having some method for planning out their writing to assure that it doesn't become aimless and unwieldy.

THE DISPOSITION TO BE SKEPTICAL. The word *skeptical* has a bit of a negative connotation. I've chosen it because it appears widely in the lists we have looked at, and people tend to know what it means. A less loaded but also less clear word might be *probing*. Being skeptical means probing below the surface of things, looking for proof and evidence, and not accepting things at face value. It needn't mean being suspicious, doubtful, or critical. Being skeptical allows us to follow others' reasoning and examine it carefully so that we can be critically discerning consumers of ideas. Media watchdogs who monitor news shows, advertisements, and politics are good examples of people who exercise this disposition. Being skeptical helps our thinking by forcing us to take an active stance toward new information rather than accept it passively. For example, being skeptical begins when we consider new information in light of our experience and knowledge base to see whether we should accommodate the information. This kind of skepticism becomes increasingly important as we must sort through more and more information.

—⚬⚬⚬— **Key Ideas for Developing Intellectual Character**

RETHINKING SMART

- *Conventional View of Smart.* The dominance of testing, grades, and IQ instruments has distorted our view of what it means to be smart. These measures value knowledge and speed disproportionately and view intelligence as something that rests inside the individual.

- *New View of Smart.* Intelligent action in the world is what counts most. Ability is only a part of performance. Of equal importance are the spotting of occasions for the use of those abilities and the inclination to put those abilities into play. We recognize smartness in the patterns of one's exhibited behavior over time.

- *Intellectual Character.* An overarching term to describe a set of dispositions that not only shape but also motivate intellectual behavior. Character implies a consistent deployment of abilities so that patterns of behavior are established over time. Character builds on beliefs, attitudes, temperaments, and tendencies but is also developable and must be nurtured by the environment.

- *Dispositions.* Acquired patterns of behavior that are under one's control and will as opposed to being automatically activated. Dispositions are overarching sets of behaviors, not just single specific behaviors. They are dynamic and idiosyncratic in their contextualized deployment rather than prescribed actions to be rigidly carried out. More than desire and will, dispositions must be coupled with the requisite ability. Dispositions motivate, activate, and direct our abilities.

- *Which Dispositions?* Curiosity, open-mindedness, metacognition, the seeking of truth and understanding, strategic thinking, and skepticism do a good job of capturing the depth and breadth of good thinking. However, they are by no means a definitive list of thinking dispositions.

CHAPTER THREE

Acting Smart

How Thinking Dispositions
Close the Ability-Action Gap

—◦◦◦— The language of dispositions is generally descriptive
and predictive in nature. We readily speak of a neighbor being friendly,
a colleague being deliberative, or a relative's quirkiness. Working with
others on a project, we notice someone's judicious nature even as we
pick up on another individual's attentiveness. In the classroom, we
take note of one child's reflectiveness in contrast to another's impulsivity. In all of these situations, we are using a label to describe what
we have observed of the individual's behavior. At the same time,
through our very use of dispositional language, we forecast our predictions regarding a particular individual's future actions. If the
expected behavior doesn't materialize, we have a dispositional way of
speaking about that as well. For instance, we make mention of someone's surprising anger or of an individual's unexpected forthrightness.
In doing so, we indicate that the observed behavior does not fit what
we anticipated.

However, dispositions can serve as more than a gross descriptive
label for a collection of behaviors. The power behind thinking dispositions or dispositions in general is that they act as both a descriptive
and an explanatory construct, making clear the mystery of how raw

ability is transformed into meaningful action.[1] It is precisely this capacity of dispositions to bridge the ability-action gap that can make the construct so compelling to all concerned with education. If schools and other educational enterprises are not developing students' dispositions to act and use their knowledge, ability, and skill, then these institutions are just wasting students' time. Inert knowledge and ability that cannot be readily put into action is of little practical benefit to anyone. We must educate students to act smart, not just to be smart.

To reveal the explanatory nature of dispositions, we must move beyond our common everyday use of dispositional language to an examination of how dispositions function and develop: their nature and their nurture. In this chapter, we examine how dispositions operate to affect our behavior. We will look at various models of how dispositions work to close the ability-action gap. These models provide us with potentially useful insights into how dispositions develop in context and how parents and teachers can work to nurture dispositional development in children.

A DISPOSITION IN ACTION

Before turning our attention to theories of how dispositions operate, let's first look at a disposition in action. By playing out a script of dispositional behavior unfolding in context, we can further clarify what it means to take a dispositional and characterological view of intelligence. At the same time, our examination of behavior in action can add meat to the bones of our theoretical models.

Scenario: In the Museum

Imagine the following scenario in which the disposition to be open-minded and its associated subdispositions come into play: you are walking through a large art museum when you stumble into a hall containing works of art you normally don't spend time viewing. Perhaps you just don't find them aesthetically appealing, or they are from a culture that you don't know much about. Rather than rush through the hall to get to another room, you take a moment to take in what is there. To make the artworks more accessible, you try to imagine yourself as an art historian. You ask yourself questions such as: What do these works say about the time and culture in which they were created? What might an art historian say about why these works are important? What things might different types of artists notice about these works?

Returning to your initial perspective, you ask yourself: Why don't these works immediately appeal to me? How do these works challenge my perceptions of what is good art? Then, just because you are worried that all of this is too sobering a way of looking at art, you ask yourself: How might children view this collection? What would I tell them to capture their interest in this room? What piece of art would it be the most fun to try and recreate?

Turning away from this questioning mode, you next seek out one particular work in the room on which to concentrate your attention. You no longer concern yourself with the entire collection but focus your perspective to avoid superficiality. Initially, you approach the work as it is presented for viewers in the hall. After taking it in from that perspective, you find an alternative angle from which to view the work. You look at it obliquely from the side, from above, from below. With each shift of your stance, you try to identify new features of the work, things you haven't noticed before, elements that become more and less salient. Finally, having felt that you have developed some appreciation, and perhaps understanding, of the collection, you move on to the next hall.

Four Aspects of Dispositional Behavior

Let's look at this incident through a dispositional lens. Seeing a disposition unfold in context, we can spot distinct elements at work in provoking the action.[2]

AWARENESS. Initially, there was an awareness of an occasion for a certain type of thinking, a spotting of an opportunity. When you first walked into the museum hall, an occasion for open-mindedness presented itself. Remember, a disposition such as open-mindedness is of a grain size large enough that it embraces a wide variety of behaviors without necessarily dictating any specific one; indicative behaviors might include considering other perspectives, examining bias, generating alternative options, and breaking out of conventional ways of operating. You recognized that this particular hall provided a good opportunity to challenge some of your assumptions about art and to try out different perspectives.

When I say that the occasion for open-mindedness presented itself when you walked into the unfamiliar exhibition hall, I do not mean that it announced itself. The occasion had to be detected. It is quite possible that many other visitors to the museum that day did not detect such an opportunity. Perhaps if you were late to meet someone for lunch, you would have raced through the hall, taking no notice. Many things can influence our detection of occasions for thinking, such as competing agendas or a general inattention to our surroundings. Our awareness of thinking occasions isn't automatic but must be developed and nurtured.

Recognizing an opportunity is a complex enterprise because it is a subtle endeavor. Stepping into the exhibition hall, there wasn't necessarily a moment in which you suddenly stopped in your tracks and were overcome with a recognition that open-mindedness would be the most appropriate course of action. The awareness we are speaking of is often more of an inkling, if it is at the conscious level at all. It may be brought on by a recognition of certain features of the situation that one has encountered before. Or it may be deliberately prompted by putting the brakes on one's tendency to react automatically and forcing oneself to take a few moments to consider alternative options for responding.

MOTIVATION. Another element at work in our scenario was the motivation to act. Having recognized the opportunity to think in a more open-minded manner in the museum hall, you made a decision to act, to do something. Other people, or even yourself at another time, might have recognized the opportunity and chosen not to act. Just as with awareness, many things can influence our motivation to act in any given situation. Acting on opportunities requires a commitment of time, energy, and resources. Having spotted an opportunity, having seen a possibility for directing our action, how motivated are we to follow through?

INCLINATION. Our motivation is often a matter of desire and will. It depends on what one values and sees as important and worthwhile. In the museum scenario, unless you saw the value of being open-minded and extending your perception of art, you would be unlikely to follow through on exploiting the opportunity even when you recognized it. Conversely, if you placed a premium on being open-minded and extending the way you looked at the world, you might find yourself more apt to spot opportunities for doing so. Thus, motivation has a primary effect in heightening awareness as well as in acting as a driver to push us into action. To distinguish these two functions, we can refer to this advance primary nature of motivation as *inclination,* reserving the word *motivation* to designate the more situation-specific driver of action.

ABILITY. The last component we saw at work in the museum scenario was ability. Having made the decision, at least at some level of consciousness, to act while you were in the museum hall, you had the requisite ability to generate questions for yourself that brought about behaviors that others generally recognize as demonstrating open-mindedness. Without such abilities, your awareness of the occasion and your motivation to act would have been for naught. Again, these dispositional components interact: the better developed and refined your abilities, the more likely you are to spot opportunities for their use and transfer across a variety of situations. A lack of awareness might, in some cases, be a factor of weak ability. Not having a rich knowledge base of specific actions and behaviors to draw from might make it more difficult to see occasions for employing the limited abilities one does have.

Dispositional behavior, then, is the marriage of

- Inclination
- Awareness
- Motivation
- Ability

One might argue that the element of ability could be left out of this equation. After all, in the last chapter, I argued that it was necessary to move away from an abilities-based notion of what it means to be smart. However, my point is not that abilities are unimportant or even that they need to take a backseat to other elements; my argument is that we must keep the role of ability in perspective. Inert ability, ability that lies dormant and must be specifically provoked, is not a very useful barometer of intelligence. Instead, we need to look at ability in action, and that means taking a characterological view of intelligence, which pays attention to the role of dispositions. We need to focus our attention on the kind of ability that transfers across a variety of contexts, that gets activated and can readily be put to use in solving problems and making decisions. The ability component of a disposition is precisely of this nature.

SOME ADDITIONAL PERSPECTIVES ON DISPOSITIONS

On first encounter, the idea that dispositions are more than a descriptive label for one's action tendencies may seem strange.[3] However, this notion of dispositions bringing about action by pulling together awareness, motivation, inclination, and ability has a rather long history. We can find references to these components in the philosophical writings of John Dewey, the popular writings of Stephen Covey, the literature on self-regulated learning, and the theories of social and cognitive psychology. A brief examination of these sources can be useful in understanding how dispositions operate in various contexts. In addition, the slightly different language and emphasis suggested by these various constituencies can help illuminate our conception of dispositional components and their role. This strong conceptualization provides the basis for our understanding of how we can best nurture and develop intellectual character.

Dewey on Dispositions

Although Dewey never put forth an explicit model of dispositions,[4] his writings on the nature of reflective thinking (1933), a broad type of thinking disposition, provide enough detail from which to infer a model. Dewey identifies three components necessary to the disposition of reflective thinking: knowledge, desire, and attitude. He describes knowledge as an awareness and recognition of the importance of certain behaviors and as specific how-to knowledge involving methods and skills. Thus, knowledge consists of practical abilities plus specific values and beliefs about the utility of those abilities. Rather than the term *motivation*, Dewey uses the words *desire* and *will* in his writings. These terms suggest that motivation consists not only of initial inclination but also determination to follow through with action. Finally, Dewey identifies three attitudes that should be cultivated to aid reflective thinking: open-mindedness toward new ideas, wholehearted interest, and intellectual responsibility. These attitudes operate at a general level and in the background to activate one's inclination, and they are different from the more specific skills considered under the component of knowledge.

From Dewey's perspective, knowledge, desire, and attitude work together to produce a general disposition of thoughtfulness, what Dewey calls reflective thinking. Though Dewey develops these three components within the context of a specific disposition, they provide a useful template for considering what is required for any type of thinking disposition to take hold: one needs a general set of productive attitudes or values about thinking, a collection of well-developed skills and strategies, a belief in the effectiveness and utility of those skills, and the motivation to both initiate behavior and stick with it. Therefore, his conception of dispositions parallels ours. Even the idea of awareness, which does not feature prominently in Dewey's conception, might be inferred since the know-how he writes of seems to include an awareness of when to use to one's abilities.

A particularly important dynamic that Dewey's writings bring forth is the role of general background values and beliefs. In our museum example, I made brief mention of the underlying attitudes you carried with you into the exhibition hall. These include a set of attitudes and beliefs about thinking in general and about this specific kind of situation that predisposed you to act in one way or another. These background beliefs served to boost your level of awareness. Once you detected the opportunity for perspective taking, your belief that this kind of intellectual endeavor was worthwhile may have motivated you to act.

Covey's Contribution

In his best-selling book, *The Seven Habits of Highly Effective People* (1989), Stephen Covey puts forth a similar model of dispositions (of course, he uses the term *habits*) employing down-to-earth language and folk wisdom. Covey's model speaks in terms of knowledge of what to do, skill in how to do it, and motivation to want to do it. This first ingredient, knowledge of what to do, is different from how we traditionally view knowledge as a set fact or bit of information. Covey sees knowledge as signaling an awareness in the situation. Thus, he signals that ability and inclination are not enough to define a disposition; an individual must also recognize when and where to call upon that ability and bring it into play.

Mindfulness and Self-Regulated Learning

We find the notion of awareness of occasions in other psychological constructs that are dispositional in nature. For example, awareness plays a major role in Ellen Langer's notion of mindfulness (1989).[5] *Mindfulness* can be described as an open and creative state in which individuals actively generate new categories, draw meaningful distinctions, consider multiple perspectives, and are open to new information. To avoid mindlessness and achieve mindfulness, one must be aware of and move beyond one's preexisting categories, automatic responses to situations, and the personal perspective one brings to new encounters.

Likewise, scholars hypothesize that awareness of occasions plays a role in *self-regulated learning,* which we can describe as the learner's effectiveness in motivating, directing, and monitoring his or her own learning. This construct is dispositional because it requires not only the cultivation of specific abilities but also the effective use of those abilities in the learning situation. Philip Winne (1995) identifies four ingredients of self-regulated learning: conditional knowledge, action knowledge, motivational knowledge, and background knowledge. Conditional knowledge permits learners to determine when certain strategies are appropriate, representing the sort of awareness of occasions we have been discussing. Motivational knowledge addresses issues of values and beliefs that support the inclination to use one's knowledge. Action knowledge and background knowledge represent types of ability. Action knowledge consists of the ability to use certain processes, strategies, and skills, whereas background knowledge includes knowledge of both the domain one is working in and the general form of tasks. These four kinds of knowledge interact in self-regulation in much the same way that inclination, awareness, motivation, and ability interact in dispositions; that is, the components don't operate in a linear fashion but are more complementary in nature.

A Triadic Model of Dispositions

David Perkins, Eileen Jay, and Shari Tishman (1993) proposed one of the most explicit models of thinking dispositions as part of the MacArthur Patterns of Thinking Project, on which I also worked for a time. The project team theorized that dispositions can be broken into three distinct, measurable elements: sensitivity, inclination, and ability (Perkins, Tishman, Ritchhart, Donis, & Andrade, 2000). This three-part model departs from the traditional view of dispositions, held by many philosophers and critical thinkers, which focuses most exclusively on issues of desire, will, and inclination. However, the triadic theory links well with other more psychologically oriented views of dispositions we have examined. In particular, the addition of sensitivity, what I have been calling an awareness of occasions, represents a recognition that abilities are put to use in context and that one must first recognize a context for appropriate use before inclination can play its part. Justifying this stance, the group wrote, "Our motive for restructuring the concept [of dispositions] lies in the failure of the conventional disposition-ability contrast to highlight the inclination-sensitivity distinction. The conventional account either collapses the two under the one label dispositions, or simply leaves out consideration of sensitivity. We urge that inclination and sensitivity are distinct and important constructs in explaining behavior" (Perkins et al., 1993, p. 4). I believe that this same argument can be applied to the distinction between inclination and motivation. I argue that these two constructs, though similar in nature, are distinct and important components in explaining behavior.

A NEW MODEL OF DISPOSITIONS EMERGES

Based on these other perspectives and on actual examples of dispositional behavior, I propose that an explanatory model of dispositions must include:

1. General inclination, consisting of fixed and developed beliefs
2. Situation-specific inclination, which we might refer to as motivation
3. Sensitivity or awareness to occasions
4. The prerequisite abilities, skills, and knowledge needed to act

Of course, the test of any such model is its capacity to account logically for the transformation of ability into action in a variety of situations and contexts, to contribute something beyond what ability alone provides, and to be useful in demonstrating the psychological reality of dispositions as a construct. In this section, we look at how this four-component model can account for volitional behavior and its development.

Looking at Dispositions from the Outside In

One means of logically validating our model is to examine intentional behavior that is not dispositional in nature. When a dispositional component fails, are there external corollaries or situational characteristics that might stand in for that weakened dispositional component in order to prompt the behavior? For instance, when an individual lacks awareness, what kind of external force or situational feature might be able to act in its stead so that the behavior still emerges? To the extent that internal mechanisms have external counterparts, the model is better able to account for a range of behavior, both fully dispositional action and action that must be supported. The external forms of the internal mechanisms also provide insight into the nature of these mechanisms, helping us to understand their role and operation. In addition, constructing such an internal-external model suggests ways in which dispositions can be developed through the internalization of external triggers.[6]

Figure 3.1 shows what such an internal-external model might look like. At the ends of the figure lie ability and action. In between reside the various mechanisms needed for bridging the divide between ability and action. At the top of the figure are external forces that can provoke action. These forces include general external motivators, such as rewards and other control mechanisms; prompts and scaffolds to assist in activating abilities; and more situation-specific motivators that affect persistence and follow-through. At the bottom of the figure are the internal mechanisms for provoking action from our model of dispositions: inclination, awareness of occasions, and motivation.

Action in the world need not progress solely on either the external or the internal track, however. Quite the contrary. In our day-to-day work, we often encounter times when we lack inclination, awareness, or motivation. When an internal mechanism fails, an external force may step in to assist in bridging the gap between ability and action. For example, I have a tendency to leave the stove on when I am cooking. I'm quite motivated to turn it off, because I am not eager to burn the house down! However, I tend not to be very aware of the burners when I am not using them. I'm often distracted by the other demands of preparing a meal. Knowing this, my partner regularly prompts me to check the burners before I sit down to dinner. Thus, my lack of awareness is compensated for by an external force, a

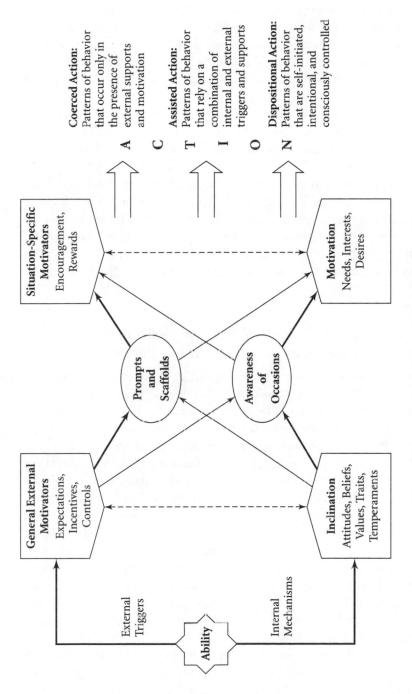

Figure 3.1. An Internal-External Model of Dispositions.

prompt by someone else to check the burners. In other instances, the external force may activate even without a failure of an internal component. For instance, we regularly encounter external incentives such as pay, rewards, or recognition that lead us to have a more favorable general impression of situations than we might otherwise experience on our own.

This movement back and forth between internal mechanisms and external forces is represented by the thin arrows in the center of Figure 3.1. At any point, the external forces can interact with the internal mechanisms that act as triggers, shown by the dashed arrows, or the general path from ability to action can jump back and forth between the internal and external. Thus, the model explains a range of behaviors from fully self-initiated, dispositional action to coerced action that is brought about completely by outside forces. Much of our behavior does not exist at either of these extremes, however. Rather, it is made of a dynamic interplay between external and internal forces.

Using the Internal-External Model to Understand How Dispositions Develop

This internal-external model of dispositional behavior also provides insights into the way dispositions develop. If we look at it from a sociocultural perspective, we see that much of children's learning is an internalization of the external, social environment around them. Over time, the individual internalizes the expectations, roles, behaviors, and modes of operating in particular circumstances so that they become a part of his or her repertoire. Such behaviors need not always be explicitly taught, however. Quite often, the lessons are implicit. For example, a child attending a new school is never explicitly taught the informal, child-dictated rules of the playground. Rather, the child participates, observes, listens, and interacts to gradually pick up the various expectations for behavior. Over time, the child quickly learns what behavior is "cool," what is acceptable and unacceptable, what the parameters of behavior are, how to talk, how teams are decided, and so on. The child develops not only skills but expectations, language, beliefs, and values as well.

In much the same way, one's general inclination develops. Through interaction with the environment and the significant people in that environment, one develops certain attitudes, values, and beliefs about what is important and worthwhile in that particular context. Although this happens generally, it occurs with regard to thinking as well. We are socialized into ways of thinking by the environment. We learn what counts as good and acceptable thinking. We learn ways of interacting with and talking about ideas. We learn what ideas are worthy of discussion and exploration in which contexts.

Facilitating Dispositional Development

Developmentally, the process of internalizing the external can be assisted by helping individuals to work at the edge of their capabilities. Vygotsky (1978) called this the zone of proximal development. Under these circumstances, external or social forces provide the scaffolding needed to boost behavior and action beyond what it might otherwise be. Such scaffolding is necessarily responsive in that it doesn't usurp the individual's preexisting capabilities but extends them beyond what they would be on their own. Thus, a set of comprehension questions that a child must answer following a reading may not boost the child's understanding of the story because the questions don't necessarily lift the child beyond where he or she might have naturally been. In some instances, such activities may even lower comprehension by interrupting a natural process. In contrast, listening to a child explain his or her understanding of the story and asking responsive or probing questions may provide the scaffolding the child needs to boost comprehension.

Similarly, when it comes to promoting children's thinking, the scaffolding we provide must be responsive. Remember my example of leaving the stove burners on while cooking? If I were to receive a reminder to turn the burners off after each episode of cooking, I would most likely become dependent on those reminders. It is the periodic intervention and the responsive reminders that are most effective. Knowing that I don't always have someone around to remind me to double-check the burners, I've developed systems for boosting my sensitivity. When an item is done cooking, I move it to another burner on the stove immediately. This way, I'm more apt to notice the lit burner if I accidentally leave it on.

Compare this kind of responsive scaffolding and self-development of awareness with much of what happens in schools. Students are routinely given assignments in which everything is spelled out for them in advance. In an effort to boost performance, extensive assignment

guidelines or project rubrics are developed. Although effective in helping students make the grade, overuse of such devices may have un-
intended results by inhibiting students' development of the kind
of internal triggers they will need to affect independent behavior. In
order for rubrics and the like to be effective, students must internalize them as expectations and values about what counts and is worthwhile rather than seeing them merely as checklists for determining an
assignment's thoroughness.

CREATING ENVIRONMENTS THAT SUPPORT THE DEVELOPMENT OF INTELLECTUAL CHARACTER

In thinking about the kind of environment in which external triggers
can best be internalized, four components emerge as important and
significant contributing forces:

1. The ongoing presence of salient models
2. Consistency of expectations
3. Explicit instruction
4. Opportunity for practice and reinforcement within
   meaningful contexts

The first two factors, and to some extent the fourth, are generally
embedded in the implicit curriculum of the classroom and social environment. In contrast, the third and fourth factors are reflected more
in the explicit intentional curriculum, making them somewhat easier
to address.

Salient Models

It is easy to see the importance of models. In learning any new behavior or skill, one often begins by attempting to replicate the actions of
someone more expert. However, when one works to acquire a disposition, models serve as more than exemplars of skills. By demonstrating congruence between attitude and behavior, a respected
models' ongoing presence also imparts values and serves to cultivate
not only one's ability but also general inclination toward a particular behavior. This dual role of the model makes it hard to cultivate a

disposition in others that one does not possess oneself. While one can easily "model" or demonstrate a specific type of thinking in a particular lesson—for example, metacognition, or thinking about thinking—modeling that type of thinking in an ongoing way that demonstrates its value and importance if one is not disposed to naturally think that way is difficult.

This is where I believe many thinking-skills programs designed to be implemented in schools fail. Such programs often call for teachers to demonstrate or model a particular type of thinking, but that type of thinking never gets a chance to take hold because its value and importance are not being adequately reinforced and may even be undermined by the teacher's other actions. In contrast, thinking dispositions can take firm root in classrooms that don't employ any type of critical-thinking program or in which there are very few explicit demonstrations as long as the teacher possesses a strong disposition toward certain types of thinking and models them in an ongoing manner.

Consistency of Expectations

Consistency of expectations alludes to the importance of sustained work over time. Whether in the home or the classroom, children read the environment for the expectations of the adults. When the expectations are inconsistent or contradictory, the environment will not be ripe for the development of the thinking dispositions associated with intellectual character. For example, take the disposition to be reflective, which includes being metacognitive and searching for truth and understanding. Although this is a disposition that most schools and teachers claim to value highly, forty-minute class periods, rapid transitions between in-class activities, and a superficial coverage of many topics send quite a different message to students.[7] When the implicit message contradicts the explicit message, the implicit message is likely to win out.

Explicit Instruction

I don't want to give the impression that dispositions somehow magically appear when conditions are ripe. Although dispositions may develop out of the natural interactions with appropriate and significant role models, there also exists a need for explicit instruction.[8] In his reference to the acquisition of "thinking frames" to organize and support thinking, David Perkins states that "simply enriching the context with modeling—the 'actions speak louder than words' theory— is not enough" (Perkins & Salomon, 1987, p. 49). Likewise, in *The Thinking Classroom,* Tishman, Perkins, and Jay (1995, p. 13) identify "the direct transmission of information relevant to good thinking" as an important cultural force in the classroom.

Keep in mind that some of the dispositions we would like to cultivate in ourselves and in others actually run against our natural tendencies as human beings. For instance, we are more naturally inclined toward egocentricism and one-sided thinking than toward open-mindedness and the consideration of options and alternative perspectives.[9] Richard Paul (1987, p. 130) refers to these nonnative types of thinking—such as a dislike of inconsistency, a love of clarity, a passion to seek reasons and evidence, and a desire to be fair to points of view other than our own—as our "secondary nature." In these instances, explicit teaching can help to develop abilities, clarify models, and direct attention to cultural values. For example, before one can effectively engage in a way of thinking, perspective taking, for example, it is helpful to know just what perspective taking is, why it is important, what it looks like in different situations, and when it is likely to be useful. Although dispositions aren't formed through such direct instruction, the presence of explicit instruction within a supportive cultural context over time supports their development. In this way, dispositions are different from even complex skills, which can be acquired through direct instruction and associated practice.

Opportunity for Meaningful Practice

To complement explicit instruction, one must also have the opportunity for practice and reinforcement of good thinking within meaningful contexts. This means that it must occur in socially interactive settings in which community members can provide feedback and support. Such settings help reinforce cultural values, scaffold individuals' actions in the moment, and supply valuable feedback about performance immediately. If classrooms do not contain such opportunities, the message sent to students is that good thinking is only marginally important and will not be needed except when specifically called for.

Practice allows the cultivation of abilities that undergird dispositions while encouraging the habituation of and inclination toward behavior. This habituation is a factor of establishing procedural precedence for behavior. We all tend to act in much the same way that we have in past circumstances. The best predictor of future performance is past behavior. At the same time, our behavior tends to be environmentally contingent. Within a particular context, we base our behavior on past actions in the same or similar context. This is why it is important to attend to good thinking practices across a variety of contexts and to the transfer of those practices to new situations.[10]

Practice is not just for the cultivation of ability, however. It is also related to the cultivation of sensitivity. There is an ability-like component to sensitivity—the ability to recognize occasions for a particular behavior across various occasions with minimal cues. By identifying opportunities for different types of thinking, or identifying thinking shortfalls in literature or in their own day-to-day experience, students can practice sensitivity to occasions. Development of such sensitivity is also an important factor in cultivating environmental triggers that can support transfer and encourage the setting of precedents.

FROM MODELS TO PRACTICE

As useful as these theoretical models of the nature of dispositions and the delineation of factors needed to support their development may be, both practice and theory benefit from the examination of actual on-the-ground examples of practice. Actual cases of teachers engaged in trying to promote thinking provide us with pictures of effective practice that illuminate theoretical ideas. At the same time, these pictures of practice help us identify the challenges involved in developing students' intellectual character, and they help us discover how best intentions can at times lead us astray. Finally, case studies help us better understand the human dimension of any effective practice. Teachers do not merely implement programs or apply instructional practices, they interpret them through the filter of their own values and beliefs. As long as we ignore the important role that teachers' background knowledge, values, and beliefs play, efforts to change what happens in classrooms are likely to be just superficial tinkering.

In the second part of this book, we examine the work of several middle school teachers as they seek to develop their students' intellectual character. This is not a study of a special program or teachers' efforts to implement a specific curriculum. Rather, it is an examination of the day-to-day instructional practice of teachers trying to cultivate students' thinking in the midst of their efforts to build understanding, cover the state and district standards, get through the textbook, and prepare students for the following year. Through these examples, we begin to see what it means to teach for intellectual character.

Key Ideas for Developing Intellectual Character

ACTING SMART:
CLOSING THE ABILITY-ACTION GAP

- *The Explanatory Nature of Dispositions.* We have a rich language of dispositions that is largely descriptive in nature. However, dispositions also explain behavior. Dispositions are the mechanisms by which we bridge the action-ability gap.

- *Inside Dispositions.* Dispositions are about more than a desire or inclination to act. They consist of a general inclination consisting of values, beliefs, and underlying temperaments; an awareness of occasions for appropriate action; motivation to carry out action; and the requisite abilities and skills needed to perform.

- *Helping Dispositions Take Hold.* Dispositions develop in a meaningful sociocultural context in which we internalize external triggers—such as prompts, scaffolds, rewards, incentives, and encouragement—over time. Dispositions aren't so much taught as they are enculturated.

- *Environmental Considerations.* Acquiring the thinking dispositions that embody intellectual character depends on the presence of ongoing salient models of thinking, consistent expectations for thinking within the environment, explicit instruction in thinking to develop ability, and the opportunity for practice and reinforcement within meaningful contexts.

PART TWO

Fostering Intellectual Character in Our Schools

CHAPTER FOUR

First Days, First Steps
Initiating a Culture of Thinking

Having spent most of my life as either a student or a teacher, I've come to mark my years according to the school calendar. For me, the official new year begins sometime between the last weeks of August and the first week of September just as the summer nights begin to cool and the days become noticeably shorter. Compared to the sense of ritual, freshness, and anticipation that mark the beginning of a new school calendar, January 1 seems a rather pale imitation of a year's beginning. I'll gladly forgo the champagne and midnight toasts in exchange for all the newness, anxiety, and expectation that accompany those first days of the school year.

For me, it is the sense of newness and possibility connected with the beginning of the school year that most excites. As a child, the need for new pencils, notebooks, and folders meant trips to the store and a seemingly endless number of choices to be made among the variety of consumer options presented. There was also the newness of textbooks and desks that, no matter how worn and used, nonetheless promised a fresh experience and opportunity. There was the newness of teachers, classmates, and seating charts that made it possible to envision a new world inside the walls of the classroom. Amidst all this newness, anything could happen; one could even become a whole new person.

Tempering this excitement and enthusiasm were the feelings of anxiety that tend to accompany all beginnings but especially school beginnings. My first days of school usually were preceded by vivid dreams accentuating all of my anxieties and insecurities: of getting lost in a new building, of being late, of being singled out, of not being smart enough, and of being under the thumb of mean and crusty teachers. Of course, buried beneath these dreams were my hopes—and the hopes of every student, I believe—of being accepted, included, encouraged, and looked after. Although anxiety is heightened by newness, it quickly becomes tempered by the establishment of routines and the growing familiarity of surroundings. Thus, as the excitement of the new wears off, it is replaced by the comfort of the familiar with its own rewards and motivations.

Nestled within and closely associated with these feelings of newness and anxiety lay a sense of expectation: What will this class be like? What is to come? What will be required here? In opening the classroom door each fall, these are the questions all teachers must answer in the first days of school. Indeed, all teachers provide answers to these questions, whether they know it or not. They answer these questions in their introductions to the class, through the routines they establish, and in the way they allocate classroom time. Often, teachers answer these questions as much by what they leave unsaid and unattended to as by what they deliberately try to convey. Although the first days of school will always be a celebration of the new and an effort at lessening anxieties, these days are first and foremost an expression of expectations that set the direction and establish the norms for the rest of the year.

In this chapter, I examine how teachers go about answering the question of expectations for their students and, in doing so, lay the foundation for enculturating thinking dispositions and developing students' intellectual character. I present four practices, emerging from the collective work of the teachers I studied, that are particularly relevant to establishing a culture of thinking at the beginning of the school year:

- Conveying a sense of the history of thought and the power of ideas

• Jumping into a big subject-matter issue

• Laying a foundation for ongoing dialogue

• Setting an agenda of understanding

Although not a definitive list of effective beginning-of-the-year practices, these four practices highlight some of the ways in which teachers' actions during the first days of school can send positive messages about thinking and its importance in the life of the classroom. As discussed in Chapter Three, these expectations initially act as external stand-ins for students' own inclination toward thinking. Over the course of the year—through ongoing reinforcement, encouragement, and repetition—students gradually internalize these expectations.

My goal here is to paint a vivid and rich picture of each practice in action so that its spirit, intent, and nature can be easily reinterpreted and applied to new situations. To do this, I have selected examples that I feel are clearest and most robust. However, in presenting my findings in this way, a bit of the context of each teacher's experience and practice is necessarily lost. I regret this because I have come to know each of these individuals as engaging teachers who deserve to be celebrated and understood in their own right and not merely as a collection of disaggregated actions. My hope is that more of the full character and personality of each teacher will emerge over the course of the next few chapters and that readers will come to appreciate the individuality and intellectual character of each of these educators as much as I have.

CONVEYING A SENSE OF THE HISTORY OF THOUGHT AND THE POWER OF IDEAS

When students first step into a classroom, they receive a series of messages about the teacher's aesthetic, organizational abilities, interests, and attitudes toward teaching and learning. The first two of these qualities are readily discernible in the arrangement of the room, strategic placement of posters on the wall, provision of supplies, use of charts and checklists for keeping track of the various rituals of school life, and finally the state of the teacher's desk. But the last two of these qualities, the teacher's interests and attitude toward teaching and learning, may not be so apparent. To discern these qualities, we look as much for what is present as what is not. We look at the content of what is up on the wall, not just its arrangement. We also look at how the physical environment of the classroom gets used and integrated into the instructional day. In this section, we look more closely at these components of the environment to better understand what a classroom that conveys an attitude and expectation of thinking actually looks like.

Questions and Quotes

Heather Woodcock's front chalkboard is ringed with messages strategically placed to engage students whose attention might be wandering. Mounted on construction paper above the chalkboard is a set of seven questions. These are big questions, universal questions, the kinds of questions that direct inquiry in the discipline, promote self-discovery, and speak to the human condition. These are Heather's guiding questions, designed to point the direction for her seventh graders' studies in humanities during the year. She has carefully crafted each question to capture the imagination, prompt discussion, and guide students' inquiry. Heather refers to these as her throughlines because they tie together all of her teaching in social studies and language arts throughout the year.[1] These seven questions are

- Why do people seek to discover what is unknown?
- How does learning about other cultures help us understand ourselves?
- What does it mean to "come of age," and how does it differ across culture, time, and gender?
- Can we all be individuals as equal parts of a whole?
- What keeps peoples of different cultures from living/working successfully together?
- How does reflection on your work and thinking help you understand?
- How do we find out the truth about things that happened long ago and far away? How do we see through bias?

While these questions outline the focus of the course, their posting serves to keep that focus alive in students' minds. With the questions so prominently displayed, students have the opportunity to ponder them at any moment.[2]

Heather also has other thinking aids posted around her room. On either side of the chalkboard, squeezed around a calendar and a homework sign-off station, is a series of quotes:

- A vision without action is a but a dream. Action without vision is a waste of time. But vision with action can change our lives. —Greg Henry Quinn

- Live in the now, and never worry alone.—Anne Nash

- You'll regret the things you don't do in life more than the things you've done wrong.—Anonymous

- Five hundred years ago a person in error was a person searching for the truth.—John Leinhard

- At times inactivity is preferable to mindless functioning. —Jenny Holzer

These quotes and many others scattered around the room speak to the mental life in some way or another. Whether they be about the relationship between thought and action, the need for taking risks both in life and in thinking, or the call for introspection and awareness, these quotes serve both to inspire and to link students with thinkers of the past.

One of Heather's first weekend homework assignments also cultivates a link with past thinkers, as well as introduces students to the power of well-crafted words to reveal insights. For the assignment, students find and copy a quote that they like and feel speaks to them. Students then share these quotes with the class and explain the reasoning behind their selections. These quotes are added to Heather's collection, and they find a home on the walls of her classroom.

The Walls Teach

As in Heather's room, the walls of Chris Elnicki's eighth-grade social studies classroom are designed to be vehicles of instruction. In one corner is a display of historical photographs chronicling the industrialization of the United States. Chris uses these pictures to teach students about making inferences, spotting bias, and noticing details. Adjacent to this set of pictures lies a series of laminated world maps that students use to trace their ancestry and learn about immigration. Around the corner, hidden behind the door, is a collection of political cartoons the students use to understand how serious public issues are often understood through analogy. Scattered throughout the room are posters that juxtapose what the Bill of Rights guarantees to U.S. citizens with pictures that show those rights being infringed on. Everywhere you look, there are maps, flags, and globes, either hanging from the ceiling or tacked on the walls.

Intermingled with these teaching displays are an assortment of personal touches: a Jiminy Cricket doll atop the chalkboard and a collection of hats covering the top of a filing cabinet. Family pictures are tacked to the wall behind Chris's desk and beside them hang a series of Colorado license plates that he has collected over the years. And as in Heather's classroom, there are quotes. Above the windows hangs the banner, "A ship in port is safe, but that's not what ships are built for." Above the chalkboard are a set of directions for learning, "When you're searching for new information, be an explorer. When you're turning your resources into new ideas, be an artist. When you're evaluating the merits of an idea, be a judge. When you're carrying your idea into action, be a warrior." Next to Chris's desk, a small poster reads, "I'd rather know some of the questions than all of the answers."

Chris's displays serve much the same purpose as Heather's guiding questions. They provide a road map for the year. Acting as a kind of visual gestalt, these bulletin board displays convey to students the kinds of issues, topics, and ideas that are going to be important in this classroom throughout the year. These displays also provide glimpses into the issues, ideas, and thinking of others, revealing the importance of perspective taking and point of view. The quotes that Chris has chosen send important messages about expectations for students' thinking, emphasizing the importance of curiosity, risk taking, and ways of constructing meaning.

How This Practice Supports the Development of Intellectual Character

On the surface, the kinds of classrooms Heather and Chris have designed are not unusual; they have not turned their rooms into spaceships or replicas of the Mayflower. However, they have created places that send important messages about both the content to be investigated and the role that thinking plays in that endeavor, a practice that is not as common as one might hope. By establishing the norms and values of the classroom, these teachers' displays represent the first steps toward developing students' general inclination toward thinking.

In contrast, most classroom displays more typically convey messages of discipline, posting the class or school rules; rote learning, displaying steps and procedures; external authority, listing district or state standards; or work motivation, inspiring messages designed to keep students going. Although these messages are not inappropriate or wrong, they do not necessarily serve an agenda of thinking and may unintentionally undermine it by promoting a "work" rather than a "learning" orientation toward the class (Marshall, 1987, 1988). A work or performance orientation is associated with a focus on obtaining external reinforcement or favorable evaluations for one's performance. Such environments focus on getting the work done, completing assignments, keeping busy, and collecting points or grades for that work. This kind of environment can become dangerous to learning when the nature of that work, its quality, and its significance are never questioned or seriously examined, when the focus becomes work for work's sake. I'll take up this issue of classroom orientations further in the last section of this chapter.

Unfortunately, more stark contrasts to the thinking-rich environment presented by Chris and Heather can also be found. I once visited a middle school classroom in which totally different messages about the importance and nature of thinking were being sent. I had come to administer an assessment of students' thinking. Walking into the room, I was struck by how barren it was. There was very little to catch the eye or spark the imagination. The exception was one poster positioned prominently in the center of the back wall. The poster was a picture of a large gorilla slumped over with its head down and eyes closed. The caption of the picture read, "Thinking makes me tired." While struck by the irony of administering an assessment of thinking in the presence of this rather disheartening sentiment about thinking, I couldn't help but wonder how this message influenced students' day-to-day actions in the class. When those responsible for engaging students intellectually view thinking as hard and boring work, it must be especially difficult for students to develop their inclination to use their thinking abilities well.

JUMPING INTO A BIG SUBJECT-MATTER ISSUE

In a sense, everything and nothing happens on the first day of school. It is possible to look at the first day as merely one of logistics and introductions: teachers pass out materials; they assign desks and lockers; and everyone puts names to faces. However, these tasks, as simple and mundane as they are, also teach. Beginning-of-the-year tasks and how they are handled convey not only the teacher's organizational abilities and confidence but his or her values and priorities. Because these tasks are not givens but represent choices on the part of the teacher, they communicate to students the teacher's passions and perspective with regard to teaching and learning. However, a logistical start is not the only way to kick off the school year. In this section, we look at what a nonlogistical type of first-day introduction looks like and what messages teachers convey when they plunge students right in to a big subject-matter issue.

Unmasking the Rules of Mathematics

There is a distinct lack of formality as John Threlkeld prepares to begin the first algebra class of the school year. He quickly introduces himself for the benefit of those students who don't know him, then calls out students' names. As he says each name, he looks around the room to locate the student and then points to him or her. Many of the faces are familiar to him. Throughout this process, John appears a bit disorganized, says he is having trouble with names and faces, comments on not being able to find his overhead projector, and in general breaks just about every rule that many so-called experts dictate for an effective start of the school year. Matter-of-factly, John presents a problem culled from the newspaper—a puzzle in which you move only one digit in the false equality $62 - 63 = 1$ in order to make it true. Without much discussion, he says that the problem is "out there." "There's something for you to ponder. Something interesting to think about," he remarks. He encourages students to bring in other interesting problems for the class, noting that this one was given to him just today by a student. He tells students that he likes problems such as these and that, over the course of the year, they will find him to be an eccentric and unabashed geek.

In this brief exchange, John has set the tone. While he appears to be disorganized and rather lax in attending to details, he also comes across as affable, good-natured, trusting, and approachable. Perhaps more importantly, he gives the impression of being on top of the content, eager to pursue mathematics with students, and ready to push their thinking. John finds mathematics engaging, and he becomes animated just talking about a problem. His passion comes through loud and clear. It also is clear that he is in charge of the class and not a slave to the textbook, which he never mentions during the hour.

John tells the class that he would like to begin with a problem from *The Phantom Tollbooth*—a book by Norton Juster that many of the students remember reading in sixth grade. John flashes a page of the book on the overhead projector and reads it quickly. In the story, the main character, Milo, explains how mathematics can make things disappear and, by way of example, presents the following problem:

$$4 + 9-2 \times 16 + 1 \div 3 \times 6-67 + 8 \times 2-3 + 26-1 \div 34 + 3 \div 7 + 2-5 =$$

Upon seeing the problem, another character, described as always first to shout out a wrong answer, says the answer is seventeen. John asks if anyone in the class is like that. A few giggles and John adds, "Don't ever be afraid to give a wrong answer. Never be afraid to give a wrong answer that you have thought about." Returning to the problem, John asks the class, "What does this equal? Work in pairs to come up with an answer." Under his breath, he adds, "I suppose that I should figure this out myself" and heads to the board.

After a few minutes, John calls out, "I want to hear what you got."

A student says that she may be wrong.

John says he doesn't care; he wants to hear it: "I really am quite serious. I want you to tell me what you get. Yeah, the bottom line is that one is right and one is wrong, at least in algebra, but I want you to try out your ideas and not be the least hesitant to say, 'Here is what I got.' And by the way, maybe we're all wrong." He writes down her solution and then quickly puts other answers up on the board. There are soon as many answers as student pairs.

Before delving into a discussion of the problem, John interjects, "I might as well add my answer to the list as well." A few students moan, and John adds, "Not that it's right but because I think it's wrong." In this gesture, John both joins the community of learners as a coparticipant and ratifies the task as an authentic problem, one in which the teacher does not secretly know the answer. John comments that most of the answers are different but hastens to add, "Math is not a democracy, and whatever gets the most votes doesn't win. There has to be a proven answer."

John leads the class in working through the arithmetic of the problem together, and immediately there is a discussion of order of operations, a topic the class has already recognized as the key to the problem. John reviews the mnemonic device, PEMDAS, used for remembering order of operations and recounts the first time he was introduced to this now familiar memory tool, thus placing himself once again in the role of a learner. Before long, students have discovered their various errors, and a communal answer begins to emerge as $-47\,{}^{143}/_{238}$.

Students begin to use their calculators to check their answers, but rather than getting confirmation, a new confusion arises as students get different answers. John uses this confusion to introduce the main point of the class, "It is interesting to notice something. Someone programmed your calculator. We have at least a dozen different kinds of calculators in here, and almost all did the same thing. Did they have to do that?" The students quickly shake their heads in disagreement, and John continues, "Mathematicians have generally adopted this agreement among themselves, scientists too, about what is meant by order of operations. If not, what would happen?"

"You'd get different answers," a student volunteers.

"Right, so there is a general agreement. In math, it is pretty important that two people doing the same problem can arrive at the same answer, so we have order of operations. We talked about those rules. What were they?" As students shout out the rules, John writes on the board: "Parentheses, Exponents, Multiplication and Division, and then Addition and Subtraction, PEMDAS."

Pausing and turning to the class, John asks quietly, "Who thought of those rules? Why all that instead of doing it Milo's way, from left to right?" There is silence, and then John begins again, "I don't know the answer to that. I don't know the answer to that, and I haven't been able to find out. But I have some places that I might look. I think that at some time in the evolution of math, Milo's way was right. . . . Could we do it another way? Could we do things in a different order?"

A student volunteers a tentative answer, "Well, it depends. If we could get everyone to agree."

"OK, it's called a grassroots effort," John adds as he expands on the student's idea. "We would have to convince others that our way is better, or we could treat ourselves as a closed society. The real point here is that that set of rules is an incredibly arbitrary thing. What does *arbitrary* mean?"

"No good reason for it," a student volunteers.

John quickly adds, "That's right. *Arbitrary* means that it doesn't really matter as long as everybody agrees on it."

From the side of the room, a student offers his evaluation of the order of operations rule: "I think that parentheses have to come first because that is the only reason to have them. It just gets too confusing otherwise."

John writes the student's assertion on the board and adds to the class, "Think about what he is saying."

The student continues with his argument, "Well, if you had another rule, like do multiplication first, and you had the problem . . . well, something like, 2 + 4 (6 + 4 × 2). If multiplication had to come first, you'd be confused because you're supposed to multiply 4 times the quantity 6 + 4 × 2, but you don't know what that is."

"Think about what he is saying," John reiterates. "His declaration was, hypothetically, multiplication first, but unless you know what *this* is, what do you do? You've got two multiplications, but which one do you do first and how? You see the dilemma, I hope. I've thought about this, and I don't see any way around having parentheses first."

Another student chimes in, "I think that parentheses only exist because we have order of operations. You wouldn't need them otherwise. That's the whole point."

"Yeah," a girl sitting in the back row adds, "they just group things for you. Like, sometimes you need to think of a group of numbers going together. If you look back at the original problem, there weren't actually any parentheses, but you could put them in to show how you grouped the operations in your head."

Still another student enters the debate, "Well, what about exponents? It seems like exponents could come first."

John tosses the student's comments back to the group, "Let's think about that. It's a good question." He then writes "2 + 4 (6 + 4 × 2)^3" and asks, "How would you do that?"

The student examines the problem and gathers her thoughts, "Oh, I guess you would still have to do the parentheses first or just not have them at all."

Another student picks up on this point and brings the conversation back around to the main point, "But the argument is why have order of operations at all, why not just go left to right and forget about parentheses?"

"Just do it Milo's way, you mean?" John clarifies and then begins to sum up the discussion, "Great stuff. You're all causing me to think about this more. I'll have to go home and see what I can come up with. That was good stuff. What I am going to ask you to do tonight is to go home and play with this some more. One of the things that you are going to play with is this kind of idea about order of operations. Instead of PEMDAS, why not PESMAD? What you are going to be doing tonight is experiment with different configurations of order of operations to see what you come up with. This was a great class. I love these kinds of discussions."

Learning About Perspective

For Susan McCray's seventh graders, humanities class is a new experience. Not only is the course title new and unfamiliar, but for many, this is their first multi-age class in which they work alongside eighth graders. For this reason, Susan uses the first day to introduce students both to each other and to the course as a whole. After a brief introduction in which students interview and introduce each other, Susan asks for an eighth-grade student to explain what humanities is all about.

A student volunteers, "It's a mix of social studies and English. Last year, we learned about the Holocaust and discrimination."

"I like how you captured the essence," Susan responds, then turns to the rest of the class, "What other kinds of work do we do in humanities?" Several students raise their hands and talk about the different kinds of projects, performances, and response journals they did last year. As Susan elaborates on each of these and begins to tell the class what new topics they will focus on this year, another teacher quietly enters the room and goes to Susan's desk. Susan continues her explanation but glances frequently at the teacher in the back of the room who is now rummaging through desk drawers. Susan stops for a moment and asks the teacher, "Can I help you?"

"No," the teacher responds, "I'm just looking for that book that I gave you."

Susan goes back to her explanations, keeping one eye on the visitor in the back of the room. She starts to explain that this year they will be exploring issues around immigration but then pauses and once again directs her attention to the teacher in the back of the room, "Can I help you out?"

"No, I'm all set. I just wanted to get the book. Dave [the principal] told me to come up and get it," the woman cheerfully replies as she continues to go through stacks of papers on Susan's desk.

A bit ruffled, Susan responds more firmly, "But I told you that I have the book. It's my book, . . . and I'm trying to teach class." Sensing Susan's growing tenseness, the class begins to follow the exchange between the two teachers more closely. Heads move back and forth between Susan at the front of the room and the other teacher in the back.

Matter-of-factly, the other teacher stops going through the desk and responds to Susan, "Yeah, I know, but Dave told me to come and get it. He gave the book to me, so . . ."

In a firm but calm tone, Susan tries to put an end to the interruption, "OK, I'd rather you not look through my desk. I'd really rather you . . . We can talk about this later."

Politely and cheerfully, the teacher heads for the door and answers Susan, "OK, no problem. Dave told me to come and get it."

With obvious displeasure, Susan responds, "Well, this has been ongoing, and we really need to work it out. But I'd rather not get into it now." The fellow teacher, still in a calm manner, responds as she exits, "OK, we can talk about it later."

With the interruption over, Susan returns to her discussion of course themes and projects but quickly stops herself. "I'm sorry. I'm distracted. This has just been an ongoing thing. I hate to pull you all into this, but what did you all just see?"

A few students eagerly volunteer, "You mean like she just totally ignored you and went through your desk!" Another student offers, "You want me to check and see if she stole anything?"

Susan shares with the students her dilemma around the incident and asks for their help, "I need to bring this up with Dave, and I don't want to have just my account. Would you all do me a favor? It would really help me out if you could just jot down what it was that you saw." After a pause, she adds, "I guess this is appropriate. I mean, it is humanities class, and we do a lot of different kinds of writing in humanities."

Students quickly get to work and ask Susan a variety of questions that show their engagement in and concern about the incident: "Do you really not like her?" "What's her name?" "Is it really your book or hers?" "How long have you been fighting?" "Is she going to get in trouble?"

A few students, sensing a setup, ask, "Did you plan this?"

Susan responds that she knows it sounds weird, but she could really use their help on this.

As the students begin to finish their writing, Susan asks if anyone would be willing to share what they saw. Most of the accounts are brief, but several students have picked up an amazing amount of detail. Susan remarks on how helpful the details are to figuring out what really happened. As students share, Susan points out some of the differences in the accounts: how the other teacher was characterized, what details were noticed, and what some people saw as fact and some saw as more ambiguous.

At the end of the discussion, a student asks, "Why did you want us to write it down?"

At this point, Susan admits that the whole incident was indeed set up. A few students are completely surprised, whereas others smile at the confirmation of what they suspected. Susan asks the students why they think she did this and what the activity might have to do with humanities.

A few students venture a guess, "Well, it was descriptive writing," one student offers.

Susan confirms this aspect of the activity and adds, "And that involves being able to look closely."

Another student offers a more down-to-earth explanation, "You wanted to teach us not to go near your desk."

Susan laughs and acknowledges that that's a reason she hadn't thought about but that the incident might have had that effect.

Susan then explains her rationale to the class: "This was a more interesting way of introducing you to what humanities is all about. Part of it is developing good observation skills: being aware of what is going on around you, being able to really describe that, to document it, but then also to be conscious of the perspective you bring to things. It seemed in this situation that you all pretty much decided that she was doing something she shouldn't do. Why do you have that perspective?"

Students offer various explanations: "Because you were yelling at her to get out of your desk." "Because you're our teacher." "Because you put it into our heads."

"How did I do that?" Susan asks.

The student elaborates by reading from his account, "When you said, 'This has been an ongoing thing, and you don't like it,' that made us think she was a bad person, that she kept doing this."

Susan picks up on this, "What else would you need to know to really analyze this situation to figure out who was right or wrong? What would you want to know?"

Several students respond in chorus, "Her side."

With this, Susan launches into a more complete explanation of the activity's purpose,

> A big piece of this activity is how much we need to always be conscious of perspective, about whose side we are seeing. History is really people's stories. It is things that happen. It is events like this. This is now

a piece of history. It is an event that happened, and the history is how people choose to record those events. We all recorded those events differently. And if she had had a group of her friends here, they might have recorded it differently than we would. So we need to be conscious of the perspective of people who are writing our history. One of the things I want you to be aware of is what is going on around you, to be critical thinkers. I want you to be willing to look at a situation, a text or a piece of writing, and look at it critically. To dig deeply into trying to understand it and understand the different perspectives represented there and the different perspectives represented in this room. We need to talk those things out. What were you thinking and why? That is what this little scenario represents.

How This Practice Supports the Development of Intellectual Character

Both John's and Susan's classes are a big departure from the way most teachers begin the school year. Instead of the usual review of rules and procedures, both teachers jump right into the middle of big subject-matter issues. For John, it is: Where does knowledge and truth come from in mathematics? What is the source of the mathematical rules we learn? For Susan, it is: How does perspective shape history and our personal understanding of events? By starting class this way, teachers give students not just a sense of what the course will cover but how the course will actually feel and how they will go about their learning.

These first-day introductions sensitize students to important subject-matter issues and ways of thinking. Susan was sensitizing students to an awareness of perspective, encouraging them to look for different sides of the story. John was sensitizing his students to the need to look beyond the surface of mathematical rules in order to develop a better understanding of and mastery over those rules. By asking his students to examine the sense of order of operations, John helps them to see that some mathematical rules are merely conventions, whereas others have a deeper basis in logical reasoning.

LAYING A FOUNDATION FOR ONGOING DIALOGUE

In addition to expectations about content and the types of thinking demanded, first days of school also establish norms of interaction between students and teachers. In these first moments, students learn how they are expected to participate in class. Is this a place where participation is limited to doing the homework, or is this a place that encourages expression of one's ideas and thinking? Is this a place where answers are shared and smartness assessed by one's contributions, or is this a place where ideas are explored? The questions teachers ask, the way they acknowledge responses, on whom they call, who is allowed to speak to whom, and when students are permitted to talk all send messages about the nature of participation and dialogue in a particular classroom. In this section, we look at how teachers encourage class dialogue that promotes full participation and supports learning and thinking.

Building a Climate of Respect

As Doug Tucker knows, encouraging a dialogue about ideas with and among students is seldom as simple as providing them the opportunity to do so. He also knows that his students face special challenges in creating and sustaining a classroom dialogue about ideas. His students' major experience of math classrooms is dominated by memory work and messages that participation means having the right answer or completing one's work quietly and on time. In addition, discipline and order have long been a major concern and focus of the faculty and administration at Doug's school. The result is that the school now exudes a sense of constant watchfulness and attention to student behavior. Staff members diligently enforce dress, language, and behavioral codes, giving the school an orderly and work-oriented feel. Although such discipline is critical to learning and reflects the dedication of the school to confront past disciplinary issues, the challenge now is maintaining order while loosening control and creating a more relaxed and comfortable climate.

The challenge Doug faces in creating and sustaining intellectual dialogue becomes fully evident the first week of school as he gives his students a warm-up problem to work on as they enter class. Not a routine type of problem, it is one that they must think about and consider carefully. They cannot simply apply an algorithmic procedure. As Doug notices the blank looks on students' faces, he tells them that they may talk about the problem with their neighbors. No one does. When Doug asks a few minutes later if anyone has a solution and is again treated to blank stares, he once again suggests that students talk about the problem. Still, the class remains silent.

It is not just that the warm-up problem is hard or that students have little experience in solving this type of problem; it is also that students are unfamiliar with how to have an open-ended, exploratory conversation. Most of their classroom conversations have been confirmatory, taking the form of sharing and confirming answers, or they have been monologues, stating one's position or opinion on a topic. Students' lack of experience in this area is compounded by the fact that an open-ended dialogue of this sort involves taking an intellectual risk in stating one's confusion or in putting forth ideas that might very well be wrong. Doug sets out early in the year to confront these challenges: his first step is establishing a relaxed and friendly climate of respect.[3]

"Let's talk about expectations," Doug says to his students the first day of class. "The number one thing is this is a safe classroom. What does that mean?"

Several students offer explanations based on safety: no fighting, no horseplay, and so on. Doug continues to push until one student, whom Doug has had before in summer school, says that it means that no one should feel bad for asking questions. Doug acknowledges the student's contribution and asks the rest of the class to think about what that means in practice, adding, "Does that mean you can call someone stupid?"

Collectively, the class responds with a series of giggles and echoes of "No."

Doug elaborates on this point to make sure that students understand its importance. "If you do say that, I will be forced to stop class and give you a five-minute lecture. It goes like this." Doug launches into an explanation of peer pressure, the effects of that pressure on inhibiting students, and the importance of not disrespecting anyone. He ends this by smiling slyly and saying, "There is only one person in the room who is allowed to tease," as he points at himself.

Students fill in the missing word, "You."

Doug adds, "And there is only one person you can make fun of."

A bit more tentatively this time, the class once again says, "You."

With a deadpan delivery, Doug completes his sentence, "And that is Theresa." The class breaks into uproarious laughter, and Doug breaks out into a big grin. He winks at Theresa, a student he also knows from summer school, to confirm the joke.

The class clearly appreciates the joke, and it helps to temper the sometimes hard edge of the first day and the serious statements of expectations. The remark also humanizes Doug and helps to establish a mutuality in the classroom. Doug sums up the discussion by saying, "Seriously, I laugh at myself occasionally, but don't make this an unsafe place for anyone."

A popular student asks, "How can you laugh at yourself? Do you look in the mirror or something and start laughing?"

Assuming the false bravado of a kid picking a fight, Doug responds in mock seriousness, "Are you calling me ugly?" Again, the class erupts in laughter, and Doug attempts to answer the student's question more seriously, "If I do something funny, I'll laugh. I know it is hard for you to understand. I was a teenager once or twice myself. As a teenager, I know it is sometimes hard to look at yourself and laugh at something you did that was silly. But you will learn you will have more fun in life if you learn to laugh at yourself." Doug caps off the discussion, which has been laced with humor and goodwill, by returning to his main point: "But this has to be a safe room. We can laugh and have fun, but if it's not safe, no education is going to happen."

In this first-day discussion, it is not just the word *safety* that students hear. They also hear a message of mutuality and respect, and they feel the beginnings of a relationship being forged between the teacher and themselves. Within this context, students begin to feel safe to be themselves and to put forth their ideas. Doug continues to build this context over time by using humor, as well as storytelling and other means, to draw out students' ideas and encourage dialogue.

Structuring the Conversation

As students enter Chris Elnicki's room on the first day of class, he informs them that they have a task to do. On the front board, under the heading "First Things" is an assignment: "Look around the room and try to figure out what you can tell about me." While students glance about, Chris quickly takes roll then asks, "OK, what did you figure out about me or questions you have about me based on the room?"

Students raise their hands and begin to call out their findings. As they do, Chris presses them to explain the basis for their conclusions, to provide some evidence and explanation for their thinking.

One student offers the observation, "You're patriotic."

"What makes you think I am patriotic? What is the evidence?" Chris asks.

Pointing around the room, the student responds, "The flag, those posters."

Chris gently pushes the student's thinking by offering an alternative explanation, "OK, so I might be patriotic, or this may be a course that tries to teach patriotism. You can probably bet that an American studies course wouldn't be anti-American."

Another student, picking up on the expectation to provide evidence, points to a quote about the ship in the port hanging above the window—"A ship in port is safe, but that's not what ships are built for"—and observes, "You want us to be determined."

Chris acknowledges the evidence and the accuracy of the student's inference, "OK, there are a lot of quotes on the wall that deal with that. I like people to take risks. I don't want you to be a ship in the port."

Yet another student comments, "You have a sense of humor," and Chris returns to the expectation of evidence, asking the student, "Why?"

The student mentions the cartoons in the back of the room.

Chris elaborates, "OK, those are political cartoons, and we are going to be learning how to make sense of those. Anyone can identify the events in a political cartoon, but being able to interpret it and make sense takes some work."

As this exchange of observations backed up with evidence continues, Chris encourages the students in a new direction: "What can you tell about me? Am I married? Do I have kids?"

"Yes," a student responds, then cites the evidence, "Those pictures over there."

"Well, I might just be good at drawing pictures of tall girls and cats," Chris counters.

"Your wedding band," offers another student with a sense of pride.

In just a few short minutes, Chris has managed to get his students to do the work of introducing him, the curriculum, and the instructional focus of the year. He also has engaged them as thinkers and active participants by tapping into the natural inferential thinking everyone does within the first few minutes of entering a new space. However, this activity is not about first impressions so much as it is about making inferences based on evidence, a distinction that Chris wants students to make. Throughout this exchange, Chris establishes his expectations for participation and sets norms for sharing ideas. He also provides a structure for the kinds of dialogues he wants students to have in his class. In addition, the episode cues and enhances students' inclination toward inferential thinking while pointing to the kinds of occasions when it is important to be sensitive to one's own impressions and aware of other points of view or possibilities.

Chris builds on this introduction and reinforces the dialogue structure he has established by asking students to analyze some photographs. He walks students through a five-step process with one of the pictures on the back wall. Step one is for students to note their first reactions or impressions. Chris warns that the process can't stop there, that these impressions are often connected to feelings, and it is important to go beyond this emotional response. The next step is to collect data, to try and see what is actually there. Then, at the heart of the process are the next two steps, to draw inferences and generalizations about what is going on based on the evidence and one's prior knowledge. Finally, students are asked to make a conclusion, to tell what they learned.

Chris hands out pictures documenting child labor conditions and informs the class that examining these pictures is a first step in answering the other question on the board, "Why are you here?" For the next seven minutes, students look at and discuss a single photo with a partner, using the structure Chris has laid out. This structure then becomes the basis for short presentations from each group. Through this opening activity, Chris not only jumps into a big subject-matter issue—How do we know what we know in history?—but he has established a structure that students will use throughout the year for talking about ideas in history.

How This Practice Supports the Development of Intellectual Character

Thinking is largely an internal process. However, we reinforce and in some cases acquire patterns, approaches, styles, and types of thinking through social interaction and participation. Classroom dialogue provides models of thinking that students can appropriate and gradually incorporate into their personal repertoires. When these norms of dialogue are sustained in classrooms over time, they provide students the opportunities to try on different types of thinking and practice them in a supportive environment. Barbara Rogoff (1990) describes this process as an apprenticeship in thinking. The power of apprentice-ships is that one learns in context. Thus, not only does one cultivate abilities but the expectations of the situation cultivate inclination, and through the authentic work, one becomes sensitive to occasions. In this way, patterns of thinking are enculturated.

These social dialogues also expose students to the language of thinking, the actual words used to describe thinking processes, prod-ucts, states, and stances. This language not only serves a communica-tive function, allowing students to express their ideas and thoughts more effectively but also provides tools for regulating and shaping thought. As Shari Tishman and David Perkins (1997, p. 371) explain, "The words we have available to us influence the way we think about the world, including the inner world of our own mental life." In this way, the language of thinking provides a tool for students' own think-ing about thinking, or metacognition. In Chapter Seven, we will fur-ther explore the role of language in cuing or prompting an awareness of opportunities for thinking and thus the activation of dispositional behavior.

SETTING AN AGENDA OF UNDERSTANDING

We might group the activities of setting up the physical classroom environment, conducting the first day of class, and encouraging dia-logue under the general heading of agenda setting. These introduc-tory practices are important precisely because they help to establish the classroom agenda by telling students what to expect and sensitiz-ing them to the important issues and questions of the course. These initial actions communicate what teachers value most and are striv-ing to accomplish with their students. Although it is clearly the teacher's agenda being communicated, that agenda can seek to involve and engage students actively. Through their actions, teachers can com-municate that they value students as contributors and shapers of a joint classroom agenda.

By its very nature, a culture of thinking has to be tied to the estab-lishment of an agenda of understanding. After all, thinking doesn't occur in a vacuum. You have to have something to think about, a pur-pose or a goal that will cause you to engage your thinking abilities. Likewise, understanding cannot be developed without thinking. I am not talking here about the loose kind of "getting it" understanding that is so often the target of school instruction; this might be better referred to as having a superficial knowledge about a given topic. Rather, I am talking about the kind of understanding that is robust and that implicates personalized sense-making and a building up of connections, applications, and associations. Such understanding is performance oriented, marked by a use of associated knowledge and skills in novel situations. Developing such understanding necessarily means digging below the surface and thinking deeply about the meaning and implications of the ideas in question.

You might suppose that an agenda of understanding is the de facto agenda of all classrooms. Unfortunately, this isn't the case. Hermine Marshall (1988) has observed that classrooms have specific orientations: learning, work, or work avoidance. In a learning-oriented classroom, the goal is to develop an understanding of the course topics. In such classrooms, the work is purposeful and directed at making sense. A work orientation focuses on completing the work of the course. You can think of this as the mentality of getting it done or covering the material. Such classrooms are driven by completing assignments and moving on to the next task. In such settings, there is an implicit assumption that doing the work will in and of itself produce the learning, which, when the goal is skill development and consolidation, can happen. However, in work-oriented classrooms, both teachers and students tend to lose sight of the larger goals of education, allowing the means to become ends in themselves. Finally, a work-avoidance orientation leads students to see how much work they can avoid doing, often resulting from the teacher's inconsistency and lack of clear instructional goals. This game of subterfuge becomes the agenda of the class. A less sinister version of this orientation can be found in classrooms where there is an unwritten compromise in which, in exchange for the teacher's not pushing too hard or asking too much, students agree to remain generally complacent and compliant.

Of course, students bring their own motivations and orientations toward school with them as well. Some may be more oriented to learning, whereas others are intent on either completing or avoiding the work. However, these basic orientations are often fostered by past school experiences, and teachers can do a lot to bend students to their will by setting and sustaining their own well-focused agenda. In this final section, we look at how, in addition to the practices mentioned in the previous sections, teachers set an agenda of understanding early in the school year.

Focusing on Guiding Questions

On the third day of school, Heather Woodcock directs her students to the seven guiding questions (see p. 58) posted above the chalkboard: "I mentioned these the other day, and I called them throughlines. What these questions are are questions we are going to return to throughout the year. All of these questions can be connected in many, many ways to what we are studying in here and to our day-to-day lives. They can be connected to history, to literature, science, and math in a lot of different ways."

Heather tells her students that she doesn't want to say any more about the questions until they have thought about them. She informs students that for the next fifteen minutes they will select a question to write about: "What I want you to start doing today is to start thinking about one of these questions. . . . The important thing in thinking about these questions is to think, to explore, and to dig deeply into them and find out more than just one answer to them. Figure out what are the different possibilities for each of these questions." To help students select a question to explore, Heather encourages students to "choose a question that interests you obviously. Don't chose one that doesn't intrigue you, and I am not expecting all of these to intrigue you. Choose the one that you think has the most depth and the most richness for you."

Before students get to work, Heather explains more about the role the questions will play in the class's studies this year, "We will go back to these questions throughout the year, and probably each of you will become a specialist in at least one of them. As the year goes on, you all will see how they connect to our studies and to the literature we are reading. But for now, I don't want you to worry about it. For now, what I want you to do is to think about how you connect or think about any one of those questions."

For the next fifteen minutes, students write their thoughts on a sheet of paper Heather has passed out just for this purpose. Occasionally, they have questions, and a few students want to be sure they are completing the assignment correctly.

One student asks Heather to read hers with the explanation, "I'm not sure if this is off the subject?"

Heather offers her assurance, suggesting, "What you want to do with these questions is let them move you in different directions. You might examine that for a while and then move to something else." To the rest of the class, Heather adds, "In answering the question you have chosen, you may want to ask more questions. That is always a part of figuring something out. Asking more questions, going further."

After fifteen minutes, Heather stops the class. "It's OK if you didn't quite finish up what you had to say. In fact, I hope you have more that you could say. . . . I'm curious what you all came up with and what direction you took these questions. Jennifer, what question did you select?"

Jennifer tells the class that she wrote about the first question, "Why do people seek to discover what is unknown?" A number of other students in the class have also selected this question, and a rapid-fire discussion ensues in which students share their thinking. Jennifer shares what initially prompted her to select the question, "Well, because if no one ever sought out new things and what they didn't know, then the world would never change. Things would just stay the same. You wouldn't have cures for sickness or anything."

Heather responds to Jennifer's take on the question, then encourages responses from others, "OK, so you are looking at outcomes. What about other people who thought about that one. Why do you think people do it? Why? What drives them. Sam?"

"If people didn't discover the unknown, then it would be boring. But discovering makes it more interesting," Sam offers.

Heather challenges Sam's response and pushes his thinking, "OK, but that takes work. Wouldn't it just be easier to sit back and not do anything, to just relax and enjoy life and not go through the bother. Wouldn't life be easier?"

Another student picks up the challenge, "But I think it is human nature to challenge yourself. And to go beyond what is there. It is just that people get things out of challenging themselves."

Heather reframes the student's response, "So you think what drives it is human nature?" The discussion moves into the role of curiosity: how it develops, how it is sustained, and what things might kill it. One student offers the observation that curiosity helped humans to evolve. Heather remarks that the role of curiosity will come up in their studies, "That's going to be very interesting as we think about the Renaissance. We'll be looking at how things changed so quickly and why."

The discussion continues for most of the period. At the end of the hour, as Heather collects students' writing, she tells the class, "You will be returning to the question you selected and to the other ones throughout this year. We'll keep thinking and writing about them."

How This Practice Supports the Development of Intellectual Character

By setting an agenda of understanding, teachers communicate an expectation of thinking that helps foster students' inclination toward thinking. A focus on understanding also encourages them to monitor their understanding, a metacognitive process. In addition, understanding tends to highlight and directly pull into play various types of thinking dispositions, such as

- Curiosity: What's this all about? What's behind this?
- Open-mindedness and perspective taking: What's another way of looking at this?
- Being skeptical and intellectually careful: What's the evidence for this? How might my understanding be wrong?

When students and the teacher know that the class will be about more than memory work, these types of thinking more naturally find their place in the day-to-day business of the classroom.

THE IMPORTANCE OF THE FIRST DAYS OF SCHOOL

The four practices I introduced in this chapter were the following: (1) conveying a sense of the history of thought and the power of ideas, (2) jumping into a big subject-matter issue, (3) laying a foundation for ongoing dialogue, and (4) setting an agenda of understanding. These represent a set of effective tools and approaches that teachers use in establishing a culture of thinking. However, the specifics of each practice is ultimately less important than its intent. All four practices help develop students' inclinations to use their thinking abilities by establishing clear expectations for thinking.

Although the four elements of dispositional behavior that we discussed in Chapter Three—ability, inclination, awareness, and motivation—interact in a dynamic way and cannot always be addressed separately in instruction, teachers aiming to build students' intellectual character tend to focus early in the school year on developing students' inclinations to think. These expectations for thinking provide a foundation on which teachers can build throughout the year.

It is a truism of education that the best predictor of how the school year will progress in any particular classroom is the first week of school. Although this adage has its basis in school effectiveness research, a program of research focused primarily on issues of classroom management conducted in the 1970s and 1980s, it seems particularly apt to the creation of a culture of thinking that supports the development of students' intellectual character. Although such a culture must be built up over time and reinforced day by day, teachers must lay claim to it during the first days of the school year. Day one is the time when expectations for social and intellectual behavior are set and when students assess the orientation of the classroom toward learning and work. It is also the time when trust is built, mutual respect is established, routines and structures for learning are introduced, and initial patterns of thinking emerge.

Because the culture of the classroom has not yet been established, virtually every action a teacher takes during the first days of school sends messages about expectations and values, which will in turn influence the development of students' inclination. Consider the simple act of giving a quiz. When John Threlkeld gives his students their first quiz of the year, it contains just four questions to be completed in twenty minutes. In contrast, the first quiz given by Karen, a teacher I observed whose classroom has a well-developed work orientation, comes from the textbook and contains eleven questions. Most of the class completes these questions in just five minutes. The point here is not that John allows more time per question but that the questions he gives require more time and thought to complete. The structure of John's quiz contains an expectation of thinking versus memorizing. Thus, the choice of what to ask on a quiz not only provides students with a chance to exercise their thinking abilities, it conveys an expectation that they do so. The feedback provided to students on the quiz also sends messages about what is valued and what gets counted. To the extent that the teacher attends to students' thinking rather than to their memorization of answers, he or she further reinforces the message that thinking matters.

As all travelers know, it is much easier to begin one's trip pointed in the right direction than to make a major correction later in the journey. It is worth noting that in each of the teaching examples I have shared, the course each teacher worked to set was shaped by introspection about the kind of classroom each wanted to have and the patterns of thinking and interaction each wanted to elicit from students. This map of the ideal classroom culture then guided each teacher in his or her choice of how to begin the school year. In Part Three of this book, we look more closely at each teacher's introspection to understand how values and beliefs shape teaching.

In the intervening chapters, we examine ways that teachers build on and sustain the culture of thinking they have worked to establish during the first weeks of school as they go about the task of developing students' intellectual character. Our examination loosely maps on to the key dimensions of dispositional development—developing ability, nurturing inclination and motivation, and cuing awareness—while highlighting key instructional practices evident in these thoughtful classrooms.

———✿——— **Key Ideas for Developing Intellectual Character**

IN THE CLASSROOM:
CREATING A CULTURE OF THINKING

- *Conveying a Sense of the History of Thought and Power of Ideas.* The physical environment of the classroom sends messages about what a teacher values, the role of thinking in the classroom, students' responsibility for learning and motivation, the types of questions and problems the class will explore, and the power of ideas. Quotes, posters, guiding questions, pictures, and tools and equipment can be used to establish the norms and values of the classroom.

- *Jumping into a Big Subject-Matter Issue.* Exploring central issues, purposes, or tensions in a subject area gives students a sense of both what and how they will learn. Such activities sensitize students to important aspects of learning in the subject. Although the teacher might explore many different types of issues, it is often useful to address what it means to know and learn in the subject: What does it mean to be a reader, to act like a scientist, or to do math?

- *Laying a Foundation for Ongoing Dialogue.* Supporting an intellectual dialogue about ideas takes work. A climate of respect must be built in which students feel comfortable sharing their thoughts and opinions. Structures and protocols need to be established that will guide the discussion, keep it focused, and direct students' thinking. Such structures might take the form of asking students to elaborate on their points, provide evidence and justification, explore the reasons that things appear the way they do, and consider implications.

- *Setting an Agenda of Understanding.* The development of understanding depends on deep thinking, and thinking itself must be purposeful and focused on some content, issue, or problem. Unfortunately, not all classrooms are focused on understanding and thinking. Developing a learning orientation involves sending messages, through the opportunities created and the discussions initiated, that the teacher's chief aim is to cultivate students' understanding.

CHAPTER FIVE

Thinking Routines
Creating the Spaces and
Structures for Thinking

A s a student teacher struggling to master the mysteries of life inside a classroom, I would spend hours poring over books and resources to devise what I hoped would be interesting and engaging lessons for the second graders in my charge. Although this planning was important and certainly necessary to my overall professional development, it prepared me less for assuming responsibility for a classroom than I imagined. No, my best preparation for stepping into the role of teacher didn't come from devising interesting lessons or designing bulletin boards but from the time I spent watching and learning the routines of the classroom of which I was about to take charge.

There was a certain way we did things in Mrs. Baker's second grade, and I, probably more than any of the students, didn't want to violate those rules of operation. I paid careful attention to how students were expected to line up, the way the day began, how and when students were allowed to talk, what movement was and was not allowed, how papers were passed out, which responsibilities were considered perks and which were deemed punishments, how materials were to be used and stored, and how we moved from one activity to another. All this watchfulness took place in anticipation of the day that I would take over the class and be the one responsible for both initiating and reinforcing those routines. Looking back, I can see that the lessons I taught in Mrs. Baker's room frequently missed the mark—either because they were too ambitious and sprawling or because they were not directed to reach students where they were in their learning. However, because I had mastered the routines of the classroom, I generally was able to sustain a learning environment that allowed me to rebound from my mistakes and to make the necessary midcourse corrections.

Routines clearly play an important role in ordering and structuring the lives of the group of individuals coexisting in the small space known as a classroom. Anyone who has spent time in classrooms can attest to this. However, for teachers concerned with developing their students' intellectual character, the importance of routines extends beyond a managerial function. By specifying the guidelines by which learning interactions take place, routines act as a major enculturating force communicating the values of a classroom. Routines not only give a classroom a sense of order and smoothness but also contribute to its unique feel as an environment for learning. In this chapter, we look more closely at how routines act to orchestrate the intellectual space of the classroom and support the development of students' intellectual character. We first examine the general nature of routines and their various types before focusing on one particularly powerful type of routine, thinking routines, that teachers use to scaffold students' dispositional development.

THE FORM AND FUNCTION OF ROUTINES

What makes something a routine? How is a classroom routine different from other types of routines we are likely to run across in our lives—such as routines for brushing our teeth, grocery shopping, or planning a vacation? These everyday routines might be better thought of as rituals or habits because they tend to emerge slowly over time from our well-developed patterns of behavior. As rituals or habits, these practices tend not to be adopted explicitly nor to be necessarily tailored to meet their ends in the most efficient manner. In fact, our way of doing things often speaks more of preference and familiarity than of efficiency. In contrast, classroom routines tend to be explicit and goal-driven in nature. Their adoption usually represents a deliberate choice on the part of the teacher. Rather than emerging over time, classroom routines are more likely to be designed and taught overtly. Routines are crafted to achieve specific ends in what is generally expected to be an efficient and workable manner. Whereas rituals and habits can be adopted without our full awareness, classroom routines tend to be well known by all participants. To test this proposition, walk into any classroom and ask the students, as well as the teacher, to tell you about the routines they use for passing out papers, lining up, speaking in class, and so on.

The explicit and goal-driven nature of classroom routines leads us to a variety of additional features of routines. First, to keep them useful and efficient, routines tend to have only a few steps. Because everyone needs to quickly go about the tasks of lining up for lunch, passing out books, getting themselves into cooperative groups, or beginning a class, lengthy or complicated procedures are counterproductive. Second, by having only a few steps, routines are easy to learn and teach. They can almost always be introduced and reinforced in context without need for extensive elaboration or pedagogy. Third, when students fail to carry out routines fully or successfully, they can also be quite easily scaffolded by simply reminding or prompting the students to carry out the next step. Fourth, to achieve their ends in efficiently directing a common behavior or task, routines have to be used over and over again so that they become ingrained and can be activated quickly in an almost automatic, though not mindless, way. All these features of routines help us not only to identify routines at work in the classroom but also to better understand how particular routines operate in context. We explore how each of these features applies to thinking routines in more depth a bit later, but first we need to make a distinction between thinking routines and the other types of routines at work in a classroom.

We can group classroom routines into four broad categories:

- Housekeeping
- Management
- Discourse
- Learning[1]

Housekeeping routines manage movement and physical materials within the classroom. For example, students might be required to raise their hands and ask permission before using the pencil sharpener, to put their book bags in a certain location, or to line up in a particular fashion. In short, housekeeping routines represent rules and guidelines for living and working together as a group.

Management routines help students prepare for learning. They include such things as getting papers passed out, forming groups, coming to attention, and preparing for a discussion. For instance, at the beginning of a lesson, the teacher might assign one student from each table to go to the shelf and collect books for everyone at the table and then appoint another student to return them. Teachers at the primary school level often use a clapping pattern to call students back to attention. This is a management routine: its effect is to prepare students for the next episode of learning, but it is not a strong learning moment in and of itself.

Discourse routines orchestrate conversations between teachers and students. Examples include the norms for a class discussion, raising one's hand before speaking, procedures for listening and responding to the contributions of others, or guidelines a teacher might establish for the "author's chair" time in writers' workshops.

Currently, many teachers have begun to use conversation protocols in their professional conversations with colleagues as a way to help them look at and understand student work.[2] These protocols structure the discussion process by establishing a series of specific focuses to which the group attends in a step-by-step manner.

Finally, learning routines focus students' attention on the specific topic being studied. They could take the form of reading the lesson in the textbook, answering the questions that follow the reading, and checking in with the teacher if there are any problems. Other examples include the use of journals or note-taking procedures, a classroom debate about the interpretation of a passage, or procedures for reviewing and discussing homework.

In all cases, these routines are instrumental, designed to achieve specific goals in an efficient and productive manner. Because teachers need to get students' attention repeatedly throughout the day, it is useful for them to establish a routine for doing so. Likewise, because classes regularly engage in discussion, go over homework, line up, and gather information from texts, these tasks can be routinized. As the examples above demonstrate, routines tend to have only a few steps, are easy to learn and teach, can be easily scaffolded, and are used over and over again.

THINKING ROUTINES
A Special Type of Routine[3]

Although thinking routines have many similarities to other classroom routines, they differ qualitatively from these other types of routines in an important way. Whereas most routines direct overt behavior, thinking routines direct and guide mental action. We might view thinking routines as a particular subset of discourse or learning routines because learning or the discussion of ideas is the larger goal. But, you might ask, don't all learning or discourse routines involve thinking? Unfortunately, the answer is no. It is quite natural for a learning routine to involve thinking, but it doesn't have to do so. There can be non-thinking or thinking-minimal learning routines that seek to direct students' actions toward learning or discourse but do little to activate and support students' mental efforts.

What does it mean to have a routine designed to support learning but not necessarily support thinking? Here's an example: a teacher establishes the routine of reading each new book chapter in a round-robin fashion. This routine's purpose is to help students learn and is thus classified as a learning routine, regardless of its effectiveness. However, it is not a thinking routine because the practice, although it might involve thinking for some students, does not serve to encourage or actively support students' thinking. It is up to the students themselves to activate their own thinking in this situation. Doing so will certainly have benefits, and the teacher might even expect that such activation will take place. However, the routine itself does little to support or encourage mental engagement.

Now, let's look at the flip side of this situation. What would a thinking-rich learning routine look like? Before beginning a new science unit, a teacher might have his or her students collectively brainstorm all of the things they know about the topic and how they think it connects to other areas of science they have studied. This brainstorm might take the form of a class web or a list. This is the way the teacher regularly begins new units, and the class knows the process and can easily participate in the practice without much additional guidance. Such a practice would be classified as both a learning and a thinking routine. The larger purpose of the routine is still learning, but now the routine is targeted to actively encourage, involve, and support students' thinking. Specifically, the brainstorming and webbing routines facilitate students' making connections, generating new ideas and possibilities, and activating prior knowledge. The odds are that any student involved in the routine will be involved in these types of thinking as well.

Thinking routines generally adhere to the same criteria as other routines. They consist of a few steps, are easy to teach and learn, are easily supported, and get used repeatedly. But what do they look like when applied to thinking routines? How can these criteria help us understand and uncover examples of thinking routines as we look at our own practice and that of others?

We initially distinguished routines from habits or ways of doing things by talking about their explicit and instrumental nature. That is, routines are known by the group of learners and are designed to serve a specific purpose. The explicit nature of thinking routines is evidenced by their having names or labels—such as brainstorming, webbing, pro and con lists, Know-Want to know-Learned (KWL)—that allow us to easily recall them and put them in play. At the broadest level, thinking routines are purposeful because their overriding goal is to encourage, involve, and support thinking. But they serve more specific purposes as well. For example, we've discussed how brainstorming is useful in generating ideas and possibilities and how webbing is used to connect ideas and identify relationships. In activating a thinking routine, whether in the classroom or in one's own day-to-day functioning, the routine's specific purpose must be suited to the task. If we want to open up our thinking, we might engage in brainstorming. If we want to choose between options, we might develop a pro and con list. Thus, while still purposeful, thinking routines are more instrumental than are other routines. That is, thinking routines act as a means for achieving broader goals rather than as goals themselves. We can see this if we contrast the webbing routine with a lining-up-for-lunch routine. Lining up for lunch is its own goal, and performing the routine achieves that goal. In contrast, webbing is not a goal in and of itself, at least it shouldn't be thought of as such; it is a tool for connecting and organizing one's thoughts and ideas.

As we've seen, routines structure actions into a series of steps, our first criteria. For ease of use and retention, the number of steps is generally kept relatively short. This economy helps increase the routine's effectiveness and encourage its use. Many routines are even named and recalled by acronyms that refer to their steps, making them even easier to activate: KWL, for example, stands for a series three questions: What do you *know?* What do you *want* to know? What did you *learn?* CSQ—for claim, support, question—is another routine designed to help students consider evidence and reasons. This routine asks students to clearly identify a truth claim that they have heard or come across in some way, consider what specific evidence they have that supports the claim, and then consider what evidence or reasons they have to question the claim.

The fact that these routines have only a few steps makes them easy to teach, learn, and remember—an important quality of all routines but of particular importance to thinking routines. Complicated routines or cumbersome processes aren't of much use in the moment. Such procedures simply tend not to get used. To be most effective, thinking supports need to be streamlined so that users can easily call them to mind as they need them. David Perkins (1999) has dubbed this ease-of-access quality "action poetry," indicating that there is a certain brevity and elegance that helps the routine stick in our minds and simplifies its recall when we want to put it into action. A problem-solving routine developed by my colleague Shari Tishman (personal communication, October 17, 2001) demonstrates the point. The routine involves three steps: Say what. Say why. Say other things to try. The routine is simple and straightforward, doesn't need a lot of elaboration, and has a certain catchiness to its wording that makes it easy to recall.

However, even if a thinking routine cannot be called up or used effectively all the time, it can be easily scaffolded or prompted into action by a teacher or coach, our third criteria for a thinking routine. A good example of this is a routine used in the Museum of Modern Art's Visual Thinking Curriculum (Tishman, MacGillvray, & Palmer, 1999). These materials help develop students' thinking through looking at art. The routine involves engaging students in a discussion centered around two simple questions: What do you think is going on in this painting? What makes you say that? Students first offer an interpretation, then back up that interpretation with evidence. The questions constitute a routine in that they are a core practice of the instructional module that is used over and over. In practice, students learn the routine quickly and begin to talk about art by spontaneously answering the questions. However, if a student offers an interpretation without evidence, the teacher or a fellow student can easily scaffold the routine by simply asking the student, "What makes you say that?" As with most routines, the routine's next step is a natural outgrowth of the previous step and acts as a natural prompt. There is no need to reteach the routine or even call attention to a dropped step. A more experienced member of the group merely cues the next step.

Although it seems axiomatic to say that routines are used over and over again in the classroom, it is worth focusing on this fourth quality of routines so as to clearly distinguish thinking routines from other efforts and strategies for promoting thinking. Teachers engage in all kinds of practices to try to get students thinking. They may ask pointed questions about a particular assignment or reading. They may propose activities that require thinking, such as comparing and contrasting two objects, writing a persuasive essay, creating an application for a new idea, and so on. Although such tasks certainly encourage thinking, they wouldn't be classified as routines because they aren't core practices that are repeated over and over again. Thus, these practices don't have a chance to become routinized for the individual or the class as a whole. When we are creating or seeking to identify thinking routines, we want to focus our attention on those practices that emerge repeatedly over time in the environment.

As we've seen, thinking routines are similar to other types of routines in that they: 1) have only a few steps, 2) are easily learned and remembered, 3) can be easily scaffolded, and 4) get used repeatedly. However, thinking routines have two additional characteristics that set them apart from other types of routines: a) thinking routines are useful across a variety of contexts and b) thinking routines exist as both public and private practices.

Routines for passing out papers or straightening up the classroom at the end of the day are clearly one-shot, situation-specific routines. These have a distinct goal and context that makes them of limited use in other situations. In contrast, much of the power of thinking routines is that they have wide applicability because of their instrumental nature. All of the thinking routines we have looked at—KWL, brainstorming, webbing, CSQ—can be useful across a variety of grade levels, subject areas, and contexts. Even some of the routines designed for specific programs, such as the Visual Thinking Curriculum questions, have this quality. Although these questions—What do you think is going on in this painting? What makes you say that?—are designed for looking at art, we can simply replace the phrase *in this painting* with the word *here* to make the routine fit easily into a science, history, reading, or math context.

Finally, thinking routines operate as public and private practices. Many of the routines we've discussed are for use only in the classroom. Thus, they get left behind once we leave the classroom; we seldom see people raising their hands to speak at a dinner party! But this is not true of thinking routines. Because of their broad applicability, thinking routines continue to be useful outside of the classroom. In addition, because thinking routines seek to activate individual as well as group thinking, individuals can use these routines to help themselves achieve better thinking. For instance, when we find ourselves in a rut, we can brainstorm new ideas on our own. Before tackling a difficult problem, we can say what, say why, and say other things to try. In trying to make a decision, we can make a list of pros and cons. Although there are times when we might prefer to engage in the thinking routine in group situations, it still can be of use to us in our private dealings.

THINKING ROUTINES IN ACTION

Having examined key characteristics of thinking routines, we want to return to the classroom to look at thinking routines in action to better understand how they get introduced, used, and enculturated into the life of a classroom. The classroom context gives us a chance to see that, although well-known thinking routines like the ones we have discussed can be useful, teachers often create their own thinking routines that can prove as powerful for them and their students as those they might adopt from outside sources.

In the classrooms I studied, thinking-rich routines tended to represent the major type of direct instruction in thinking that the teachers used. This was the way they attended to the development of students' ability in thinking. Therefore, it was not uncommon for teachers to introduce new routines throughout the year to serve specific purposes. However, a large number of the thinking routines at work in these classrooms were introduced quite early in the school year. Doing so helped to clarify the teacher's expectations for students and to send clear messages about what learning in a particular classroom was going to be like. Consequently, one way to group thinking routines is as the answers to certain key questions about learning that students bring with them to any new classroom:

1. How are ideas discussed and explored within this class?

2. How are ideas, thinking, and learning managed and documented here?

3. How do we find out new things and come to know in this class?

To one extent or another, all teachers provide students with answers to these questions. The answers may be fuzzy, unclear, and always changing in some circumstances, in which case students will respond with confusion and uncertainty. Or the answers may be sharp and accessible, providing students with a clear sense of how to be a productive member of the classroom. In the following examples, notice how the routines not only provide sharp answers to the questions but also give students useful tools, structures, and guidelines that they can use to be successful in a new classroom.

Routines for Discussing and Exploring Ideas

For classrooms to become intellectual environments in which students develop their ability to think, they must also be places where ideas are regularly discussed and explored. Thinking is not content neutral: we need something about which to think, something that will engage us mentally and motivationally enough to warrant the hard work of thinking. However, if students are to think well about ideas, that is, to use their ability to reason, to connect, and to expand on ideas, they will need support in doing so. Furthermore, if this kind of intellectual activity is to take place as part of a collaborative group working together to build understanding and explore the meaning of new ideas, then processes and routines for such collaborative work must be established. How do teachers teach students to discuss and explore ideas in a way that engages them actively and brings out their best thinking? In the next subsections, we look at two such routines. The first is from Susan McCray's humanities class, the second from John Threlkeld's algebra course. Although each of these routines is embedded into the fabric of the classroom, we will look at their introduction to see how the teachers first expose students to each of the routines.

THE WHY ROUTINE. In the middle of Susan McCray's blackboard is a sentence—well, kind of a sentence:

susan sighed cause I was so nurvous I couldnt slept last knight

Off to the side of the would-be sentence, written at a slant, are the words *Daily Edit*. As the combined class of seventh and eighth graders enter Susan's room, she tells them to open their composition books and get to work fixing the sentence. This is a routine for beginning the class that Susan established the first week of school. It ensures that students know exactly what to do when they come to class and promotes a smooth opening. As such, this is a learning routine that also serves as a management routine. While the class works on the sentence, Susan checks in with students individually and passes back homework. After a few minutes, Susan positions herself at the blackboard, and discussion of the sentence begins. Notice that throughout the discussion, Susan is working to embed another routine, a thinking routine focused on the discussion of ideas.

"All right," Susan begins. "Can I have everybody's attention, please. Is everybody done with the daily edit? Rachel, give us the first one."

With complete confidence, Rachel offers, "Capitalize Susan."

"Why is that?" Susan asks as she makes the correction on the blackboard.

"Because it is the beginning of someone's name."

"Very good," Susan responds as she quickly moves on, looking around the room for raised hands. "Next. Matthew."

"A comma after sighed."

"Why is that?"

Matthew responds, "Because she's talking, and she's taking a breath."

"OK." Susan nods and then clarifies, "She is taking a breath or pausing. You do pause after a sigh." Susan lets out an exaggerated sigh to make the point and then adds, "You also said she was talking. We're beginning a quotation. Before introducing a quotation, you always need some kind of punctuation, like a comma."

Before Susan can ask for the next edit, a bilingual student still struggling with English offers a change to be made, "You need to change *'cause.*"

"OK, what's wrong with it?" Susan asks him.

"It's kind of slang and not right," he answers.

"What should it be then?"

"Because."

"How do you want me to write it?" Susan pushes, watching to see if he will also catch that the word needs a capital letter.

"b-e-c-a-u-s-e," the young man offers.

Susan records his response on the board and then adds, "There's something that needs to come before, though. What is it?"

The same student quickly responds, "The quotation mark." And without prompting, he adds, "Because it's the beginning of what she is saying."

The offending lowercase *b* is next changed to uppercase, and then questions erupt about possibly changing the sentence.

"Couldn't you leave out the word *because* altogether?" a student asks.

"Couldn't you change the *Is* to *she* so that you don't have to have quotations at all?" offers another.

As each of these issues is discussed, Susan asks why. "Why would that make a difference? Why do you do that? Yes, you can pause there, but why else might that need a comma?" Through her constant questioning about the reasons for each editing choice, Susan conveys to her students that she is interested in more than answers; she is interested in the justification of those answers. At one point in the lesson, she explicitly addresses one student's frustration at having to provide a justification for a correct edit by telling him, "Yes, it's right, but we are also trying to learn the reasons."

At this point in the year, Susan's active questioning teaches students a simple routine about providing answers and explanation. She conveys to them how they need to talk about this particular task as well as her expectations for them. Over the next couple of weeks, there is a subtle shift in Susan's handling of the daily edit. When she asks students for their edits, she begins to take a very slight pause, allowing students to jump in with their reasons on their own. Often, students respond readily, but when Susan senses the justifications are not forthcoming, she prompts the student, "Why is that?" As the weeks progress, more and more students take on the why routine themselves.

This may seem so simple and straightforward that you may wonder if is a routine at all. Let's examine it briefly through our criteria. Is it purposeful, that is, does it serve to activate and promote thinking? Yes, specifically reasoning and justification. Does it have only a few steps? It has two steps: first provide an answer and then a justification. Is it easy to learn and scaffold? Absolutely. Is it used over and over again? In Susan's case, it is. It became part of the class's standard way of operating. Can the routine operate both privately and publicly? Yes, thinking of the reasons for one's answers and justifying things to oneself can be very helpful in determining whether one is correct.

Finally, is the why routine useful across a variety of contexts? More than any other single word or question, *why* dominates the discourse of the thoughtful classrooms I have encountered. It was present in all subject areas, from art to mathematics, and at all grade levels. From the first days, the teachers I observed used the simple question, *Why?*, to push students to give explanations and evidence for their opinions, answers, solutions, and ideas in mathematical computation, grammar and punctuation, historical interpretation, and so on. Thus, from the outset, these teachers established a routine of discourse in which they expected evidence, complete accounts, and depth in students' talk. The why routine forces students to think in evidential ways, look for connections, and see that all ideas have roots. When students have difficulty responding to the question, teachers use the occasion to develop students' abilities through probing questions that help students uncover the evidence behind their thoughts.

Although it is a fairly simple routine to establish, the why routine is missing in too many classrooms. Too often, the answer to a student's question about how ideas will be discussed and explored is that they won't be. Rather than exploring and discussing ideas in some way, information in some classrooms is predigested for students by either the teacher or the text. Such practices not only do little to develop students' understanding of ideas, but they also do nothing to promote students' abilities or inclinations to think. Let's now look at another example of how teachers use routines to help students discuss and explore ideas.

MATHEMATICAL ARGUMENTS. It's the fourth day of school, and John Threlkeld's students have run into a roadblock. They've been sharpening their arithmetic skills and working on lots of order of operations problems within the broader context of understanding how mathematics operates as a discipline. Along the way, John has presented his eighth graders with the following problem as part of a homework sheet:

$$x^2 \qquad (x)^2 \qquad -x^2 \qquad -(x)^2$$

Although this is the kind of arithmetic convention that most textbooks would handle perfunctorily by providing a set of rules, in John's class it is an opportunity to develop mathematical ideas, explore one's thinking, and learn how to work together as a community of learners seeking to understand mathematics. The ambiguity of the problem also provides a context for John to introduce the routine of mathematical arguments to his class.

After quickly agreeing to the meaning of each of the expressions listed above when x equals two, John asks the class what x^2 means when x equals negative two.

The classroom erupts in opinions as students shout both "Negative four!" and "Four!" with equal conviction.

John asks for a show of hands as to who believes what and prods those reluctant to be counted: "You have to vote. You need to have an opinion. Which camp are you in?"

The voting is split down the middle with nine students voting for four and eight for negative four. Once again, the class spontaneously erupts into discussion and conversation. At this point, the discussion is a bit chaotic, but John allows the free-flowing conversation to continue for a while. Some students are arguing with their neighbors, and others are trying to make their points to the larger group. One student shouts, "Do it on the calculator!" as a surefire solution to the confusion. John just smiles and lets the students proceed. Shortly, the triumphant expressions of the two students working on the calculators turn to puzzlement. Each has come up with a different answer—so much for using technology as the arbiter.

"OK," John tells the class, "here we enter a real dilemma because, not surprisingly, your calculator does something different than her calculator does. How are we going to settle this argument?" Without any formal introduction, John begins a process of calling on one student at a time to present his or her position. For John as a teacher, the challenge is not in getting students to express their viewpoints and give their reasons, however. The challenge in this mathematical debate is getting students to listen to and respond to each other's arguments.

One of the strongest students in the class raises his hand to begin the debate. "Well, it's like we were doing with order of operations. You have to do the exponent first."

"So what camp are you in? What are you arguing for?" John asks to clarify the position the student is taking.

"Oh, I say it is negative four because you do the squaring first and then you take the opposite of it."

Another student erupts, "But that just proves the opposite side. If you take a negative number and multiply it times itself, you get a positive."

"Why are you saying take a negative times itself?" John asks.

The student elaborates on his point, "Because that's what you're doing. You're taking negative two times negative two. You're not taking the opposite of x."

Quickly, there's disagreement from another student, "But you're just substituting negative two for x and when you do that it's the same thing as $-x^2$."

"Let's continue to listen to people's versions and then make some decisions," John adds. With repeated calls for patience and listening, John continues to call on students to express not their answer but the justification for their beliefs. Throughout, John encourages students to listen to one another and build upon or contradict other's arguments. Interestingly, the girls dominate the discussion.

After a few minutes, he calls for a new vote, and the majority of the class is now convinced the answer is negative four. A more timid teacher might take this as a defeat of the argumentation process, but John is unfazed and doesn't reveal any hint of frustration or surprise. Instead, he sees an opportunity to get down to fundamentals. "Where we're getting bogged down is that we're trying to remember a rule rather than think about what is going on. I need you to think about what is going on here. Let's go back to something that was brought up in the discussion. What does x^2 mean?" John carefully draws out the point that a variable has to be treated as an entity just as an expression in parentheses is treated, thus, x^2 equals $(x)^2$.

Exasperated, a girl in the second row asks, "Why didn't you just put the parentheses in the problem, then?"

John turns the question back, "Why didn't I?"

With a sigh, the girl responds, "To make us think?"

John responds and concludes the class with a final message, "Yes, that's the main reason. This isn't something just to memorize. I need you to understand it."

In this short fifty-minute period the first week of school, John has stressed the importance of understanding and thinking in mathematics. But he has done more than that: he has introduced a thinking routine that the students will use throughout the year in their exploration of mathematics. But was the routine effective? After all, didn't students get more confused by listening to each other's arguments? Remember, first and foremost, that thinking routines should activate and encourage thinking. In this episode, the students were thinking and engaging deeply with the ideas. Yes, some of their reasoning was flawed, but a thinking routine can't produce perfect reasoning, answers, or results. What such routines can do is provide a context in which the kinds of thinking and results we are after as teachers are more likely to emerge. In a case such as this one in John's classroom, students' thinking and understanding ultimately is enhanced as students become aware of the flaws in their reasoning.

Routines for Managing and Documenting Thinking and Learning

For the most part, the thinking routines we have discussed facilitate better thinking and performance in the moment. These routines push students into specific modes of thinking, such as evidential reasoning in the case of the why routine or logical reasoning in the mathematical argument, that serve immediate ends. In this respect, they are similar to housekeeping, management, discourse, or learning routines: they facilitate getting the job of the moment done. However, thinking routines do not have to be directed to such immediate goals. In this section, we look at how routines facilitate the long-term goals of managing and documenting thinking and learning as they unfold over time. These types or routines are much more macro in nature, assuming an overarching character in terms of students' interactions with course content. Consequently, the success of these macro-level routines as pedagogical practices depends entirely on their ongoing use and development. This is in contrast to the more focused routines we discussed in which the core practice itself could be successfully employed on a single occasion. For instance, one could engage students in brainstorming or in the process of argumentation as part of a particular lesson with relatively good results without actually making the practice a routine of the classroom, but a macro-level routine would fall apart and become much less effective if it was not repeated and routinized.

Macro-level thinking routines are useful to students because thinking is difficult work, and the job of building understanding is a long and complex process. When no classroom routines for managing or dealing with this ongoing intellectual work exist, students may struggle and fail to find the coherence and meaning behind what they are learning. More importantly, they may find it difficult to do their best thinking because of cognitive overload, that is, because the thinking demands exceed their capacity. When our thinking is distributed, when we do not have to rely solely on our internal mental resources, we free ourselves up to engage in more challenging thinking.[4] For instance, in writing this book, I have made use of distributed cognition by using notes, outlines, videotapes, computer programs, and paper files to help me store and organize both my data and my thoughts. By not having to keep everything in my head at once, I free up important mental space for thinking.

A standard way of looking at these distribution devices is as tools or strategies: the teacher provides initial training in their use, and the learner subsequently masters them for self-use. However, if we approach and use them in a way that better reflects our criteria for what makes something a thinking routine, these same devices could be considered thinking routines. Principally, that means that the practices must be relatively streamlined and easy to teach, that they be used on an ongoing basis, and that they activate and help direct thinking. By returning to these criteria, we can see that whereas a computer database can act as a tool for distributed cognition, it is unlikely to be used repeatedly in most classes and doesn't focus on thinking directly. In contrast, mind mapping (Buzan, 1993)—a method of note taking that emphasizes imagery, connection making, and an individualized, nonlinear organizational structure—could be considered a thinking routine in some situations. Mind mapping asks note takers to draw images for key concepts they want to remember and then to connect those images in an associative web, rather than in an outline form. Although the process of mind mapping can be complex, this complexity can be built up over time. Thus, entry into the practice can be somewhat streamlined. In addition, mind mapping is a tool with broad applicability across many contexts. Most importantly, the process helps to direct and activate associative, aesthetic, and creative thinking in the service of advancing memory and understanding. How do teachers introduce and get students to use such macro-level routines? Below, we look at two such routines for documenting and managing thinking that teachers Chris Elnicki and Heather Woodcock introduced.

DOCUMENTING THINKING WITH A JOURNAL ROUTINE. There is nothing distinctive about the spiral-bound notebooks Chris Elnicki asks his seventh-grade social studies class to bring to class. For the most part, they are standard issue eighty-page notebooks of college-ruled paper. However, the process of personalizing the notebooks begins right away. On the overhead projector, Chris displays a sample cover containing four key pieces of information:

[Title]: A Citizen's Journal
By [Your Name]
2001–2002
How Organized: [?]

Chris quickly moves students through each of these elements, first explaining the role of the title: "You can name your journal anything you want. You could call it 'Things Elnicki Made Me Do' or 'Bob.' It really doesn't matter because it is yours. The second part of the title is a subtitle, 'A Citizen's Journal.' You are a citizen of this class, and this is your history of involvement with this class. It will document your learning, and you will use it to help you make sense of what we are studying. If you want, you can just let the subtitle be your title."

Soon, questions come up about what "organization of the journal" means. Chris elaborates by way of example:

You have to make a choice about how you are going to organize things. I've only seen two ways that students have done this. One is to put things in order. I'll show you some examples of that, but basically you organize things by date, chronological order. Another way to organize it would be by section. You could have a section for "First Things" and then a section for assignments and notes or homework. Most people, about 80 percent, do sections. I don't see any difference in the good and the better journals according to which way they are done. I don't have a preference. Do it whichever way you feel most comfortable with.

With this managerial task out of the way, Chris moves on to helping students develop a sense of how they will use the journals to document their learning and deepen their understanding. He does this by showing examples of former students' journal entries. Putting a copy of a student's response on the overhead projector for the entire class to see, Chris tells the class, "When you write your responses, you need to make sure that you communicate fully. That means when you pick it up or I pick it up five years from now, you know what it is saying. So let's test and see if this person is doing that."

Chris then moves into the example, reading to the class from the journal entry, "9/25. If I could go back in time and live with any Native

American group, I would select the Anasazis because they have a lot of land and their homes are well built." Turning to the class, Chris asks, "OK, what do you think the question was?"

A student volunteers, "If you could go back in time and live with a Native American group, who would you choose?"

"Right. That was the question," Chris responds. "This person communicated fully. We know what the question is. They didn't have to write the question, but we still know what it was."

Next, Chris asks students to assess the response itself. Using his school district's grading scheme, Chris asks the students how they would characterize the response, "Is it proficient, basic, or advanced?"

"Basic," a student in the front row responds.

"Does that mean you think it is below grade level?" Chris pushes.

"No," the student backs down. "Maybe proficient?"

"How many of you think it is proficient?" Chris asks the class. Most of the hands go up, and Chris pushes forward to the real intent of his questioning, "What would it take to make this an advanced response? What could be added?"

"More detail," a student answers.

"More detail about their homes, what they were like," another student elaborates.

"Maybe who you wouldn't want to live with and why?" offers another.

"OK, you kind of reversed it then and have taken a different angle. That shows some advanced thinking." Chris then adds, "Maybe if you compare it to something else. Maybe if you add some new information that we didn't talk about in class. How about if this person talks about what other people said? 'I heard someone in the class say this during the discussion,' or 'I heard Mr. Elnicki added that . . .' That would probably be more advanced because they are including some more information."

In this first example of a journal entry based on a first-things prompt, Chris emphasizes the two key elements of the journal-writing routine that he will reinforce throughout the year. First, there is the need to communicate fully so that one's notes can be understood, to both oneself and others. Second, it is important to go beyond one's first thoughts and initial response to elaborate and add information. Chris specifically mentions the process of adding to one's response based on the class discussion. In this way, the journal is not just a record of one's response or a compendium of classroom assignments; it is a vehicle for building connections and developing understanding.

In a later class in which Chris asks students to construct a web of the American Revolution, the use of the journal to build connections becomes clear. Before the students begin their unit, Chris shows the basic structure of a web—with nodes for such things as battles, British views, causes, impact, people, and results—and asks students to copy it into their journals and begin the process of elaborating upon it. As the class discusses their initial ideas, Chris encourages students to add to their webs and make note of these new additions, "When you add something I say or something anyone else adds, make a star or underline it. We want to keep it clear what were the first things you had on your own and then what you added." Thus, Chris emphasizes that the journal is a process for developing and extending one's learning.

The importance of these two steps also is reinforced when Chris assesses his students' journals. Although he often makes note of missing items and admonishes students about organization and structure, his most frequent comments to students are, "Communicate completely! Be sure to explain what you are doing," and "Go beyond your first thoughts and strive to do some deep thinking." It is in these two elements that keeping the journal most acts as a thinking routine. By asking students to clarify questions and go beyond initial thoughts, Chris promotes connections and the continual elaboration of ideas.

GUIDING QUESTIONS AS A ROUTINE FOR MANAGING THINKING. In the last chapter, we saw how Heather Woodcock used a set of seven guiding throughline questions to convey a sense of the power of ideas and to set an agenda of understanding for her seventh-grade humanities class. (Refer to p. 58 for a list of the questions.) At the outset, Heather's posting of these questions worked as an advance organizer of students' thinking by highlighting the most important themes and questions of the course and orienting students' expectations. However, it is Heather's ongoing use of the questions rather than the questions themselves that actually establish what we now understand as a thinking routine.

By activating a process by which students regularly engage the throughline questions, Heather establishes a thinking routine centering on connection making. Heather's initial introduction of the throughlines to her students first hints at the connection-making emphasis: "What these questions are are questions we are going to return to throughout the year. All of these questions can be connected in many, many ways to what we are studying in here and to our day-to-day lives. They can be connected to history, literature, science, and math in a lot of different ways." She then asks students to begin the process of connection making in a very general way by selecting a throughline question to think and write about in an early paper. However, because the class has not yet begun its studies, the actual connection-making routine isn't activated in this introduction. The routine itself emerges later in a formal writing assignment related to the class's first unit of study. In this unit, students are reading *A Wizard of Earthsea,* by Ursula Le Guin, and studying European explorers. As part of this study, Heather gives students the following writing assignment:

Throughline Connections

Choose a throughline that you think connects to either our study of *A Wizard of Earthsea* or our study of Explorers.

- In your first paragraph, explain the throughline you have chosen and discuss its implications and meanings.

- In your second paragraph, connect that throughline to *A Wizard of Earthsea* or the Explorers by pointing out how the throughline can inform, clarify, or expand your thinking about what you studied.

These two questions—which might be generalized as: What does the throughline mean to you now? How does the throughline connect to and inform what you are studying?—essentially make up the thinking routine. It is a routine because the questions are asked over and over and become a part of the life of the classroom. At times, Heather stops class and holds an impromptu discussion using the questions, or she asks the questions more formally as part of a writing assignment. The questions effectively guide students' individual thinking as well. Asking oneself these questions in the midst of study facilitates the process of making connections and deepening understanding. In both the public and private realms, this connection-making routine, when coupled with the throughline questions, helps students manage and direct their thinking in the course by constantly pulling them toward the bigger picture and ideas.

Routines for Finding Out New Things
and Coming to Know

I'm observing the first day of school as it unfolds in a fairly traditional suburban high school's mathematics classroom. The room is neat and orderly, and Karen White is a well-prepared veteran. She has organized this first day to emphasize the housekeeping and management routines that will help her maintain the decorum she feels is important to learning. Unbeknownst to her, she is also instructing her students in a routine about how the students will come to know and find things out in her class. She does this through a brief lesson on perfect numbers, which provides the only mathematical content of this first day. Seeking to engage students in an open-ended and non-threatening way, the teacher asks her students to devise and share their own definitions of what a perfect number is. A few students gamely participate, while many others hold back. Perhaps they are confused by the lack of context for the question. Perhaps they sense that guessing at the right answer is the best they will be able to do. The few students who actually do take up the challenge do so with a sense of humor:

"A perfect number is any number with a dollar sign in front of it."

"A perfect number is infinity because it goes on forever."

"Fourteen is a perfect number because that's my birthday."

Pleased with these humorous, if not mathematical, responses, this experienced and well-respected teacher smiles at the class and gamely asks, "Would you like to know how mathematicians define a perfect number?"

Off to the side, a student who has watched the exchange quite passively up until now responds in a resigned manner, "It doesn't matter whether we want to know or not, you're going to tell us anyway."

In his comment, this student reveals that he has recognized the futility of the classroom exchange and seen through its hidden subtext. There may be opportunities to participate in this class if you are willing to be a good sport about it and just play the game, but in the end the teacher will deliver the information she expects you to know. To play the game of school, you will try and hold on to that information just long enough to return it to its rightful owner on the day of the test. At that time, the staunchness of one's informational stewardship will be judged. Through his comment, this student also acknowledges what he feels is the de facto routine by which students find out new things in this and most other classrooms: they are told them, either by the teacher or the textbook.

Of course, a routine such as being told affords students little opportunity to develop their skills in thinking. Furthermore, when this routine dominates the life of a classroom, students' inclination to think is not only neglected but also suppressed. When all one needs to do is wait for the teacher to deliver the goods, thinking seems to have little payoff. Fortunately, there are other responses to the question of how students come to know and find out new things. Below we look at two routines used by Heather Woodcock and Chris Elnicki to help their students engage with reading and develop an understanding of the past.

WRITING: A ROUTINE FOR COMING TO KNOW. A few pages of lined paper, folded over and stapled, serve as an impromptu journal for Heather Woodcock's students. Although not fancy in its construction, the simple journal becomes the core of a routine for students as they read *A Wizard of Earthsea* together. Heather explains, "This is a journal just for *A Wizard of Earthsea*. You're not going to put anything other than *Wizard of Earthsea* thoughts in it. The way this is going to work is this: starting today, you are going to do a little bit of writing in class. We're going to start and end class with time for you all to think and write, because I find that it helps me before a discussion to write a little bit to get my thoughts in order."

This simple routine, giving time for thoughts before and after reading, needs little more instruction than that. When a few students question what they should write about before they read, Heather suggests, "Write any questions you have about the book so far. What are you wondering about?" This prewriting activates students' thinking and identifies what students are confused about. It also brings the group together as a learning community seeking to develop an understanding of the book. This quality emerges when Heather asks students to share any questions or confusions they have about the book thus far.

One students offers, "Why do some people [in the book] have magic and others don't?"

"Great question, Johnny," Heather responds. She begins to answer his question and then pulls back, "I want someone else to answer. It doesn't matter what I think. What do you all think?"

Several students offer their thoughts. Some suggest that the magic has to be developed and comes from a desire to cultivate it. Others feel that the magic is something some of the characters are born with.

After several such theories, Heather tells the class, " What I'd like for you to think about as you are reading is, Where does that magic come from?" Thus, the brief prewriting period helps shape students' reading of the text by focusing their attention on certain questions or puzzles.

After students have read, the follow-up writing helps students reconnect with their initial thinking and record their developing understanding. In addition, the writing prepares students for speaking and sharing their ideas in the class discussion. By giving students time to organize their thoughts, Heather ensures that all students are more ready to participate in a discussion. In this way, the writing is a routine to facilitate students' metacognition. As students become more comfortable with the routine of using writing to think about their thinking, the routine can move from the external realm of the notebook to the internal world of the mind.

The routine itself, as well as Heather's guiding of the discussions it prompts, sends students a message about what it means to learn and find things out that is very different than that of traditional classrooms. Rather than being spoon-fed information to memorize, students learn that understanding is an iterative process of constantly examining what one knows and doesn't know, posing working hypotheses that one can investigate, and discussing ideas as part of a group. Students also learn the power of self-questioning for focusing one's attention and efforts. Through class discussions, students learn that in this class questions aren't so much answered as they are investigated. This gives the work of the classroom an active sense of energy that can carry it forward.

A ROUTINE FOR MAKING INTERPRETATIONS. As part of their exploration into the question, "Why are you here [in school]?" Chris Elnicki passes out old photographs, taken by Lewis Hine and other photojournalists, of child labor conditions in the early 1900s. Each pair of students receives a photo and is asked to engage in the process of historical interpretation. This exercise offers students their first opportunity to practice a routine to which Chris has just introduced them on this first day of school.

Having had students make interpretations about himself and the course based on the evidence they can see in the classroom, Chris next introduces students to a more formalized process of interpretation using a photograph pinned to the back wall of the classroom. In the photograph, a person on the back of a horse plummets toward a small tank of water while a sea of upturned faces watches, spellbound. Directing students to the picture, Chris explains, "These five steps help us to find things in photographs that we may sometimes overlook and maybe to help us learn more things about it."

Chris then walks students through the steps, carefully explaining each one in the context of the photograph the class is observing: "The first step is our first reaction. You can't stop this. It immediately comes up in your brain. Your brain does this automatically when you see it. It could be, 'Ugh, black-and-white photograph, I don't like it.' Or it could be 'I didn't know horses could fly.' But it is usually connected to a feeling.

"Our next step would be to collect data," Chris continues. "We are going to count some stuff. We're going to look to see what kind of detail there is." Moving closer to the photograph, Chris begins the process of noticing details out loud while the class watches, "Here's men with suits and men without suits. Here's a cowboy and a number of people wearing hats. I can count the number of horses in the air. I can look at her clothing and see what I can discover. Well, she has a bow in her hair. She has a belt around her waist. She's wearing some interesting shoes. I can count about eight pieces of lace." Chris adds, "I can count support beams. I can maybe make some guesses about the distance here. Oh, hey, what's this? There's another horse there. I never noticed that before."

Moving toward the front of the room and away from the picture, Chris tells the class, "The data will generate questions for me, and I can make some overall generalizations from that data. What can we say about the picture?"

A student interjects, "Like it's a picture of people watching a woman and a horse jump."

"Right," Chris continues. "That generalization is very provable from that evidence." He adds, "Inference is the next step. You've been doing that with me. You made inferences about who I am and what this class is like from my symbols and the evidence around the room. We could make inferences about the picture. Why was it taken? Are the people happy, sad, excited? What am I going to find outside of this stadium?"

Again, students begin to offer ideas: "A parking lot." "Cars." "A field."

Wrapping up the process, Chris introduces the last stage, "The final stage is conclusions. What did you learn from this?"

It's been a quick introduction and a somewhat truncated example in practice, but Chris is anxious to get students engaged in the process themselves, knowing that learning the routine requires doing the routine and not watching it be done. Chris also knows that the students will repeat this process throughout the year—sometimes in a formal manner by going through each step and writing responses, sometimes informally by moving quickly through the first steps to focus more specifically on interpretation. In teaching and practicing this routine early on, Chris conveys to students that his class is not just about getting answers, it is about finding out answers. He wants his students to know that the history they read is based on the process of interpretation of evidence and that it is the evidence that must be kept front and center, not the interpretation.

THE IMPORTANCE OF THINKING ROUTINES

Routines dominate the life of classrooms. From passing out papers to checking homework to dismissal at the end of the day, the routines of each classroom are unique. Although these housekeeping, management, and discourse routines contribute a great deal to the overall feel and decorum of a classroom, it is the thinking routines, or their absence, that give a classroom its intellectual life. Through these thinking routines, students are enculturated into thinking, developing both their ability and their inclination to think. In every thoughtful classroom I have visited, thinking routines, rather than direct instruction or the use of any thinking-skills program, were the principal means by which teachers developed students' skill and ability in thinking.

Thinking routines provide us with a new way of looking at critical-thinking instruction. When administrators, parents, or teachers are concerned about getting students to think, it is not unusual for them to seek out programs or curricula on critical and creative thinking. These lessons may be good; they may even be effective at developing students' skill. But what these materials often fail to do is to enculturate a disposition to think. When we look at the process of enculturation closely, this fact is not surprising. Enculturation depends on immersion into a way of doing things over an extended period. This immersion process is accompanied by a fair amount of ongoing mediation, support, and nurturing from more experienced members of the culture. Although some direct instruction may occur as one learns how to operate in a new culture, it is only through ongoing participation in and practice of the culture's routines that one gradually comes to feel a part of that new culture. The problem with most prepackaged thinking-skills programs designed by outside experts is that they sit outside the culture of the classroom, never really becoming a part of it.

In contrast, thinking routines form a unique bridge in the process of enculturating students. On the one hand, because of their ongoing use and broad applicability, thinking routines embody a class's way of doing things when it comes to thinking and learning. They are a part of the cultural fabric that communicates the values, intent, and feel of a classroom. In this way, thinking routines play an important role in developing a culture of thinking. You may have noticed that the teachers introduced many of the routines shared in this chapter early in the school year, often during the first week. This is no accident. You also may have noticed that some of the examples of first-days practices in Chapter Four could be looked at from the perspective of thinking routines. It is precisely this ubiquitous and embedded nature of thinking routines that makes them such powerful cultural forces. On the other hand, thinking routines act as the means of enculturation themselves. Because they are so easily taught and scaffolded, thinking routines become the way that teachers build students' capacity and commitment toward thinking. Thus, thinking routines are both the tools of instruction into the culture and part of the culture itself.

—wwv— **Key Ideas for Developing Intellectual Character**
IN THE CLASSROOM: THINKING ROUTINES

- *The Form and Function of Routines.* Classrooms are dominated by routines for accomplishing housekeeping chores,
  securing classroom management, facilitating discourse, and
  directing learning. Such routines are explicit and goal-driven.
  For these routines to be effective, they usually consist of only
  a few steps, are easy to learn and teach, can be scaffolded or
  supported by others, and get used over and over again in the
  classroom.

- *Criteria for Thinking Routines.* Although thinking routines
  often can be characterized as learning or discourse routines,
  the converse is not always true. Some routines for guiding
  learning are far from thinking-rich and do little to engage
  students mentally. First and foremost, thinking routines must
  activate and help direct students' thinking. Because this thinking is not necessarily the goal but usually a means to a larger
  purpose such as understanding, we say that thinking routines
  are more instrumental in nature. In addition to the criteria for
  other types of routines, good thinking routines must also be
  useful across a wide variety of contexts and be able to operate
  as both public and private practices.

- *Some Examples of Thinking Routines.* Many familiar classroom practices and instructional strategies can be thought of
  as thinking routines if they are used over and over again in a
  way that makes them a core practice of the classroom. For
  example, KWL (What do you know? What do you want to
  know? What did you learn?), brainstorming, pushing students
  to give evidence and to reason by asking them Why? classroom
  arguments or debates, journal writing, questioning techniques
  or patterns that are used repeatedly, and so on.

- *Thinking Routines as an Enculturating Force.* Thinking
  routines act as a major enculturating force by communicating
  expectations for thinking as well as providing students the
  tools they need to engage in that thinking. Thinking routines

(continued)

IN THE CLASSROOM: THINKING ROUTINES
(continued)

help students answer questions they have: How are ideas discussed and explored within this class? How are ideas, thinking, and learning managed and documented here? How do we find out new things and come to know in this class? As educators, we need to uncover the various thinking routines that will support students as they go about this kind of intellectual work or enact new ones if such routines are not readily present in our practice.

CHAPTER SIX

Language and Thinking

Prompting, Priming, and Patterning

D‍o you recall the teacher in Charles Schulz's *Peanuts* cartoon strip? Her face was never shown, giving her both a generic and ubiquitous feel. Her faceless dominance was further emphasized by the words she spoke: "Blah, blah, blah, blah, blah." These utterances, which were always the same whether presented in a comic strip or animated feature, would float above the students in their own cloud as if preparing to rain down upon the class. And yet for all their oppressiveness and foreboding, the words themselves lacked substance, having no real meaning or sense of import for Charlie Brown or his friends.

I've been in classrooms like that myself, both as a student and as an observer, and I expect you have as well. Classrooms in which the teacher's words seem to hang in the air, circling above the heads of the students, statically locked in their own orbit. Classrooms in which the dialogue is so one-sided that the voices of the students answering pointed questions can be heard only as a staccato punctuation against the more dominant droning of teacher talk. Classrooms in which dialogue and conversation are completely usurped by teacher monologues. In such environments, language is, often unwittingly, being used to create distance. Distance between the students and the teacher. Distance between the student and the subject. In these classrooms, language is also used to shape students' thinking, in this case not in a productive sense perhaps, but shaped all the same.

This rather dark scenario of the use of language need not be the case. Language in and of itself need not create distance or depress students' engagement with ideas and thinking. In fact, language can be a powerful vehicle for activating thought, and as teachers we need to be aware of the role it is playing. Language is the principal medium of instruction in classrooms. Even in classrooms where students engage mostly in hands-on work or performance-based tasks, language mediates the experience students have. Consequently, language is a strong enculturating force shaping students' interaction and thinking. In this chapter, we look at how teachers seeking to cultivate students' intellectual character use language to its best effect. Specifically, we examine how language shapes thinking and how patterns of talk help to establish and develop certain kinds of cognitive processes. We also explore how language cues thinking, both explicit types of cuing as well as ways that language can operate more implicitly. This discussion leads us into looking at the language of thinking itself and how best to use it in the classroom.

Behind this examination of language and its role in classrooms is a rich history of linguistic theory and practice that can help us better understand how language and thought interact. Most instructive for our purpose is the seminal work of Benjamin Whorf (Carroll, 1956). Whorf is perhaps best known for his linguistic relativity principle, often referred to as the Sapir-Whorf hypothesis.[1] The basic premise is that the language we speak structures and influences our interpretation and understanding of the world. Although this principle is generally studied and applied within the broader context of understanding distinct cultural groups who speak different languages or to understand the effect of bi- or multilingualism, the principle also has much to say about the effects of language in cognition more generally. Three key ideas from Whorf's work in linguistics and cognition relate to our examination of language and thinking in the classroom. First is the emphasis Whorf placed on patterns and "patternment." Second is the idea of linguistic thinking, in which our individual ways of talking, expressing, seeing, and thinking are viewed as being grounded in the process of socialization. It is through socialization that we incorporate linguistic activity into cognitive activity. Third is the notion that language gives us the means by which we can isolate bits of our experiences, thus sharpening our attention and allowing us to engage in abstraction. As we discuss and explore the way teachers use language to foster students' thinking, we will return to examine these points in more depth.

LEARNING TO THINK BY TALKING

Talk, whether internalized self-talk, overt conversation, or writing, is one of our principal mechanisms for organizing our thoughts, making sense of new ideas, and pushing our thinking in new directions. At the same time, our ability to think grows and expands through our exposure to other people's thinking, ideas, and knowledge, which become available to us through their talk and writings. Given the importance of such talk to thinking, it's not surprising that thoughtful classroom environments are dominated by discussion, writing, and a general sense of reciprocity in conversation.

But there is more to using language to facilitate students' thinking than just getting students to talk and write. At the core, there must first be something that engages students mentally, something that necessitates a discussion, something that exposes students to new ideas, uncovers other perspectives, and pushes thinking forward. This need for substantive and meaty content requires teachers to go beyond skill development and memorization of facts to examine how they can embed skills and information in issues, problems, and experiences that will engage students and give them something to both talk and think about. Some examples of such substance that I observed in the classrooms I studied include power, magic, equality, kinship, string theory, connections between mathematics and baseball, puzzles, laws about citizenship, infinity, limits, and negative powers—just to name a few. Although not all of these topics may grab your attention immediately, in the hands of a skilled facilitator, each can be the basis for a lively exploration in which students must continually think, express their thinking, interact, and listen to the thinking of others. This ability to engage students in the lively exploration of a powerful topic is well demonstrated by Chris Elnicki's exploration of the American Dream in his social studies class.

Talking and Thinking about the American Dream

To spark the class discussion, Chris first has students explore the topic through an aesthetic lens by creating posters that capture what the American Dream means to them. Individually, these small construction-paper posters aren't too impressive, but collectively the 130-some images from all four of his classes pack quite a punch as they are combined to create a giant collage across the front wall of the classroom. The words *American, Dream, Freedom,* and *Equality* feature prominently in the display, as do dollar signs, pictures of famous Americans, and flags. As students enter the room and confront the display for the first time, they can hear Simon and Garfunkel's *America* playing in the background.

Chris quickly directs the class to the first-things notice he has squeezed into one corner of the blackboard: "Record in your journals what this collection tells you about the American Dream." Grabbing their journals, the thirty-five students of period five move along the wall laughing, discussing, pointing, and commenting on the collection.

After they have written their initial thoughts in their journals, Chris prepares to engage the class in discussion. As students share their ideas, the role of language and talk in making this assignment a real opportunity to develop students' thinking is clearly evident.

"This is like a museum exhibit. I want you to take the position that you are trying to understand this display about the American Dream and begin to identify themes in the posters and interpret what the posters say about the group," Chris tells the class.

Immediately, a girl in the back of the room mentions the theme of freedom. Chris asks her how she would define *freedom.* Tentatively, she responds, "The freedom to do what you want to."

Chris then pushes further to expose other perspectives, "Did all the people who used the word *freedom* in their posters mean that same thing by it?"

Other students point out that some posters talk about religious freedom and that voting is a kind of freedom. When a student shifts gears and mentions that a lot of the posters mention fame and fortune, Chris asks how those words connect to freedom. This sparks an excited debate about whether the rich or the poor have more freedom. At the core of the discussion are notions of obligation and commitment versus being unencumbered.

"When you have money, you have a lot of stuff to tie you down, like you have to make house payments and stuff, so that makes you not feel so free," a student comments.

"Yeah, if you don't own a house, you're freer to just move anytime you want," another student adds.

"But if you don't have money and have to worry about it all the time, that's not being very free," a third student counters.

This discussion of the meanings and intent of words continues for most of the period as students identify key issues or themes emerging from the posters and then examine various perspectives that people have on those themes. There are no pat answers or easy statements to be made. At every turn, there is complexity, controversy, and nuance. What does it mean to seek a better life? What does equality look like in practice? What role does diversity play in the United States? Can people's dreams be in conflict?

At the close of the discussion, Chris continues to push students' thinking by engaging them in talking about the American Dream itself. He asks the class, "How do you think the American Dream may be changing over time?"

A student responds, "Well, I think it is probably expanding and becoming even more diverse than it was initially."

Another student concurs and elaborates, "Yeah, because so many people keep coming to America, and they probably don't all come for the same reasons as people used to. Like with the Pilgrims, their dream was mostly about religious freedom."

A student counters, "But that comes back to freedom. Freedom is really key." With that comment, the period ends.

Developing Dialogical Thinking

Throughout this exchange, students are involved not only in expressing their ideas but also in listening to, incorporating, projecting, and responding to the perspective of other students. In this process, students learn to consider multiple perspectives and engage in what Richard Paul (1987) calls dialogical thinking. Dialogical thinking moves outside of the narrow internalized world of the individual into a more reciprocal space where other positions are actively explored. Bakhtin (1981) argued that reasoning itself is fundamentally a dialogical process through which the thinker hears several voices within his or her own head that represent various contrasting perspectives on an issue. Such reasoning is a move from the monologue to the dialogue that permits students to engage in building understanding by incorporating both the ideas and thinking of others. We see this shift when we compare the beginning of the conversation in Chris Elnicki's classroom with the end. At the beginning, the first student response was a personal statement about the meaning of freedom, "The freedom to do what you want to." The student wasn't thinking about what freedom might mean to others. However, though Chris's questioning, students were prompted to actually consider the meaning of freedom from other points of view. By the end of the conversation, students became aware of various perspectives on freedom and had come to see freedom from a social and historical perspective, as exemplified by one student's comment, "I think it is probably expanding and becoming even more diverse than it was initially."

Thus, the discussion of the American Dream and of the meaning of freedom in particular has served several purposes. First, the discussion pushed students to clarify their thoughts and ideas as they put them into language and expressed them to the group. Second, the exposure to other perspectives served to move students from the monologic to the dialogic. This does not mean that students have become dialogic thinkers, however, only that they have engaged in dialogic thought. To become more dialogic thinkers, that is, individuals who are likely to look for and consider alternative perspectives, students need ongoing exposure to other ideas as they explore and seek to formulate their own positions, ideas, and meanings. As Paul (1987, p. 135) states, "They need to discover opposing points of view in nonthreatening situations. They need to put their ideas into words, advance conclusions, and justify them. They need to discover their own assumptions as well as the assumptions of others, advance conclusions other than their own, and construct reasons to support them." This means that students must go beyond listening to the contributions of others to actively soliciting, responding to, and incorporating others' ideas into their own talk and thinking. This ability to seek out, anticipate, and address alternative points of view is a foundation for developing effective counterarguments.

Developing dialogical thinking can seem like a tall order, particularly given typical patterns of classroom discourse in which students give individual responses to a teacher leading the discussion. What is needed is a pattern of classroom discourse that not only sensitizes students to the presence of alternative points of view but also forces them to confront and address those perspectives actively. In this next section, we look at how teachers develop patterns of thinking in their students by initiating patterns of talk in the classroom.

WAYS OF TALKING, WAYS OF THINKING

One develops patterns of thought through learning language in a social context. As Whorf argued, "Every language is a vast pattern-system, different from others, in which are culturally ordained the forms and categories by which the personality not only communicates, but also analyzes nature, notices or neglects types of relationship and phenomena, channels his reasoning and builds the house of his consciousness"(Whorf, 1956, p. 252). Although Whorf was specifically writing about the inherent differences across the spoken languages of the world, his statement holds true for the language of subcultures, including that of classrooms as well. Penny Lee (1997, p. 462) points this out in her discussion of experts and novices practicing within a given field: "The process of learning specific terminology and ways of talking about phenomena helps learners direct their attention to subtle features of their art that they have to learn to isolate consistently. Expert and novice experience and understanding of the same phenomena can be so different that where language is a significant factor in mediating that difference, we are warranted in saying that the linguistic relativity principle is at work even within a single language." Thus, for our purposes, we might edit Whorf's statement to say that the language of every classroom is a vast pattern-system that culturally ordains the forms and categories by which students not only communicate, but also analyze, notice or neglect types of relationship and phenomena, channel their reasoning, and build the house of their consciousness.

Examining the language of the classroom through this lens, we can see that how we talk in our classrooms, the patterns of dialogue we set up and reinforce, can be as important as what we actually talk about. Through the patterns of talk that dominate the classroom, we focus students' attention on key features and attributes of a thinking-based discussion, such as responding to others' ideas, attending to the other side of the case, generating alternative explanations, and weighing evidence. We establish the norms for the kinds of thinking that are valuable and appropriate, and we help students internalize these ways of thinking as part of their own self-talk. Through practicing new ways of talking, students develop new ways of thinking.[2] This idea that private thinking mirrors public argument has a long history going back to the Greek and Roman philosophers (Billing, 1987). It can also be seen in more recent studies of how reasoning and rhetorical strategies quickly become adopted by students in classrooms (Anderson et al., 2001).

We can see this process of development happening in the mathematical argument from John Threlkeld's classroom (Chapter Five). We saw how students were forced to take a position, present evidence and logic to defend that position, weigh the evidence and logic presented by others, respond to flaws they perceived in others' reasoning, and ultimately reach a new understanding of the problem. Although this argument was conducted orally as part of a whole-group discussion, the process mirrors what John wants his students to do independently as they confront new problems and issues in mathematics. That is, rather than rely on a memorized rule, students must reach for understanding as they construct their own logical arguments and weigh those arguments against alternative perspectives and rationales.

Of course, one episode or encounter does not constitute a pattern of talking, and a single episode is certainly insufficient to develop new ways of thinking. To act as an enculturating force, ways of talking must be established and carried out over time. In this respect, these discourse patterns are quite similar to the routines we explored in the previous chapters. Another shared characteristic is that these patterns of talking tend to be taught in context and in the moment. However, this need not always be the case. Teachers sometimes find it helpful to set up specific situations in which they lay out a new set of verbal rules and protocols for the group to practice across several occasions. These explicit structures can then be integrated more informally into the ongoing conversation of the classroom and eventually into students' thinking. This internalization is the goal of reciprocal teaching, a discourse routine developed by Annemarie Palinscar and Ann Brown (1984). Reciprocal teaching promotes students' metacognition by focusing their attention on asking questions of clarification, summarizing what others have said, and posing new questions to stimulate thought and discussion. Two additional examples of explicitly developing new ways of talking are Heather Woodcock's leaderless discussion and Chris Elnicki's public issue discussion, which we now look at more closely.

A Leaderless Discussion

Heather Woodcock challenges the typical pattern of teacher-directed classroom discourse by using a structure she calls a leaderless discussion. This technique forces students to be more active listeners, to incorporate their own ideas and perspectives with those of their classmates, and to take more initiative and ownership. In addition, it frees the teacher to listen more carefully to students and to assess their responses. In the midst of a classroom discussion, Heather sometimes becomes aware of her role in dominating the flow of conversation and ideas and suddenly declares, "Could you hold that thought? Let's do a leaderless discussion without me so that you're not all looking at me every time you talk. Do the hands with the fingers, and I want you to raise this issue to see what people say. You can use this issue as a discussion question."

With this redirection, students shift their focus from the teacher to each other, applying the guidelines for a leaderless discussion that they have previously learned. These rules are relatively simple: students take turns throwing out an issue, question, or puzzle related to the topic under discussion—often a book the class is reading or a particular historical event they are studying. The person initiating the question then calls on a fellow student to respond. When that student is finished, he or she has the responsibility of calling on the next contributor. Thus, the leading of the discussion is passed from student to student. Students signal their desire to participate by raising their hands, using their fingers to indicate how many times they have already contributed to the discussion. This simple method of record keeping ensures that a few students don't dominate the discussion. Once interest in the question has died down, a new student may ask the group if it is OK to pose a new question for discussion.

These logistics help the discussion move along smoothly. However, the real pattern of talk being developed has to do with how Heather has coached students to respond to each other. We can see this in the students' discussion of the book, *War Comes to Willy Freeman*, by James and Christopher Collier. Sitting in a semicircle so that everyone can see everyone else, students explore questions of race, politics, gender, and war as they relate to the American Revolution and to today. A girl asks the group, "Why does it seem like the blacks were more sympathetic towards each other even though they were on different sides? And are we more racist or less racist today than in the book?"

A boy opposite the questioner raises his hand and is called on. He begins by restating the question, signaling that he has listened closely to what is being asked, "Well, the reason I think they were sympathetic towards each other even though they were on different sides is because it was really hard for them either way. They had been brought from, almost kidnapped from, their country and just brought over here, and it was like, 'What's going on?' They really had to work together. They just had different views on the war but they all wanted to come together. Everybody was, like, more racist then and all this other stuff."

Another student presents his opinion, "I think, like also, they may have been more sympathetic to each other because they wanted them to join their side. If I wanted someone to join my side, being mean to them isn't exactly the best way to go about it. I think in one way there is [sic] more racism then than there is now. There was slavery, and any white person would feel free to do whatever they wanted to them."

A third student adds her comments, again relying on her experience, "I think it has changed from the 1700s to now because half of my friends are white and half of my friends are black, and it doesn't really matter what race you are."

Because no hands go up to continue the discussion, a student asks the group if she can pose a new question. The group agrees, and she asks, "Why do you think that Willy's father grabbed her to help take the horse back?"

Another student quickly raises her hand and asks, "Can I add to that? Why did he take Willy instead of taking her mother?"

Students have many ideas related to this question of motive, and responses flow quickly. However, Heather notices that the responses aren't grounded in the particulars of the story. Rather, students offer hedged possibilities, "Maybe it was because . . ." "It could have been to . . ." To focus students back on evidence and information from the book, Heather raises her hand to join the discussion. She's quickly called on as she has not yet made a contribution to the discussion.

Heather begins her response by referring to the book, "On page 17, this is reminding me of what you said, Steve. This is real interesting, I think probably why Pa took Willy, which I thought was really stupid of him. Willy's mom said, 'She's just a child, Jordan.' And he says, 'No, she ain't. She's thirteen.' And then the mom says, 'She's a girl. She's not a man.' And that stops him for a minute, and then he says, 'Willy, get me one of my hats.' And I'm wondering if he wasn't thinking of

Willy as a child anymore, and does he not care whether she is a girl or a boy?"

Heather's modeling seems to work, and the responses that follow make more references to the text. One student adds, "Well, it says that the mother is wearing a dress, and Willy is wearing breeches. So if they need to hurry and get the horse and ride it back, he's not going to want to wait for her to change into pants. Willy already has them on, and she can just put on a hat and pass for a boy."

Another student contributes, "I agree. I think that the mom is more vulnerable than Willy. 'Cause if Willy looks like a boy, then they are just going to be, like, 'Son, where are your parents?' It says in the book that the men command more respect."

The discussion moves along in this fashion for another ten minutes, lively on occasion and moving more slowly at other times. All members of the class participate, including Heather, who raises her fingers and waits to be called on like any other member of the group.

The leaderless discussion promotes three elements of good talk and good thinking. First is an emphasis on responding directly and in a focused way to the question being asked. By restating the question, students are forced to clarify their understanding of what is being asked and focus their response on the question. Second is the importance of tying ideas together by referring to and building on the responses of others. We see this when one student adds to another's question or a student makes a direct statement of agreement with another's response. This way of talking facilitates the making of mental connections. Third is the role of evidence in making arguments. Although Heather's students often feel more comfortable expressing opinions and sharing personal stories, she chooses to enter the discussion to subtly remind students of the need to support their opinions with evidence from their reading. Clarity, connections, and evidence play an important role in the leaderless discussion, and through the discussion students can internalize these elements in their thinking.

A Public Issue Discussion

When the thirty-five seventh graders in Chris Elnicki's social studies class enter the room, they immediately notice that their desks have been rearranged into a large circle. Quickly finding a seat, they prepare to discuss the question written in large block letters on the blackboard: "What kind of policy should the USA have concerning immigration?"

Michelle has been appointed the moderator for the discussion, and she quickly gets to work, calling on the first brave student to raise his hand.

Josh makes his initial contribution, "The policy I think we should have is to have background checks on all the people who come from everywhere to make sure they are clean. No warrants, no drug smuggling and stuff."

Still quite new at this and a bit nervous, Michelle quickly turns to the next student offering to participate.

Sean offers a different perspective: "I think we should let people into America like we did in the 1900s. In the 1900s, we didn't have restrictions all that much, and it was a big technological advancement time when all these machines were coming into use, and everything was, like, being made better, and if we let more people in now, maybe that would happen again."

Chris interjects to point out the different character of Sean's remark, "OK, we could call that factual information, and if someone disagreed with Sean, we could look for information that either proved or disproved that."

On the opposite side of the room, Denise raises her hand with the intent of redirecting the conversation, "Going back to Josh, are you saying that people who are living in the United States already who have warrants, to get rid of them?"

Without waiting for the moderator, Josh responds, "No, I'm just saying that, like, drugs that are in the United States mostly come from Mexico. And, like, we should do a background check because we don't want bad people coming to the United States."

Once again, Chris quickly labels the exchange that has just taken place, "Denise with a clarifying question. Nice job."

Another student jumps in, "This is still going on that point. Well, some people make mistakes. Like, if they live in another country and they make a mistake and they pay for it. But they have family members living in here or something. What do you say about that?"

"I don't understand the question. Could you say it again?" Josh asks.

The student expands on her initial comment, "Like if somebody from Germany wanted to come here, but they had a background where they smuggled drugs or they were caught with drugs once or twice, but they cleaned up their act. And they've been drug free for ten or fifteen years. Would you allow them into the United States?

"Yeah, I'd allow them into the United States," Josh states, then adds, "But it's like recent warrants I'm talking about. But if they cleaned up their act, I'd say, 'Yeah, come on in.'"

The class isn't quite finished with Josh, and they ask him a few more questions before the discussion begins to move to the more general issue of the intersection between immigration and drugs and the feasibility of background checks. This happens as a student makes a connection to an earlier comment that has yet to receive any attention: "I want to go back to Sean's comments. You said to open it back up like it used to be before, but the whole reason why we have a border is because of drugs, and if we opened up, it would be even worse."

Chris labels the comment, "OK, there could be a factual-issue disagreement here. We could do a check on those facts and see if the boundary is really about drugs."

Sean clarifies and expands his original position, "Well, I kind of agree with what Josh is saying about background checks and all, even though that may seem contradictory to what I said before. We shouldn't completely open our borders, and the background checks are good ideas." Sean continues, responding to another student's earlier assertion that background checks are too time-consuming and therefore not feasible: "What I was reading last night said there was [sic] only about 700,000 people a year that come in as immigrants, and there is [sic] about [that] many that also come in illegally. So it wouldn't take that much to do background checks on 700,000."

"OK," Chris interjects, "Sean's bringing in evidence to support his position, and he's also dealing with a definitional issue. He says 700,000 isn't that many, and others are saying it is."

Over the forty-minute period, the discussion remains lively, weaving across additional issues related to immigration, including the contributions of immigrants historically, the plight of refugees, and the importance of access to freedom. Throughout, students are making connections and spontaneously relating their comments to previous contributions in one way or another. The sophistication and ease with which students contribute and the facts they bring to support their positions are quite impressive. But the students aren't so much innately adept at this kind of thinking and discussing as they are well prepared. How did Chris set the stage for such an effective performance? Why did he choose this forum and instructional vehicle, and what does he hope students will gain from it?

Chris Elnicki engages his class in a series of public issue discussions throughout the year to get his students used to presenting opinions based on evidence, listening to others, and expanding their understanding of issues by considering alternative perspectives and making connections. He introduces students to the discussions by explaining their connection to their ongoing study of what it means to be an American:

> Tomorrow, we're going to have a public issue discussion. So the question is, What is a public issue discussion? First, let me tell you what it is going to look like in here. When you come in tomorrow, there will be a giant circle. All of the desks will be in a ring. And we are going to discuss these issues [points to the blackboard]. We're going to talk about the United States and whether we should restrict immigration policy. We're going to deal with the general question of what kind of policy should we have concerning immigration. So when you come back tomorrow after you've gone through these readings and highlighted things and made questions for yourself, you're going to come in tomorrow with some kind of opinion about what the immigration policy should be. Without even knowing exactly what it is at the moment, you'll have an opinion about whether it should remain how it is, be made more restrictive, or be loosened up a bit to allow more people in.

Chris goes on to clarify the purposes and goals of the discussion by explaining that the discussion is not like a debate in which someone tries to prove a point or to win an argument. Rather, he says, "The goal is to expand our thinking about some issues and to review things that are in our own minds. We're going to think about controversial topics. We're going to see how other people feel and relate to those topics." Chris breaks down this overarching goal into more discrete actions that both guide students' participation and direct his assessment of students' performance during the discussion. These actions, set out in Exhibit 6.1, consist of mental and verbal moves, each with a corresponding point value, that students should strive to make as a part of their participation in the discussion.

As Chris goes over each move, he gives examples of what it might look like in the midst of the actual discussion and tells why and how

2 points	Taking a position
1 point	Making a relevant comment based on others' responses
2 points	Supporting a position with evidence
1 point	Presenting factual information
2 points	Drawing other people into the discussion
1–2 points	Helping to move the discussion along
2 points	Recognizing contradictions in other people's arguments
2 points	Recognizing others' irrelevant comments
2 points	Making an analogy
1–2 points	Asking clarifying questions

Exhibit 6.1. Public Issue Discussion Assessment.
Source: Elnicki (1998).

each is important within the overall purpose of the discussion. For instance, in explaining the role of analogies, Chris offers the class an off-the-cuff example, "You know, this immigration thing is just like my mom making cookies. You get all these different ingredients all over the place, and you make something new, and everyone benefits because everybody gets a cookie." Chuckling with the rest of the class, Chris adds, "OK, it might not be a very good analogy, but I tried. You're going to have better analogies." Chris then explains why analogies are useful in deepening understanding: "What I find is that when somebody starts to say, 'This is like this' in these conversations, that sometimes becomes some of the most fun and some of the best thinking that we do. We start to use those symbols, and that takes us in a little bit of a different direction, and often we discover some interesting things in terms of people's arguments."

We can see that Chris's list of actions not only constitutes a useful set of moves for a group discussion but also embodies much of the kinds of thinking Chris is trying to encourage generally. Asking clarifying questions, looking for supporting evidence, weighing the evidence one comes across, making connections and analogies are precisely the kinds of mental moves that can support students in their ongoing efforts to think, reason, and develop understanding. By explicitly naming each of these mental moves and providing students with a list of them, Chris raises students' awareness of them. In essence, naming the thinking moves helps create a new mental category that can foster new perceptions. We discuss this role of language further in the next section.

The actual format of the public issue discussion is similar to that of Heather's leaderless discussion in that Chris takes somewhat of a backseat and has students actually lead the discussion. However, it differs in that one student is in charge of the facilitation and has the responsibility for calling on others, clarifying comments, making connections, and asking others to respond to points being made. In this respect, the skills that the student moderator needs are similar to those taught in the reciprocal teaching discussed previously (Palinscar & Brown, 1984).[3] The student in charge is coached to be careful about various types of bias—specifically, gender bias, favoritism toward one's friends, and bias against calling on oneself—in carrying out his or her role. Another contrast with Heather's approach is that Chris takes on a metalinguistic and metacognitive role in the conversation, actively commenting on the discussion itself and labeling its various parts. For students still learning to take on new mental and verbal moves, this commentary identifies the moves and makes it easier for students to try on and replicate them in their own contributions.

THE LANGUAGE OF THINKING

We all know that some words carry a lot of baggage. When we hear those words in a certain context or when they are spoken by particular individuals, they trigger a mental and often an emotional charge that helps us interpret the situation and infuse it with meaning. The presence of these words not only directs how we see the situation but also affects our response and the shape of our thinking. You can see these emotion-based responses easily when slurs or epithets are used. These words tend to heighten our awareness and our ire. On a less emotional level, such words also help us frame the situation as confrontational, polarized, and biased. Thus, they tell us something about the thinking of the speaker and point a direction for our own thinking and response, perhaps by causing us to confront the bias and one-sided perspective being displayed.

Let's consider a less loaded instance of how words can shape thinking. Consider having a discussion in which a friend says to you, "I'd be cautious about that." How would the use of the word *cautious* shape your thinking? It might cause you to pull back and reconsider the situation from a new perspective or to look more closely at the situation. It might make you more metacognitive, leading you to be more aware of your thinking and to avoid automatic responses. It might cause you to probe your friend's perspective and see what she is noticing that you aren't. The use of the word *cautious* tells us something about the speaker's thinking as well. The word indicates a level of skepticism and suggests that not enough evidence exists in the speaker's mind.

Now, consider the different reaction you might have if your friend simply had said, "I'd think about that." Here, the word *think* seems almost too general to interpret. It could mean various things from "make sure that's what you want to do" to "I think you're wrong, and I want you to see that." The word *think* is so general that it really doesn't direct our action in the same way the word *cautious* does. Of course, this generality is fine in some instances, particularly when we have enough contextual information or personal wherewithal to provide our own specificity and direction to the word. However, this often isn't the case for our students or ourselves. When we tell students to think, I imagine that many of them are completely puzzled about what we are asking them to do. For many students, the word *think* seems to be interpreted as: Be quiet for about ten seconds, look downward in the general direction of the floor, then look up and nod when the teacher asks, "Well, did you think about it?" If we want students to do more than fall silent at the word *think,* we need to be more directive and explicit in our use of language. We can use the language of thinking itself.

What Is the Language of Thinking?

What exactly do I mean by the language of thinking? Simply put, the language of thinking consists of all the words we use to refer to thinking processes, products, states, or stances.[4] For instance, words like *examine, justify, elaborate, ponder, reflect, infer,* and *consider* refer to thinking processes. These words describe ways of thinking or kinds of mental activity in which we might engage. We can think of these words basically as synonyms for the word *to think.* Words such as *theory, idea, conjecture, hypothesis, summary, deduction,* and *guess* identify products or outcomes of thinking. As you can see, there is clearly a connection between thinking processes and products, and most thinking verbs can be reframed as thinking nouns. The process of justifying yields a justification. The result of reflecting is a reflection. In addition, some words can be both processes and products, depending on how we use them. For example, you can question a statement, or you can ask a question. Process and product words represent the bulk of the language of thinking, and there are literally hundreds of them.[5]

Stance and state words, although fewer in number, are no less important. Stance words signal one's attitude toward thinking products. For instance, when we hear a particular claim, point, or idea, the words to describe our response can be *agree, disagree, question, concur, doubt, dispute,* or *resonate with,* just to name a few examples. Although these words also represent verbs or thinking actions, they differ from the other thinking processes I described earlier in that they clearly signal one's reaction or stance toward the thinking product on which attention is focused. You certainly could consider these words a subset of thinking processes if you like, but they differ from most thinking processes in an important way: being responses to stimuli, stances are more like products than are other process words. As such, they represent the stuff of thinking itself rather than a description of the act of thinking. David Perkins (personal communication, 2001) has called this "stuff" *ideons,* from the Greek word for idea. Both thinking products and thinking stances would be considered ideons.

State words describe one's mind-set or overarching mental reaction to events and ideas, such as *confusion, wonderment,* and *awe,* or feeling *overwhelmed, open, questioning,* or *dumbstruck.* These words, too, appear to be somewhat like products. However, they aren't necessarily the deliberate products of thinking; they aren't something that the process of thinking brings about. We wouldn't normally consider confusion a result of thinking, nor would we seek to create confusion for ourselves by thinking, but we recognize that confusion may characterize one's understanding and thinking at a particular time. In this way, state words operate more like adjectives in describing our mental functioning, understanding, and comprehension rather than as objects of thinking, or ideons, that we have sought to produce.

The Language of Thinking at Work

We have lots of thinking-related words, and those words can be grouped into categories, so what? How does this aspect of language relate to getting students to think and to promoting their intellectual character? Let's first look at two lists of thinking language to get a sense of the difference the language of thinking makes to the overall feel of a classroom. The two lists in Table 6.1 represent thinking-related words—processes, products, states, or stances—that two teachers used during the first week of school.[6] Both teachers teach the same course in the same subject area.

Classroom A	Classroom B
advocate	appreciate
agree, agreement	assume
ambiguous	aware of, being aware
argument	believe
assertion	challenge
assume, assumption	check
believe	clue
challenge	compared
conjecture	concept
convinced	concerned
curious	confused
declaration	conscious
dilemma	crazy
disagree	discover
dispute	distracted
dissenting	evidence
explain	expect
explore	explain
fundamentals	figure out
hypothetically	find out
interesting	focused
intuitive	forget
justification, justify	get a thought in their head
legitimate	get stuck
logical	getting it
observations	impression
opinion	inspire
play with	intentions
ponder	logic
position	mind
prediction	notice
proof	observation
question, questioning	presupposition
random	pretend
reasoning, reason, reasonable	question, questioning
respond	realize
rethink	reflect
revelation	remember
theory	settled in your brain
understand, understanding	understand, understanding
valid	visualization
	wondering
	worried

Table 6.1. Language of Thinking Lists from Two Classrooms.

One list comes from what I would characterize as a very thoughtful classroom, whereas the other is from a room where the teacher has a strong desire to promote thinking but the environment tends to be less rich in thinking overall.[7] Read over each list to see what kind of a feel you get for the classroom environment. Is it possible to pick out the list from the more thoughtful classroom? What differences in tone, generality, and direction do you detect across the lists?

The list for classroom A belongs to John Threlkeld and that for classroom B belongs to Karen White, both of whom teach beginning algebra. Overall, I consider John's classroom to be much more thoughtful and thinking-oriented than Karen's. However, the lists don't necessarily reveal a stark contrast, and you may have been left with some ambiguity about which was more thoughtful overall. This is to be expected; the language of thinking is only one component of the culture of thinking. We'd be surprised and probably a bit skeptical if creating thoughtful classrooms required us only to use a different vocabulary. Still, there are some differences between the lists that are worth pointing out.

You may have noticed that the words in John's list tend toward greater specificity than those in Karen's list. For instance, Karen uses words and expressions such as *being aware of, figure out, find out, getting it, get stuck, get a thought in your head, mind,* and *settled in your brain.* This kind of everyday talk may be accessible to students, but it isn't very pointed as far as telling students what kind of thinking to do or what the product of their thinking should be. John's list exhibits some of these expressions as well—*play with, rethink*—but they are far fewer in number. Greater specificity may be useful in facilitating specific thinking processes—such as argumentation, proof, and exploring ideas—and indicates clearer expectations for doing so. Another issue is the manner in which Karen sometimes used the words, though this certainly won't be clear from a list of words out of context. For instance, Karen explains to a student who has been absent that "Yesterday, we had a really cool class where we *worried* about perfect numbers." On another occasion, she speaks energetically and with pleasure about course goals that students had listed: "This makes me *crazy.* There are people who are concerned with actually understanding the math." The choice of these words made me, as an observer, feel somewhat confused both about what Karen means and the types of thinking processes and states she is alluding to in her use of language.

Another difference that you may detect across the lists has to do with the focus of instruction. When I shared these two lists with a group of teachers I was working with in Denver, Colorado, one woman remarked that John's list reminded her of a trial or investigation. It seemed to her that there was a lot of arguing or debate going on in the class. We can see this in words like *advocate, agree, argument, assertion, assumption, challenge, declaration, disagree, dispute, justification, legitimate, position,* and *valid.* This impression squared well with my own experience of the class. It was a place where ideas were debated and argued about and where students were expected to take and defend positions. Karen's list seems to indicate a focus on acquiring knowledge, skills, and answers. We can see this through such words as *aware of, believe, check, clue, discover, figure out, find out, get a thought, getting it, get stuck, mind, realize,* and *remember.* There are also quite a few words in Karen's list that deal with attitude, affect, and things to avoid or watch out for: *concerned, confused, conscious, distracted, focused, forget, intentions,* and *worried.*

THE POWER OF IDEONS. Looking at the two lists of thinking words in terms of the four categories—process, products, states, and stances—another difference between the two lists emerges, (see Tables 6.2 and 6.3). Although Karen used many words associated with thinking processes and stances, John's words made more mention of very specific products of thinking and thinking stances. In fact, John used such ideons, that is, product and stance words, more than twice as much as Karen did. In contrast, Karen used three times as many state words as John.

Use of ideons may be more helpful in that these words indicate to students not only what they must do, thinking processes, but also what they must produce. Asking a student for a justification of an answer is perhaps more likely to provoke thinking than a more general admonition to check his or her answer. Product words clearly implicate thinking processes, but the converse is not always true; processes are not always clearly tied to products. This can be particularly true in classrooms where students are inclined to do only what teachers demand of them. It is one thing for a teacher to ask students, as a general admonition, to reflect on their progress or to work on developing understanding as they read. It is quite another to ask students to produce a reflection regarding their progress or to write a summation.

Process	State	Product	Stance
assume	bogged down	argument	advocate
explain, explaining	convinced	agreement	agree
explore, exploring	curious	assertion	ambiguous
justify	understand	assumption	believe
memorize		declaration	challenge
play with		fundamentals	dilemma
questioning		justification	disagree
reasoning		observations	hypothetically
remember		opinion	interesting
respond		prediction	intuitive
rethink		proof	legitimate
understand,		question	logical
understanding		reason	position
		revelation	question
		rule	random
		theory	reasonable
		understanding	valid

Table 6.2. The Language of Thinking in John Threlkeld's Classroom.

The mention of thinking stances might play a similar role in directing students to think. By asking students to take a stance or by labeling the stances that students spontaneously offer, John points out the thinking that is going on and indicates his expectation for thinking. In comparison, Karen seldom alludes to taking a stance toward particular ideas or comments. As a result, her students might be less inclined to engage with the ideas because such engagement is not so much a part of the way of talking about ideas in her classroom. As previously mentioned, another difference in the two classrooms is Karen's use of words to describe thinking states. This reflects her concern with students' feelings, comfort, and perceptions. However, the states she refers to are often linked to students' attention and basic comprehension, such as *focused* or *distracted* and *getting it* or *confused*, rather than implicating deeper and more complex ways of thinking.

CREATING NEW THINKING WITH WORDS. The language of thinking also works to promote students' thinking by creating new categories of thought and experience. When we give a name to something, we create a new reality that previously didn't exist for ourselves. These new labels and categories foster new perceptions and new responses by allowing us to draw out *isolates of experience* or *isolates of meaning* (Carroll, 1956). They help sensitize us to thinking occasions and the

Process	State	Product	Stance
being aware	aware of	clue	appreciate
check	concerned	concept	assume
compare	confused	evidence	believe
discover	conscious	impression	challenge
expect	crazy	intentions	
explain	distracted	logic	
figure out	focused	observation	
find out	get stuck	presupposition	
forget	getting it	question	
get a thought in their head	settled in your brain	understanding	
notice	understand	visualization	
pretend	worried		
question			
realize			
reflect			
remember			
understand			
wondering			

Table 6.3. The Language of Thinking in Karen White's Classroom.

particular types of thinking called for in those occasions. For instance, because the Dätiwuy language of northern Australia has more precise words for describing certain body movements, such as looking about while seated, looking back over one's shoulder, and stumbling upon something unexpected, speakers of that language are more adept at noticing, picking out, and replicating these movements than are English speakers, even though the movements are equally observable to all (Lee, 1997). The presence of these words indicates the importance of the categories to the group and helps to direct attention and perception.

The same principle of using language to call attention to important subtleties and differences applies to thinking. A guess is different from a conjecture, which is different from a hypothesis, which is different from a theory. Assuming is different from inferring, which is different from deducing, which is different from generalizing. By knowing and being comfortable with the nuanced language of thinking and by being in an environment where that language is used, students come to think more often and more deeply. Janet Astington and David Olson (1990) found that knowing and correctly applying thinking language in appropriate situations is related to students' critical-thinking abilities.

It is not surprising, then, that in thoughtful classrooms teachers not only use but also teach the language of thinking. Remember Chris Elnicki's public issue discussion? One of the things he did throughout that discussion was to label students' responses:

- "Denise with a clarifying question."
- "There could be a factual-issue disagreement here."
- "Sean's bringing in evidence to support his position, and he's also dealing with a definitional issue."
- "John, are you trying to point out a contradiction?"
- "OK, that's an ethical value issue."
- "Max is doing something no one has done today, presenting an analogy."

By putting names to the thinking occurring in the discussion, Chris helps students in their ongoing efforts to isolate the thinking moves from the flow of the discussion. The students then have a chance to try out these new ways of thinking and verbal framing as a way of putting into practice the new conceptual categories. Instruction also can take a less formal approach. When John Threlkeld first uses a word like *ambiguous* or *conjecture,* he pauses and asks students if they know what it means. Once someone defines the word, he then uses it quite naturally as part of the language of the classroom. In a lesson on bias, Heather Woodcock has her students read a portion of text on the Middle Ages and then look for words that indicate the perspective of the author and any possible bias. This brief activity helps sensitize her students to language and how it conveys attitudes and stances. At the same time, it helps students focus on the more specific language of bias itself.

THE LANGUAGE OF MINDFULNESS

The language of thinking emphasizes the important role that explicit language plays in shaping and directing thinking. However, language can play a much more subtle role in shaping thinking. An example will help to demonstrate this point.

A few years ago, I had the opportunity of viewing an exhibit of René Magritte paintings. If you are familiar with his surrealist work, you know that his paintings are anything but ordinary, frequently juxtaposing unlikely objects or putting objects in unusual settings to surprise the viewer. Turning a corner in the exhibition hall, I was confronted with an austere canvas two by three feet. Painted in tones of brown and black was a very large tobacco pipe of a simple and old-fashioned variety. The pipe had a large bowler-shaped cup and stem that curved upward in a sensuous *S* shape. Below the image of the pipe, painted in the perfect script of a sign painter, were the French words, "Çeci n'est pas une pipe," meaning "This is not a pipe" (Magritte, 1928a). My first reaction was to chuckle to myself. My second reaction was to engage more fully with the painting. If this isn't a pipe, what is it? Some kind of a tool, perhaps? A painting of a pipe rather than the pipe itself? Upside down, it looked a bit like it could be used as a hat. After playing Magritte's game for a few minutes and enjoying it, I continued my way through the rest of the exhibit, only later to come across "This is not an apple!"

"This is not a pipe" would not come under the heading of a phrase from the language of thinking. The words themselves didn't even ask me to think or to engage with the painting in any way. Yet the words were quite effective at prompting my thinking. Why would this happen? When I first viewed the painting, my mind recognized the image instantly as a tobacco pipe. There was nothing unusual or startling about the image to force my mind to process it further. Having achieved a sense of closure, my mind was ready to disengage and move on to the next painting in the gallery. However, reading the words arrested that disengagement, that desire to tune out. Rather than closing down my thinking, Magritte's words opened it up. If this isn't a pipe, what is it? What else might it be? What else does it look like? What have I assumed that I shouldn't? Language often has this effect of producing or forestalling closure. When something is labeled, decided, listed, or given in an absolute fashion, one's mind often takes it in without questioning. In contrast, when even a small bit of ambiguity is introduced, allowing for the possibility of interpretation and change based on context and conditions, the mind is more likely to remain open. This open, flexible state in which new categories are created can be termed mindfulness (Langer, 1989).

Conditional Instruction and Mindfulness

A key principle of mindfulness is that one should cultivate an openness to distinctions and differences in context rather than seeking early closure. This openness to distinctions permits greater creativity and helps to avoid rigid and narrow thinking. Under conditional instruction, that is, instruction that focuses on the situated and conditional nature of facts and knowledge, participants encounter information in an open rather than absolute format. Therefore, we predict that the mind will remain open to adapting or altering that information when conditions changed.

A study by Langer and Piper (1987) first introduced the idea of using conditional, as opposed to absolute, instruction as a means of cultivating greater mindfulness in specific situations. In the study, subjects casually encountered a rubber object in a room where they were working with an experimenter. The experimenter commented to the subject either that this could be a dog's chew toy (a conditional instruction) or that this was a dog's chew toy (an absolute instruction). The subjects who received the conditional instruction were much more likely than their counterparts to consider using the rubber object as an eraser when, later in the experiment, the experimenter artificially created the need for something to erase a pencil mark. By being told that the object could be a dog's chew toy, the participants were able to remain mentally open and consider using the object in a new way once the conditions changed. In contrast, labeling the object definitively tended to produce cognitive closure.

Conditional instruction has also been tested in more routine learning situations, such as in reading factual material in preparation for a test on urban planning. Conditional instruction in these settings took the form of presenting the facts in a more open way: "this may be the cause of the evolution of city neighborhoods" instead of "the cause of [the] evolution of city neighborhoods is . . ." In these studies, participants who were conditionally instructed demonstrated equal retention of information but more flexibility and creativity in using that information to solve problems (Langer, Hatem, Joss, & Howell, 1989; Langer & Piper, 1987; Ritchhart & Perkins, 2000).

But why should the simple alteration of language have such a large effect? Although it may seem as if the conditional words—*could be, might be, one possibility is*—somehow magically keep the mind open, I think something else is going on, something more akin to what happened when I saw the Magritte painting. The introduction of openness and a degree of ambiguity through conditional instruction or circumstance prompts a shift from a passive to an active role. The student becomes engaged not in memorizing information but in making sense of the situation. As the student takes charge to fill in the gaps, his or her authority and autonomy as a learner are strengthened also.

In the process of making sense of something, even in brief perceptual instances, alternatives get explored because the learner isn't just striving for a correct answer but rather is building a series of connections and abstractions that will facilitate later transfer to new situations (Salomon & Perkins, 1989). When learners take a single correct answer as the goal, they are likely to narrow quickly their examination of possibilities, resulting in less flexible use of their knowledge (Langer & Piper, 1987).

The thoughtful teachers I studied weren't aware of mindfulness theory or conditional instruction. Nonetheless, they tended to teach in mindful ways using conditional instruction. Teachers presented ideas as open, using phrases such as "some people think," "one explanation is," "no one knows for sure, but most think," "it could be," and "usually it is that way but not always." One area where we might not expect to see conditional instruction is in mathematics. After all, isn't math just a bunch of rules to memorize? However, both Doug Tucker and John Threlkeld often use conditional instruction when helping students solve problems. In debriefing a particular problem, both teachers would frequently ask, "Who solved it another way? Who has a different approach? OK, that's one way to tackle it." Similarly, when they were showing students new techniques or procedures for solving problems, they would frequently present more than one way. When a teacher presents only one way of solving a problem, students close off and work to memorize that method, often ignoring their own intuitive understandings. When a teacher presents more than one method, students are more likely to activate their understanding and reconcile and use that understanding with the methods that have been presented.

The overall effect of such open and active instruction is to make students more aware of and sensitive to the ambiguous or conditional nature of the world and to help them see that knowledge and understanding are always in flux. In addition, such instruction draws on our natural inclination to fill in the gaps and make sense of the world. Honoring this natural inclination in the classroom by creating situations that are both engaging and ambiguous helps students develop a sense of their own agency as learners.

THE POWER OF LANGUAGE

Language wraps itself around, in, through, and between everything that we teachers and learners do in the classroom. Because it is omnipresent, we can easily take the role of language for granted, considering it only as a tool for delivering our content. Yet in many ways language acts as both the medium and the message in the cultivation of intellectual character. Through language, we expose students to new ideas, alternative perspectives, and opportunities to participate in dialogue. This external dialogue can then be internalized in the form of self-talk, through which individuals spontaneously anticipate, project, and consider alternative perspectives. Students try on new ways of thinking that they have been exposed to through the language of others. The language of the classroom is used to carve paths and lay down patterns of conversation to guide the thinking of the group. These paths highlight what is most important in a given context and enculturate students into new ways of talking and thinking. The specific words we use allow students to isolate elements of their experience, attend to them, reflect on them, and respond to them. These words act as cues that can prime students to engage in certain kinds of thinking. The language we use in the classroom can produce a response of openness and encouragement of autonomy, or it can act to close off and restrict our own and our students' thinking.

As an important cultural force, we teachers need to increase our understanding of the role that language is playing and can play in our individual classrooms. We need to look at our practice and think about the opportunities we provide for students to engage in meaningful dialogue. We need to examine the discourse routines of our classroom to see if we have created structures that can both direct conversation and guide students' thinking. We need to examine the language of thinking that we use to see where we might sharpen and focus it. Do we speak only in general terms of thinking, feeling, and having ideas, or do we ask students for specific products of thinking and ask them to take stances toward ideas? At the same time, we must not let our concern with language paralyze us or make us too self-conscious. Language is a flexible medium, and we should pull and push at its edges to expand and better capitalize on its power to prompt, prime, and pattern thinking.

~~~~~ **Key Ideas for Developing Intellectual Character**
IN THE CLASSROOM: LANGUAGE AND THINKING

- *Something to Talk and Think About.* Issues, problems, or experiences that engage students give them something to think about as well as a meaningful way to explore facts, ideas, and skills. Creating controversy, ambiguity, or conflict around a topic can enhance discussion and thinking. Language needs something to wrap itself around: some content, focus, or topic to which it can grab hold.

- *Reasoning as Dialogue and Argumentation.* The social world becomes the internal world. The act of reasoning can be thought of as carrying on an internalized dialogue with oneself. Through experiencing dialogue and argument in the group, students not only are exposed to other points of view but also come to actively anticipate and consider alternative perspectives, not only of others but from within themselves.

- *Creating Patterns of Talking and Thinking.* Students develop modes of thinking by internalizing classroom patterns for discussing ideas. Sometimes these patterns are explicit, as in reciprocal teaching, the leaderless discussion, or the public issue discussion. These structured interactions teach specific mental moves, such as asking clarifying questions or connecting ideas, that students can adapt for use in their own thinking.

- *The Language of Thinking.* Words related to processes, products, states, and stances of thinking form a language of thinking. This language helps us to isolate bits of experience, which increases our sensitivity to thinking occasions and metacognitive awareness. Because product and stance words specify thinking outcomes, they may be the most useful in activating thinking.

- *Conditional Instruction.* Language can help keep the mind open and flexible. When we take in new information and facts conditionally, as something that "might be" or as "one way" rather than as absolutes, the mind engages more actively with the data and is more able to remember, adapt, and use it in new contexts.

CHAPTER SEVEN

Thought-Full Environments

Sustaining a Culture of Thinking

T ry this little thought experiment: recall a classroom you recently have been in or seen, perhaps on videotape or television, that you would describe as a thinking-rich learning environment. Generate a vivid image of that classroom in your mind's eye. Work to bring up and experience the feelings you felt while being in or viewing that environment. Once you have a good sense of that classroom physically, intellectually, and emotionally, think of five spirited adjectives or descriptive phrases to describe that classroom. Work to capture the essence of the classroom and give others a good sense of what it would be like to actually be in that environment. You can make either a quick mental list of your words or write them down.

What adjectives best describe a thinking-rich classroom? Having done this experiment with teachers all over the world, I can share some common responses: passionate, engaging, fun, exciting, warm, responsive, trusting, safe, flexible, unique, outside the norm, pushing the envelope, spirited, active, hands-on, cool, focused, rich, beyond the status quo, textured, challenging, highly independent, student-centered, hardworking, energetic, inspiring, meaningful, connected, purposeful, rigorous, open, joyful, full of risk taking, and resourceful.

Quite an impressive set of descriptors; perhaps some of your adjectives are in this list. Clearly, these words paint a picture of the type of classrooms that we would like to be in, both as teachers and as students. An interesting aspect of such lists, either the one you made or the one here, is the feeling they produce. When I read over this list or create a mind picture of one of these classrooms, I can't help but smile, feeling excited and energized. These classrooms aren't dry and restrained environments; they are places brimming with interest and life. They are places that are full of thought—thoughtful in the most literal sense.

With your list of adjectives still in mind, continue the thought experiment by connecting the adjectives you identified to specific features or aspects of the classroom you were recalling. For instance, if you described the classroom as passionate, what is it that you saw or picked up on in the classroom that made you choose that word? Perhaps it was the way the teacher talked and expressed herself, or maybe the passion was visible in the interaction between the teacher and students as they discussed ideas. Whatever the aspect, push beyond your overall feelings or impressions to identify that aspect concretely. Try to point toward some general feature that others could see or attend to if they were to visit the classroom. Be aware that there isn't necessarily a one-to-one correspondence between your list of adjectives and these features, as it often takes several different things in combination to give us a sense of a place.

What you have identified in this second list is a collection of what I call *cultural forces,* that is, those aspects of a classroom responsible for giving it its unique flavor and feel. Although you might have worded them differently than I have, perhaps more concretely and better grounded in particulars, I suspect that most of the items you listed would fit under one of the following eight cultural forces:

- The expectations for students' thinking and learning that the teacher conveys
- The routines and structures that guide the life of the classroom
- The language that the teacher and students use and the conversations they engage in
- The opportunities, work, or activities the teacher creates for students

- How the teacher acts and what the teacher models for students
- The attitudes that the teacher and students convey
- The interactions and relationships between the teacher and the students as well as among the students themselves
- The physical environment and artifacts present in the room

I contend that our impression of any classroom, thoughtful or otherwise, is based on our quick assessment of these eight cultural forces at work. For all of us who have spent time in educational settings, which is virtually everyone, these eight elements represent natural categories. Based on your experience, you had these categories in the back of your mind before I provided them to you in a list. That is not to say that having the list before us, even though it is not exhaustive or definitive, isn't quite useful. Indeed, having a list of cultural forces can help us focus our attention more directly on how to build and sustain thoughtful environments, whether those environments are classrooms, schools, other educational settings, or the home.

I've already explored some of these forces at length in earlier chapters. Chapter Four focused on the initial process of building a culture of thinking by conveying expectations for thinking during the first days of school. Chapter Five discussed the role of routines in structuring the life of the classroom and developing students' thinking abilities. Chapter Six took a detailed look at how language operates to pattern, prime, and prompt thinking. In this chapter, I focus on those cultural forces I haven't yet touched on. I've grouped these forces together because collectively they help to paint a good portrait of what a thoughtful classroom looks and feels like. This grouping also provides us with an understanding of what it takes to sustain a culture of thinking over time. As I explore this remaining cluster of forces, I often loop back to examples of practices and instructional moves that I have mentioned previously. I do this to show that the cultural forces are not always discrete elements that can be isolated from one another.

OPPORTUNITIES FOR THINKING

In classrooms that are effective in nurturing students' intellectual character, you're unlikely to find the development of thinking skills listed in teachers' plan books. In my observations, I never witnessed a teacher teaching what might be considered an actual thinking-skills lesson, though several did talk with students explicitly about thinking-related issues such as developing understanding, taking responsibility for one's own learning, and the role of reflecting on one's thinking. Instead of thinking-skills lessons, what I found in teachers' practice was an abundance of rich thinking opportunities woven throughout the year that were carefully timed and supported. Through these opportunities, students learned thinking skills and were given a chance to practice them.

The thinking opportunities I witnessed varied widely in terms of the thinking and dispositions they sought to activate. Some activities focused on perspective taking, others on generating new possibilities and divergent thinking. Not surprisingly, opportunities for reflection and developing understanding often dominated. Usually, a teacher would weave together various types of thinking dispositions within a given project or activity. Whatever their focus, these rich thinking opportunities shared three important characteristics.

1. They focused on big ideas that were important to the discipline and worth the time and effort the class spent on them.

2. The opportunities themselves were engaging to students, capturing their interest and attention.

3. The opportunities provided the students some degree of autonomy, independence, and choice.

In this section, we take a look at how each of these characteristics operates to help ensure that the thinking opportunities teachers create are powerful and effective.

Focusing on Big Ideas

With the current political focus on standards and assessment, it is easy for classroom instruction to become centered on disconnected skills and isolated bits of knowledge. It takes work for teachers to step back from these objectives and think about how to reach them by connecting to bigger ideas and more important purposes. It takes even more work to make sure that these big ideas remain at the core of our teaching. We need to make sure that we remain aware of the forest even as we look at individual trees.

Heather Woodcock manages to do this by using a set of guiding throughline questions. These questions, presented in Chapter Four, identify the big disciplinary issues around which Heather's curriculum travels: the role of exploration and discovery in human existence, the importance of culture in shaping who we are and what we think, the origins of conflict, the significance and rituals of coming of age, and what it takes to search out the truth about events. Having the questions posted in the room helps to make sure that both teacher and students keep the larger goals and purposes front and center. However, the real focusing power of the questions comes not by merely making the big ideas present but by constantly asking students to make connections between the questions and what they are learning. This crucial activity is possible because Heather has framed the questions in a way that allows students to consider them as ongoing concerns that they can answer in different ways under different circumstances. Thus, by regularly tying students' work and activity back to the guiding questions, Heather ensures that students keep in mind the big ideas of the course.

Like Heather, John Threlkeld recognizes that big ideas need not only to be named but also to become an ongoing part of the classroom dialogue. Consequently, John is always asking his students to make connections, think about the purposes of their work, and search for the big ideas embedded within the problems and exercises they tackle. For instance, consider the two quiz problems presented in Exhibit 7.1. Although the problems themselves focus on making sure that students are acquiring basic computational skills, the accompanying questions ask students to connect these skills to bigger ideas in mathematics, in this case the distributive property and significance of parentheses in order of operations rules.

Developing course themes and generative topics is yet another way of making sure that the opportunities created for students will address big ideas. Both Susan McCray and Chris Elnicki organized their classes around the theme of the American Dream and the question, What makes an American an American? The American Dream is a generative topic in that it is central to the discipline, rich in connections, and accessible to students.[1] Its centrality to U.S. history is easy to see as the topic addresses the fundamental values of democracy, issues of national identity, and reasons behind our diverse and changing population. The topic's richness can be found in its connections to issues

A. Evaluate each of the following using the given values.

1. $x = 2$ $\qquad$ x^2 $\qquad$ $(x)^2$ $\qquad$ $-x^2$ $\qquad$ $(-x)^2$

2. $x = 2$ $\qquad$ $3x^2$ $\qquad$ $(3x)^2$ $\qquad$ $-3x^2$ $\qquad$ $(-3x)^2$

3. $x = -2$ $\qquad$ x^2 $\qquad$ $(x)^2$ $\qquad$ $-x^2$ $\qquad$ $(-x)^2$

4. $x = -2$ $\qquad$ $3x^2$ $\qquad$ $(3x)^2$ $\qquad$ $-3x^2$ $\qquad$ $(-3x)^2$

What very important point is being made by the above 4 problems?
Be as specific and clear as possible! THINK ABOUT IT—CAREFULLY!!

B. Evaluate each of the following using the given values:

1. $x = 2, y = 5$ $\qquad$ $5(x + y)$ $\qquad$ $5x + 5y$

2. $x = 2, y = 7$ $\qquad$ $-4(x - y)$ $\qquad$ $-4x - 4y$

3. $x = -2, y = 7$ $\qquad$ $-4(x - y)$ $\qquad$ $-4x - 4y$

What is the point of the 3 problems here? Can you write a rule down
without using any numbers?

Exhibit 7.l. Connecting Skills to Bigger Ideas in Mathematics.
Source: John Threlkeld.

of personal and group identity, immigration, nationalism, founding
ideals, and freedom. This richness makes it possible to explore the
topic through a variety of angles. For instance, Chris highlights issues
of immigration policies and practices, the Revolutionary War, and the
Bill of Rights, whereas Susan focuses on immigrant stories and experiences, slavery, westward expansion, racism, and the Civil War. Students find the topic accessible because they can approach it on both a
personal and a national level. Also, teacher and students can easily
connect the topic to questions surrounding current issues and con-
troversies such as: Who gets to be a U.S. citizen? Where does your freedom end? How do we reconcile a history of slavery and racism with
the idea of the American Dream?

All of these examples of connecting course activity to big ideas
accomplish the same thing: they enhance the purpose and meaning
of the work for students. Through a focus on big ideas, students
become clear about the larger purpose of the class and what the
teacher wants them to understand and learn more about. This makes
it easier to engage students in thinking because the work itself

demands thinking and active exploration. Students see that simple memorization of material or practice of skills is insufficient to meet the demands of the class. Furthermore, the thinking demanded of students is authentic in that it serves particular ends, unlike certain one-size-fits-all thinking-skills programs that might introduce a thinking skill in a discrete context disconnected from anything else students might be doing.

Fostering Engagement

Focusing activities on big ideas helps ensure that the thinking connected to these opportunities will be important and worthwhile to students. However, it is still necessary to get students engaged in these activities in the first place for that thinking to occur. The teachers I observed did this by situating the big ideas within a context that students could care about and find interesting or one that would grab their attention. Susan McCray's exploration of the roots of racism and Heather Woodcock's project on unanswerable questions provide some examples.

THE ROOTS OF RACISM. Susan McCray creates student engagement by personalizing the history of immigration in the United States through the actual stories of immigrants. Bringing history to the level of the ordinary individual, not just the famous or influential, makes the issues more real and accessible to students. In addition, because many of Susan's students are new immigrants themselves, they get a sense that their own experiences are recognized and honored. The stories Susan selects bring up issues of racism and inequality, issues that are close to the surface and full of passion for these adolescents. We can see these factors coming together to create student engagement as Susan's class begins to discuss Julius Lester's book of first-person accounts of slavery, *To Be a Slave.*

The class began reading the book the previous night as homework, and Susan opens up the day's discussion by asking, "What do you think of the book so far?"

Students, seated together informally in a circle on the floor, shout out a variety of responses: "Interesting." "Different." "I like it."

Susan follows up, "What's interesting about it?"

Joan elaborates, "There are different points of view, so you're not just getting one side of things or being told that this is the way it was."

Pushing Joan and the group further, Susan asks, "Why do you think [the author] did that?"

A student responds bluntly, "Because he likes to write books that way?"

Another student offers a more complex reason, "Because it gives you a better feel for what it was like, and you get to see how not everyone thinks the same way."

Still another student adds, "It makes you think about it more, too. You consider what you think or how you might feel. Like about racism and slavery and stuff."

Susan picks up on this theme and asks a new question of the group, "This is a huge question, but why do some people have these thoughts [about racism, blacks, and slavery] and others not? Where do people get these ideas? Why did some think blacks were inferior?"

Taking the question in a different direction, Marcus asks Susan and the group, "What I'm wondering about is how did the whites get the power to begin with? Over the blacks?"

"Good question," Susan responds, looking out at the group and inviting a student to respond.

"How did it get started?" a student asks back, then adds, "Nobody really knows. I know they came on boats, but when before that did it start? Nobody [in the materials they have been reading] has really answered it."

A few students begin talking about the whites taking over Africa and enslaving everybody. Susan interjects to correct this misconception, informing students that whites never actually took over all of Africa and that this didn't account for slavery. Another student offers up a confusion around voodoo, the topic of another book the class has recently read, and asks why voodoo didn't work for blacks to keep power.

This new question is left hanging when a student returns to the original question Susan asked about people's thinking toward blacks.

Marcia points out that in one of the accounts they read, the white owner didn't really want to have a slave but needed one to get by. Also, the owner didn't treat his slave badly, so maybe not everybody thought of blacks as inferior.

Susan asks Marcia to supply the evidence for her assertion, "Can you point out that passage? How did they treat him differently?"

Marcia thumbs through her book and reads a short passage.

"OK," Susan remarks, "He's the slave being treated better, but what is he still losing?"

The class responds with a chorus of "Freedom," "His home," "His family."

Susan prepares to close the discussion, which, while rambling, has readily engaged students with a variety of issues. Susan gives the class a final question to think about, "So what would you have done [if you were white and in that same situation]?" Then she adds, "I have to say, I ask myself these questions a lot. What would I have done? What causes people to do these things? How does it happen?"

The issues that Susan introduced in this discussion are raw, complex, and nuanced. The emotions they evoke are close to the surface and passionately held. These factors work to create students' engagement with the content and involvement in the kinds of thinking that can lead to understanding: considering different perspectives on the situation, looking for root causes, exploring the implications of actions on various scales and over time, and connecting ideas and themes.

UNANSWERABLE QUESTIONS. Another example of thinking opportunities that foster student engagement is Heather Woodcock's project on what she calls unanswerable questions. These questions are the kinds of universal, philosophical quandaries that humankind has always pursued, not exactly the typical fare for a middle school humanities class. On a visit to Heather's class in late March, I first noticed the questions. On cardstock sentence strips, written in an assortment of different hands and reflecting various levels of penmanship, were a collection of questions the students had generated:

- How did the world begin?
- Is there a God?
- Why do hate and evil exist?
- What is my mind?
- Are there parallel universes?
- Why do we judge?
- How do emotions work?
- Do humans have extra-sensory perception?
- Why is there a need to change our identity to fit into society?

- Why do we smile when we are happy?
- What is space? How far does it go before there are no more stars, planets, or darkness? And once we get there, what will we find?
- Is destiny predetermined, or do we determine our own? Or both?
- Who/what is God?
- Why do people commit suicide?
- Is there life on other planets?
- Is there a heaven?
- Why do good people suffer?

I couldn't help but be intrigued. I asked Heather about the origins of the assignment and its purpose. She explained, "I was doing some writing in my journal, and I started asking myself some of these [kinds of] questions and was intrigued by them. I thought, Well, why can't seventh graders do this?" She elaborates on the goals and purposes she thought the activity of contemplating these questions afforded students and how it fit within the course itself:

> I wanted them to think about being inquisitive outside of the classroom. . . . I was trying to get them to really focus on something that they were curious about and then bring that into school a little bit and make it more formal. Make them more aware of the bigger questions. Because there are so many answers to things we do in school. We don't necessarily ask the big questions very often. And there's no reason not to. So, it wasn't really based on Colonial America or any, you know, course content per se, other than I think the overarching goal of our curriculum is just to get kids to think more broadly. To think about life in an interesting way. . . . Another thing I'm trying to work on with this particular class is risk taking. And this certainly, not only in the writing and in the reading of these, but also in the performing of these, is a great way for them to take a risk in a structured environment.

Heather designed the assignment in a way that fostered engagement and personalization on several fronts. First, the generation of questions themselves created engagement. As homework, Heather asked students to generate three or four big questions that didn't have obvious responses or answers. Then the class had a general discussion about these kinds of questions, exploring the following issues: What makes a question unanswerable? Are they important questions if you can't find the answers? Are these kinds of questions the most important questions to be asking? Are they important at all? Why? As further homework, each student formulated a question that really intrigued him or her, writing about why he or she was drawn to that question, what was interesting about it, and initial thoughts on the question. This personalization ensured that the students had a high degree of engagement with their particular questions. Students shared these preliminary writings in small groups and received comments and suggestions on how to improve the response papers in a second draft. The final step of the project was for each student to use his or her response paper as the basis for a performance piece, perhaps a poem, a dramatic reading, or a piece of visual art. As with the beginning of the assignment, this final performance offered students a lot of choice and opportunity for personalization.

In reflecting on the assignment, Heather felt the level of engagement for students was not only high but also ongoing: "The kids are definitely intrigued. They're enjoying it. They thought it was a little bit strange to be doing in school, but they really liked hearing each other's questions and their responses to the questions. And it's been great to have the questions up in the classroom, because so many people come in and say, 'What's up with those questions? That's so interesting.'"

The thinking opportunities that Heather's assignment affords are numerous. First, there is the initial formulation of one's personal wonderings into formal questions. Then, there is discussion of the role of such questions in contrast with other more definitely answered questions. Next, the exploration of the questions themselves requires each student to think in terms of possibilities, options, probabilities, and consequences. Finally, there is reinterpretation of the questions through an aesthetic lens. Clearly, this is a rich assignment made powerful because of the high level of student engagement it elicits.

PROVIDING FOR CHOICE AND INDEPENDENCE. Meaningful student choice and the accompanying encouragement of autonomy are important components of rich thinking opportunities. These factors not only support student engagement and interest but also encourage greater independence and self-direction in thinking. When I speak of meaningful student choice, I am referring to those choices that actually have an impact on student motivation, sense of ownership, autonomy, and learning. Teachers often allow students limited choice within a very narrow range of options. In these instances, the teacher very much retains control of the learning rather than giving that control to the student, which constitutes a much bigger instructional risk. However, when assignments truly are open-ended and afford students choice, the required decision making is more likely to involve students deeply with the content in a way that encourages thinking.

Heather Woodcock's project on unanswerable questions demonstrates how choice can nurture not only students' independence and risk taking as learners but also their curiosity. From start to finish, the project entails a high degree of student choice and decision making. Students select a question that interests them, explore their own thoughts and feelings about the question, then make a decision about how they will share this content with others in an engaging, thoughtful way. Heather explains that this degree of autonomy wasn't easy for all of her students: "Some kids were able to think of a lot of possibilities. They really opened up. Other kids had a very difficult time coming up with a lengthy response. They weren't necessarily so good at thinking about all the options. Those are the literal kids. The kids who tend to like, you know, look at page 55 and tell me what you think the third paragraph down means." Heather went on to say how one student avoided the level of autonomy and risk taking she was trying to cultivate by simply choosing an example that Heather had given in class for his question.

I asked Heather if she thought the assignment was still effective for these more literal students. Did they become less literal? Did their thinking change over the course of the assignment? She responded, "I think that the first draft came in, and it wasn't as well resolved as it could have been. I think the second draft did help them see how they could have pushed their ideas a little bit more. I read the drafts, but the kids also commented on each other's, so there were kids telling those kids, 'Oh, you might want to do this. . . . And I wonder about this. . . .' And I think it pushed them a little bit."

The unanswerable questions ultimately had a larger impact on the class than Heather imagined. By posting the questions on the walls, they became on ongoing part of the discourse of the classroom.

Heather remarks, "The kids bring them up every now and then. And I do too, in conversations. For instance, 'Why do we judge?' has come up. . . . Hate and evil [have] come up. 'Why do hate and evil exist?' Someone referred to that in a discussion about slavery a few weeks ago. So the kids are doing it." Thus, the assignment helped to create a greater sense of ownership and connection to class content, even though that was not its ultimate goal.

A very different example of fostering student ownership can be found in Chris Elnicki's end-of-semester evaluation. He provides students with a set of eight assessment options from which to choose: a traditional test with or without notes, a short-answer test with or without notes, an essay exam in or out of class, an oral exam, or a Web-based exam. In offering these choices, Chris wants students to think about what kinds of forums provide them with the best opportunity to show what they know. In making their final decision, students have to weigh the pros and cons of each option carefully: an essay outside of class provides time for revision and access to resources, but the performance expectations will be higher; a traditional test without notes will be over quickly and perhaps not too demanding in terms of the expected responses, but it will require a lot of preparation and memorization.

Setting up these choices is also quite demanding for Chris. He has to balance all the variables to make sure the time commitment that students need in order to do well on each is approximately equal. He also has to educate students on the options so that they can make informed choices. However, knowing that their evaluations are a matter of personal choice helps students buy into the process and take the evaluation seriously. This helps motivate students to do the thinking required of them as they prepare. To enhance expectations and support students' motivation further, Chris gives students two weeks to prepare for the evaluation and offers regular after-school help sessions.

By infusing thinking opportunities with choice, whether that be choosing the direction an assignment might take, selecting among options for demonstrating one's understanding, or asking questions that will guide one's exploration, teachers support student engagement in and motivation toward thinking. These opportunities also send a signal to students that teachers expect them to be independent thinkers, take risks, and show initiative. Such expectations help to cultivate students' inclination toward thinking.

Thinking Opportunities Must Be Coupled with Time and Support

Each of the characteristics highlighted in this section independently enriches the thinking opportunities present in activities and is therefore worth consideration individually when developing activities for students. However, when considered collectively, these three characteristics can help to ensure that thinking will happen, that it will be worthwhile, and that the thinking that takes place will have an effect beyond the immediate occasion. Two additional factors related to the actual implementation of thinking opportunities are worth mentioning: (1) teachers must provide adequate time for thinking to take place; and (2) thinking needs to be appropriately scaffolded to ensure student progress.[2] These factors can be seen in the examples from John Threlkeld and Heather Woodcock's classrooms. For example, John had to structure his quiz (see Exhibit 7.1) to provide students with enough time to prepare thoughtful responses, and Heather had to provide students with the time and support that would allow them to go deeper into their unanswerable questions. As a means of offering additional commentary on these two factors, I want to present a new example from Susan McCray's humanities class. This lesson comes from the beginning of the school year and is designed specifically to teach students about the importance of writing drafts, revising, and taking time to produce quality work and understanding.

TIME AND SCAFFOLDING IN THE DRAFTING PROCESS. To introduce her students to the process of revision, Susan uses a nonthreatening art project. Over the course of a week, students create covers for their reading response journals, working through various drafts until a final cover is created. Susan defines the task: "The first thing we are going to do for our Reading Response Journals is design the covers. What you want to try and represent is what reading means to you."

She then elaborates on the assignment by showing the class some examples of previous students' journals: "The reason I've chosen these samples is that I think they are nice representations of how you can do this." Holding up three journals for the class to see, Susan interprets each cover for the class,

> What she is trying to show here is, this is a book, and this is her, and the book is like a whirlpool. And she said, when she described it, that

she gets sucked into what she is reading and becomes drawn into the book and becomes part of the world of the book. This one, he said that reading helped him to see all these different worlds. So he used the symbol of eye. This one is 'open your imagination': the idea that when you open a book, all these worlds appear to you, and there is a picture of a brain with all these thought bubbles going. So you want to think of what is a way to symbolize this to you. You can try to represent the different things that reading does for you, the different kinds of books you like to read. But try to be a little more creative with what you are expressing instead of just the things you like to do or read. You represent your reading.

There are several protests from students who claim they can't draw, but Susan reassures them that they will be successful: "You'll work at [it], and you'll see. It will get better and better."

Students spend the rest of the class period generating ideas for a first draft. As students sketch their ideas, Susan wanders around the room and checks in with those who are having difficulty getting started. Rather than tell them what to draw or how to start, Susan's approach is to help them engage in a process of self-questioning, "What do you read? What happens for you when you read? How do you feel when you are reading? What do you like about reading? What does reading do for you?" Susan encourages them to think about their answers and the images that might go along with them. Susan's questioning technique helps to scaffold students' thinking. That is, her questions provide just the right amount of support to move students' thinking to the next level without taking the control and responsibility away from the students themselves. It is this kind of guiding and directing of thinking, rather than imposing a structure, that is the hallmark of effective scaffolding.

At the end of the period, Susan reminds students, "Your homework is to bring in a first draft. But it is just a draft. We will be doing drafting. Remember, don't come in here thinking it's perfect, it's done, because there will definitely be critique and feedback. We're going to make these beautiful." These words communicate to students that they have time to think, to plan, and to take risks. Teachers often bemoan the fact that students stick to what is safe rather than taking risks. However, one must have time to take a risk. When time is limited, we typically fall back into the familiar because we recognize that we might not have time to recover from a misstep born of taking a risk.

Over the course of the week, the class gives feedback, and the students make new drafts. With each draft, the covers of students' reading response journals grow in sophistication and detail. By the end of the week, students have completed their third or, in some cases, fourth covers. To show students what can happen when they revise their work based on feedback, Susan collects all of the drafts and final covers to create a display of the drafting process that will fill the room. Using project display boards set up on desks and tables, she turns the room into a virtual art gallery of students' work. As the class enters and prepares to do a walkabout, Susan remarks, "I just love seeing the drafting process, seeing how things get better. The drafting process—it works, it works. I love this. I love seeing what happens with the criteria and feedback. This is why I want you to save the drafts so that you can see what happens over time. Isn't it dramatic? This is why I push the drafting process. This is why we will do drafts on everything."

By giving students time to work and emphasizing the process of refinement, Susan creates an expectation for in-depth thinking, that is, thinking that goes beyond one's immediate response. Just as a few seconds of wait time after posing a question allows students to develop more sophisticated responses, adding time to the thinking opportunities provided in larger projects and activities allows students to elaborate on their thinking, to build on others' ideas, and to make new connections.

Students' thinking is further fostered by the careful scaffolding that Susan provides. Rather than impose a structure to explicitly direct students' work, she asked questions that would help to move them along. These questions activated the types of thinking students needed to do to advance their work rather than channeling their activity along a prescribed set of steps. When teachers scaffold students' thinking, they provide just enough support and push to move the thinking to the next level while still keeping it in the students' control.[3] Scaffolding shouldn't be confused with structuring. When tasks are overly structured, that is, when assignments lay out every action that students are to take in an almost lockstep fashion, students tend to stop thinking and begin to operate mindlessly (Ritchhart & Perkins, 2000). When trying to decide whether you are providing a scaffold or a structure, ask yourself, Am I helping students to activate their thinking and make appropriate decisions about next steps, or am I telling students what step or action I want them to do next? The former actions are a scaffold for students' thinking; the latter provide a structure for students' work.

THE TEACHER AS A MODEL OF THINKING

A truism about parenting says, "Children learn what they live with." The saying, which can as easily be applied to teaching as to parenting, implies that interests, values, and ways of acting are not so much taught as they are caught, or enculturated, to stick with the term I've been using. The implication of the saying is that even when we don't think we are parenting or teaching or instructing, we are. Our children and our students are learning from us all the time.

One of the things they are learning is what thinking looks like. In thoughtful classrooms, a disposition toward thinking is always on display. Teachers show their curiosity and interest. They display open-mindedness and the willingness to consider alternative perspectives. Teachers model their own process of seeking truth and understanding. They show a healthy skepticism and demonstrate what it looks like to be strategic in one's thinking. They frequently put their own thinking on display and model what it means to be reflective. This demonstration of thinking sets the tone for the classroom, establishing both the expectations for thought and fostering students' inclination toward thinking.

But I'm Not Modeling

During my final interview with Chris Elnicki, we watched and discussed a portion of videotape from the previous day's class. I was interested in getting Chris's perspective on one episode in which he returned to an off-the-cuff question a student had asked the day before. The class was discussing British harassment of the U.S. colonists, and a student, Jake, asked, "Who was the traitor who got hung? He said, 'I regret that I have but one life to give?'" When Jake asked the question, Chris responded that he was drawing a blank and would have to look it up. The next day, Chris began the class with the correct version of the Nathan Hale quotation written on the board, "I regret that I have but one life to lose for my country," as well as Patrick Henry's words, "Give me liberty or give me death." Chris then shared with the class some background on the quotes and explained why Jake's question and the quote had initially confused him: "I want to follow up on the question that Jake asked at the end of class yesterday. He was asking about this quote. . . . Nobody knows if Nathan Hale actually said that. Supposedly, he did, but the likelihood is pretty slim.

Probably somebody built up the situation and used that line to motivate people in the war. The one I confused it with was this one. I've had this confusion for a long time. I've kind of confused these two lines in my own mind and even merged these two people to some extent."

When I asked Chris about the incident, he looked at me and said, "Oh, I wasn't trying to model anything by doing that. It was just something that came up." Although Chris and many others might think of modeling as a demonstration conducted by a teacher to instruct students in a particular behavior, the most powerful form of modeling is the kind that just comes up. In fact, I would argue that modeling as a demonstration may be useful in developing ability, but it is actually quite weak when it comes to developing students' inclination and sensitivity. Demonstration modeling often feels artificial and lacks the real conviction of someone engaged in a spontaneous act. In contrast, authentic modeling enculturates values by showing students what the teacher deems important and worthwhile, sensitizes students to thinking by pointing out occasions, and fosters ability by showing a technique in context. When I speak of modeling, it is more in the context of the teacher acting as a role model, someone worth emulating, than as a demonstrator. When you are in the presence of such models, you get the sense of the teacher as a thinker and not as a teacher of thinking.

Chris was modeling curiosity by showing his engagement with the content of the class. He was also modeling metacognition by demonstrating and explaining how he came to spot his own confusion of the issue. Finally, he was demonstrating skepticism in the context of the particular quotes he was discussing. It was a brief moment, but a culture is comprised of an abundance of just such brief moments.

A Culture of Moments

This culture of moments is highly evident in John Threlkeld's math class. John is a strong model of the disposition to be curious, to be skeptical, to seek truth and understanding, and to be strategic. Consider what kind of image you get of John as a thinker from the following brief statements:

- "The reason I am showing you this problem is that I don't agree with the solution."

- "I don't know the answer to that, but I know where we might start looking."
- "You are causing me to think about this more. I'll have to go home and see what I can come up with. This is good stuff."
- "Interesting idea. I'm not sure I agree or disagree. I haven't thought about it yet."
- "Now you've got me curious. I want to follow up on what Rick said. I need to think about this."
- "Great questions. I don't know the answers."
- "Oh, that's interesting. I wonder why it is doing that? I may have to rethink this."
- "I'm not as convinced as I was."
- "I did spend time thinking [about yesterday's problem], but I don't want to say anything yet."
- "This problem comes from my bedtime reading."

As you can see, the power of modeling doesn't come from any one instance. Instead, it is the pervasiveness and naturalism of the modeling that makes it such an important enculturative force for promoting thinking.

Effective Modeling of Thinking

When we examine these teachers' modeling, certain commonalities and themes emerge. For instance, teachers' modeling often takes the form of relating nonschool readings and activities to what the class is exploring. This type of modeling conveys teachers' interest in continuing to explore the content of the course and provides students with models of curiosity and seeking understanding. Teachers also model their confusion and lack of understanding in front of students. Although some might argue that teachers must be the experts, the effect of modeling confusion is to convey to students the complexity of the issues rather than any lack of teacher competence. For example, Heather Woodcock comments about a passage in a book the class is reading, "I don't understand this, and what I find most interesting is what I don't understand." A third stimulus for modeling is students' questions and comments. By displaying a genuine curiosity and interest in students' questions, teachers indicate that the students' comments have caused them to think further or in new ways about an issue. These responses convey a sense of reciprocity in the interactions between students and teachers, a cultural force we will take up in the next section.

CLASSROOM ATTITUDES AND INTERACTIONS

Few things speak louder than the attitudes and interactions on display in a classroom. The way teachers treat students, the way students treat teachers, and the way students treat each other say volumes about the overall ethos of a classroom. But how do these interactions relate to the ideal of developing intellectual character? What does it mean to have positive attitudes and interactions around thinking?

For students to engage in their best thinking, the environment must first be respectful and safe. Students need to feel comfortable before they are willing to take the risk of offering up new ideas, challenging assumptions, or putting their thinking processes on display. Because thinking often is a process of refining ideas, possibilities, solutions, strategies, and understandings, students need to know that mistakes are not only acceptable but also encouraged. A safe and respectful environment may make the sharing of thinking and ideas possible, but safety and respect in and of themselves aren't enough to actively encourage thinking. Students need to know that their thinking efforts are valued. The classroom must cultivate a shared sense of discovery, excitement, and enjoyment in the act of thinking. Finally, the classroom must provide forums and structures that can facilitate positive interactions around thinking.

Honoring Students' Disposition Toward Thinking

Acknowledging and honoring students' disposition toward thinking provides students with positive feedback that reinforces their actions. Such acknowledgment communicates the teacher's values and reinforces the inclination of students to repeat the behavior. However, as in the case of modeling, the honoring that these teachers do is less "teacherly" and more authentic than our traditional view of what it means to honor. The typical perception of honor at school might include such practices as praising students' contributions, providing recognition, or calling special attention to the behavior. In contrast, the way these thoughtful teachers tend to honor students is by showing interest in their thinking, using it as a springboard for class discussions, or giving students the time and space to pursue their thinking.

You see this kind of honoring when John Threlkeld enthusiastically responds to students' comments with "Great question." He uses this phrase a lot, and his teaching is punctuated with an endless series of "great questions" being called out in John's booming voice. In explaining what makes a question great, John offers this perspective:

> What makes a great question in my mind is perhaps that moment of doubt that may have occurred in even one more person's mind that might have been, "Oh, wait a minute. Is she right? I hadn't thought about that before." That's what I am hearing. It's that question that we hadn't thought about before. . . . It's an opportunity for me to, at one level, set the record straight . . . to really clarify what is an important idea. And I can't keep track of all the good things I want to say all the time, so when kids ask me something they don't know, that's why I think it's a great question.

For John, great questions aren't just those that engage him or that he has never thought about. They are also those questions that show that students are thinking and that help others to think about the material. When students regularly see their questions and confusions honored in this way and treated as important opportunities to learn and explore, students are more inclined to engage in thinking deeply about the material and are less afraid to show both their curiosity and their confusion.

Teachers also honor students' disposition toward thinking when they indicate that students' ideas and opinions count and that the teacher is not the sole intellectual authority in the classroom. While discussing *A Wizard of Earthsea,* a student asks Heather, "Why do some people have magic and others don't?" Heather responds by saying, "I want someone else to answer. It's not what I think, but what you all think." When teachers don't rescue students by answering all their questions and when they treat seriously the notion that the classroom is a learning community, students begin to feel that their thinking is respected and valued and that they play an important role. This respect is motivating and helps to foster an inclination toward thinking.

Helping Students Experience Cognitive Emotions

Describing an instance of understanding and coming to know, William James once stated, "The transition from a state of puzzle and perplexity to rational comprehension is full of lively relief and pleasure" (as quoted in Tishman, 1997, p. 369). The kind of pleasure James refers to is a uniquely cognitive one. Israel Scheffler (1991) refers to this particular feeling as the *joy of verification*. Scheffler has described feelings such as this as *cognitive emotions* because they have their basis in and are a response to the cognitive functions of the mind. Other cognitive emotions include surprise in unexpected outcomes, aesthetic appreciation, and thrill in discovery. The presence of such positive emotions with regard to thinking can help to incline students toward thinking. These emotions are a crucial basis for intrinsic motivation, that is, motivation that is based on enjoyment and engagement in the task itself rather than on the prospect of external punishment or reward.

In these thoughtful classrooms, teachers seek to provide students with opportunities to experience cognitive emotions. This often means that teachers must first create situations that are complex, ambiguous, and challenging for students in order for students to experience "the transition from a state of puzzle and perplexity to rational comprehension" that James describes. You can see this in the daily warm-ups that Doug Tucker gives to his students. Because the problems are challenging and often require students to expend considerable time and energy to solve, students feel a great deal of satisfaction when they discover solutions. Of course, the problems have to be at the right level of challenge so that students feel like the task is indeed possible for them to accomplish.

John Threlkeld also displays this ability to pull students in to difficult problems. At the beginning of the year, John creates situations through which he can exploit mathematical ambiguity and engage students in discussions of fundamental ideas. After a particularly heated class spent exploring one problem, John comments to the class, "Can you believe that we talked about that problem for almost forty-five minutes? Isn't that great?" John is not only expressing and modeling his own joy in the exploration of ideas, but he is calling students' attention to the fact that such work is filled with intrinsic emotional satisfaction.

Another example of cognitive emotions at work comes from a homework problem that John gives his class. The problem asks students: "Using only the digits 1, 2, 3, and 4, and the operations of +, −, ×, ÷ and parentheses, write expressions for each of the whole numbers from 1 to 30." Now, some might argue that this problem is rather contrived. After all, there is no real-life application here, and the problem is completely decontextualized. How can students buy in to this? Why should they care about solving the problem? All that is true. However, what the problem has going for it is that it is able to exploit the cognitive emotions. Upon writing an expression for one of the numbers, particularly a number that others might be having difficulty with, a student experiences a great sense of accomplishment. Thrill at discovery, delight in verifying that a solution works, and aesthetic appreciation for the variety of outcomes possible occurs by using just these four numbers.

My assumptions about the role of cognitive emotions in making this problem work are borne out the next day when students come to class with their homework in hand, sharing and comparing answers even before the class begins. John asks the class, "Did you spend more time on this than you normally would on homework for a whole week?"

The class answers that indeed they did, and one student elaborates, "This was fun because we were motivated."

What is the motivation that the student is referring to? There is no prize, no extra credit. The homework is not even to be graded, only checked. So the motivation has to come from within, as does the fun. The source of the students' motivation can be found in the cognitive emotions they experienced as an ongoing part of solving the problem. Helping students to experience these feelings and ultimately to tap into them as a source of intrinsic motivation is the real contribution of such problems.

Student-to-Student Interactions

Although it is not simple, it is relatively easy for teachers to attend to their interactions with students. After all, these interactions are under their direct control. More challenging and perhaps more telling when it comes to the culture of the classroom are the interactions among the students themselves, interactions that the teacher does not directly control and sometimes does not even observe. Therefore, teachers have to exhibit a special vigilance in attending to and laying the foundation for positive interactions. Although some of these practices might fall under general classroom management techniques, promoting student-to-student interactions that support thinking is more than learning to be civil toward and respectful of one another. Students must learn how to engage one another in the discussion of ideas.

We have discussed several practices for encouraging such thinking-based interactions. In Chapter Five, I presented the mathematical argument as a routine for discussing and exploring ideas. Through the argument context, students learn to present their positions and offer evidence to support that position. The formal argument format ensures that students are speaking to each other about the ideas rather than trying to push one another around verbally. In Chapter Six, I discussed the use of language to pattern ways of talking and ways of thinking, and I presented the leaderless discussion and the public issue discussion as examples. In both these contexts, a premium is placed on learning to listen to and respond to others' ideas by looking for connections and opportunity to build on or expand those ideas.

Another example of structuring students' interactions is the critique process used by Susan McCray. She initially introduces this process to her students in the context of developing their reading response journal covers during the first week of school. Susan initiates this process by using her own reading response journal cover as an example. "What I have here is my first draft, and I wanted to get your feedback on it. I thought we could do this all together as a group and then work in small groups at your table to give each other feedback."

To structure this process, Susan presents the class with a set of guidelines for critiquing and offering feedback. The first step is for the group to review the criteria that will guide the feedback. Because Susan has just initiated the project, the group still has to develop the criteria, so she begins this process by asking students to think about what makes a good reading response journal cover. Students offer a variety of suggestions: "Good use of color and space," "Imagination," "Sense of humor," "Neat," "Meaningful," and "Shows what reading can do for you." For each criterion offered, Susan asks students to explain what they mean and why the criterion matters. In the process, some criteria emerge as more important than others. For instance, all agree that a sense of humor can be a nice thing to have, but it doesn't have to be on the reading journal cover. Susan summarizes the list the students have developed: "These criteria are what make something good.

These are what we want to be looking for and commenting on. How can you improve or make something better if you don't know what makes something good?"

With the criteria in place, students are ready to continue the critique process. The second step in the process is for students to listen to the creator's questions about his or her work, that is, the things that he or she wants specific feedback on. Holding up her journal cover and walking it around the room, Susan demonstrates: "One thing I would like to know is do you get it. Do you get the message I'm trying to convey here? The other thing I want to know has to do with the lettering and its placement."

Next is the asking of clarifying questions about Susan's journal cover. The first student asks, "Is it supposed to be like a bunch of different pictures, or is it supposed to be a comic strip?"

Laughing, Susan responds, "My intention was that this is a window, and I'm on one side of the window, and the world is on the other side. This image here is the mountains. And what reading does for me is it's like smashing my hand through the window and taking me out into the world. Reading pulls me, but I didn't intend the violent element of it. It's through reading I get to clarity and to the real world, and I get to go out there."

This explanation seems to answer most students' questions of clarification, and Susan directs the class to the fourth step, which is providing positive comments. A few students are ready to offer suggestions, but when they do, Susan quickly reminds them that they are only to give positive comments at this point. Several students comment on liking the overall concept. Another says that the hand is well drawn.

Finally, the class is ready to attend to the last step in the process: offering comments and suggestions. These are numerous and pointed, often referring directly to elements of the criteria: "There could be more color." "Maybe you could turn it the other way so the lettering isn't so crowded." "You could add more background color to give it more depth." "The broken window seems rather violent; it doesn't really convey escape." "You could just have two windows instead of four." "Maybe you could open the window instead of smashing it." "More details would help."

Although the students are still new at this process at this early point in the year and need to have the guidelines posted in front of them, they catch on pretty quickly, and the conversation moves along. When students repeat the process in their small groups, it's clear that they are already internalizing the steps and are comfortable making the transition from one to the other without Susan's prompting. Later in the year, when students share essays they have written, the core process of listening to the creator's questions about the work, asking clarifying questions, providing positive comments, and offering suggestions based on the criteria seems almost seamless.

Practices for structuring students' interactions, such as those presented here, give students tools that can guide their interactions with peers, even in informal contexts. Researchers have found that the use of such rhetorical devices and strategies in classrooms tends to snowball so that more and more students over different and varied contexts gradually adopt these ways of speaking and interacting (Anderson et al., 2001). These devices add a certain level of predictability to the discussion and exploration of ideas while ensuring that students know what to expect when they present their thoughts and work to the group.

MAKING THINKING VISIBLE IN THE ENVIRONMENT

Documents of learning serve as both an individual and an institutional memory of learning and thinking. Such artifacts and remembrances are important in establishing any culture, and the culture of thinking is no different. By collecting, displaying, and saving artifacts of individual and collective thought, the classroom quite literally becomes thought-full. Furthermore, the presence of students' thinking products in the room encourages ongoing reflection and revisiting of ideas. When no procedures and practices for documenting learning exist, students may struggle to identify and remember the joy and excitement of learning. These uniquely cognitive emotions, like all positive feelings, are self-reinforcing to the extent that we are more inclined to do things that give us pleasure.

Pictures and Portfolios

Procedures for documenting learning can be rather informal. For instance, when I was conducting my screening interviews to identify teachers for inclusion in this study, I was struck by how often the more thoughtful classrooms I visited contained pictures of students engaged in some sort of classroom endeavor. These weren't just pictures of class field trips; these pictures provided documentation of classroom work as well. In one classroom, a walk around the room provided me with a panorama of the thinking and work the class had been involved in over the course of the year. I could literally see how students worked together and on what kinds of projects. When Susan McCray created a display of all of the drafts students had completed for their reading response journal covers, she was providing similar documentation of students' thinking. This visual display helped students to take pride in their progress and development over time and to see how their thinking and ideas had grown and changed.

In contrast to this informality, portfolios provide a more formal tool for documenting learning. When they are used to help students set goals, revisit and revise past projects, or make new connections, portfolios can be useful as tools for managing learning and thinking as well. Both Chris Elnicki and Susan McCray use portfolios in this way and employ student-led conferences with those portfolios as a way of further engaging students in their learning. For Susan, this takes the form of rounding up community members to come in and meet with her students one on one to review their work. Students prepare for these meetings by putting together a collection of work that will show an outsider who they are as a learner, what they have gotten out of the class, and where they hope to go next. Visitors listen as the students explain their work and then ask questions about the meaning of the work for the students. Through the process, students develop an increasing sense of themselves as learners based on the review of their work.

Reflecting on Work

Reflecting on work is a way of grounding the learning experience for students. It is also a way of pulling out the thinking that has occurred in producing the work for more careful examination. This is particularly important when the work is ephemeral, such as in a discussion or play. In these cases, students' reflections become the record or artifact of the event. However, a reflection has to be more than a recollection of what happened or what was done. When reflections are no more than reports of events, they serve little purpose for teacher or student. Furthermore, such accounts fail to engage students in thinking about the events in a way that will help them improve in the future. Similarly, merely asking students how they felt about the work, the project, or the event is unlikely to have much long-term impact. Although identifying feelings can be important, it is useful for developing intellectual character only when they can connect it to thinking about how to handle future events.

The reflection following Chris Elnicki's public issues discussion demonstrates one way to structure students' reflections to focus on and improve future learning. Immediately following the discussion, Chris gives his students ten minutes to reflect on the experience and assess both their individual and group performance. First, he asks students to rate their preparedness for and participation in the discussion on a scale of one to ten and to explain why they chose that particular rating. Students then write an improvement goal for themselves for future discussions. Chris also asks them to identify things that went particularly well in the discussion at the group level, provide comments on the facilitator's performance, and write a goal for the class's improvement. Finally, to anchor the discussion as a vehicle for learning more about the issue, Chris asks students to formally state their opinions on the issue and support them with points of evidence introduced in the discussion.

IDENTIFYING THE THOUGHT-FULL CLASSROOM

Although thoughtful classrooms aren't as common as we might like them to be, they aren't necessarily rare either. In this chapter, I've laid out a means of spotting them by attending to the cultural forces at work and examining the relationship between these forces and thinking. By looking at the work students are doing to see if it is providing them with thinking opportunities, by examining what kinds of thinking the teacher models, by observing the artifacts of the classroom to see what they reveal about thinking, and by paying attention to the interactions and attitudes on display in the classroom, we can identify thoughtful classrooms and continue to learn from them. We can also use the cultural forces as a tool for our own self-reflection. What does our practice reveal about the level of thoughtfulness in our classrooms? What are the leverage points that we might best capitalize on as we seek to create a more thoughtful classroom? In the last part of this book, we turn our attention to these kinds of practical questions more directly, examining how we can collectively and individually best go about realizing intellectual character in our own classrooms and schools.

~~~~ **Key Ideas for Developing Intellectual Character**

IN THE CLASSROOM: THE CULTURAL FORCES

- *The Opportunities Created.* In thoughtful classrooms, students have an abundance of rich and powerful opportunities for thinking. This richness and power comes from focusing students' activity on big ideas, making sure there is a high level of engagement, and providing for student choice and the exercise of independent and autonomous thinking. In addition, in implementing these opportunities, teachers must give adequate time for thinking to take place, and they need to scaffold students' thinking in a way that will push it to higher levels.

- *The Thinking Modeled.* Teachers are modeling every moment of the day. We are constantly sending students messages about what good thinking looks like, where thinking can take you, and what kinds of thinking are important. Some of the most influential modeling we do is the incidental modeling that shows our students who we are as people. This modeling reveals our curiosity, our interest, our passions, our deliberateness, and our level of thoughtfulness.

- *The Attitudes and Interactions Promoted.* The attitudes of the students and teacher in a classroom are one of the best indicators of a thoughtful environment. In such environments, the cognitive emotions, such as the joy of verification or thrill at the unexpected, are readily evident in both the teacher and the students. Teachers must directly attend to positive thinking interactions among students by providing structures and ways of talking about ideas and thinking that they can readily adopt.

- *The Artifacts Presented.* The products of thinking and reflections on thoughtful work are the kinds of artifacts that can make thinking visible and salient in classrooms. When the teacher and students put energy into documenting thinking through portfolios, pictures, and reflections, students receive the message that thinking matters. In addition, these artifacts remind students of the joy, work, processes, and results of thinking, which may increase their inclination toward future thinking endeavors.

PART THREE

Moving Toward the Ideal of Intellectual Character

Beyond Technique

Where Teaching for
Intellectual Character Begins

A few years ago, I was teaching a math methods course to a group of preservice teachers in training. We were using case studies to explore some of the common dilemmas teachers face in helping students develop an understanding of mathematical concepts and procedures. One particular case presented background information on an elementary class's experience with fractions, and described a current lesson focused on adding fractions. The case was written up by the teacher and detailed both her efforts and the concerns she had about what students were understanding. At the end of the case, the teacher expressed her unease about how to deal with some of her students' confusion about fractions.

My group of teachers in training had all read the case before class, and we quickly divided ourselves into small groups for the discussion. Each group examined the dilemmas evident in the case, talked about what kinds of things the teacher might try in her next lesson, and explored what assumptions about students' understanding she might want to explore further. The discussions were lively, and these students preparing to teach enjoyed the opportunity to talk about real teaching and learn from an actual classroom example. As we debriefed our small-group discussions within the larger group and talked about the issues, Carol raised her hand. The discussion was very interesting, she said, and it had made her think about teaching fractions, but what was the correct answer? What is it that the teacher should do next? Carol's question struck a chord with the group, and soon they added other questions: Were there things the teacher in the case had done that were wrong? Could the confusions have been prevented? What is the correct way to teach fractions?

Most of the preservice teachers viewed the case as some kind of a test with a clear and exact answer. Furthermore, most of them viewed teaching and teacher training as a matter of finding the right answers to the dilemmas of instruction. They wanted to know the correct way to teach, how it should be done. Their learning focused on acquiring a set of specific techniques that they could then apply. This view of teaching as a matter of gathering and honing techniques certainly isn't unique to preservice teachers. We see it all the time in in-service training for experienced teachers as well. Sometimes, we even clamor for it, "Give me something practical I can take back to my classroom, something I can use right away." But technique can only take us so far. The act of teaching is more complex than merely selecting the right tool for the job or prescribing the correct antidote for students' ills. As Maggie Lampert (1985) points out in her writings about her own practice, teaching isn't so much about solving problems of instruction as it is about managing dilemmas. Parker Palmer (1998, p. 5) puts it even more bluntly: "Technique is what teachers use until the real teacher arrives."

In this chapter, I move the discussion of teaching for intellectual character beyond and in some ways behind the techniques and practices I have documented in earlier chapters to uncover the foundation, to find the source. Where does teaching for intellectual character actually begin? If the masterful teaching presented thus far isn't the result of teachers skillfully applying teaching tips and techniques they have picked up in workshops along the way, where does it come from? What is the basis for the on-the-spot decisions teachers must make and the dilemmas they must manage? This examination of foundations is necessary in order for us to better understand not only the teaching examples in this book but also our own practice as teachers. Through better understanding, we begin the process of moving our practice toward supporting the development of students' intellectual character. Therefore, as you read this chapter, it is important for you to look back on the examples of teaching that have been discussed. At the same time, it is important for you to look inward at your own teaching and around at the practice of those with whom you work. What motivates and drives your work and shapes who you are as a teacher?

EXPLORING FOUNDATIONS

The foundations of a teacher's practice, the way he or she makes decisions and manages dilemmas, can't be uncovered by looking at its outward manifestations. Nor can its source be discerned by merely aggregating some combination of experience and training. To get to the root of teaching, we have to look inside the teacher at the various values, beliefs, theories, and knowledge that person holds: values about what is important to teach; beliefs about the nature of teaching, learning, and the subject matter; theories of instruction; and knowledge about the subject matter, curriculum, and pedagogical practices.[1] Uncovering these roots isn't always easy. Beliefs, values, and implicit theories can be elusive things, difficult for both the researcher and the teacher to grab hold of and hang on to. Furthermore, it isn't always clear what information we can consider reliable and trustworthy. How do we know when we have tapped into core beliefs? How do we know when these elements are affecting a teacher's practice?[2]

In my study, I chose to approach the challenge of identifying the foundations of teachers' practices from two angles. First, I sought to identify the core beliefs and instructional goals guiding teachers' practices, what I call the red thread of their practice. Second, I assessed teachers' knowledge of thinking as revealed through their mental model of thinking. Both of these processes were ongoing and occurred simultaneously with my classroom observations. To ground your reading and to understand the foundations that shape teachers' practices, it is helpful to know a bit about my methods. Readers who are interested in the research perspective can find a more complete account in the Appendix.

The Red Thread

The red thread is used in a variety of cultures as a metaphor for connecting, binding, and uniting. I was first introduced to it by Swedish colleagues who used the expression in the context of finding a central commonality across different situations. In Hebrew, the word *theme* translates literally as "the red thread." In Chinese culture, the red thread represents the invisible connections that bind every newborn to all of the important people in that child's life. In Buddhism, the red thread signifies passion. Thus, I feel the red thread is an apt metaphor for describing the beliefs, passions, values, and goals that tie together and unite a teacher's practice over time and contexts. The red thread does not represent a single belief, however, but a set of deeply held beliefs. Thus, I was not looking to find a single core value or belief but a core collection that would aptly capture each teacher's agenda. The development of intellectual character suggests a teaching agenda in which the fostering of students' disposition toward thinking is a high priority, a passion, and a part of the teacher's red thread. In fact, this was one of the working hypotheses of my study: teachers who are adept at creating thoughtful classrooms have the teaching of thinking as a core value in their practice. A related hypothesis, connected to a second aspect of my exploration of foundations, is that these teachers would have a well-developed mental model of thinking. I'll address the issue of mental models in the next section.

To unearth teachers' red threads, I interviewed them about their goals, values, and beliefs, and I observed their classrooms in order to uncover the implicit messages in their instruction. I analyzed the interviews for recurring themes that appeared in both the interviews and the teacher's instruction. This ensures that the theme is not just a philosophical stance the teacher took during an interview but one that the teacher's practice embodies. In naming these themes, I sought those recurring constructs, metaphors, and ideas that teachers themselves repeatedly expressed.[3] When I talk about a teacher's red threads in the sketches to follow, I stick closely to that person's language whenever possible. To ensure that I was accurately capturing teachers' red threads of practice, I shared my initial written interpretations with the teachers individually and solicited their comments and reactions.

Mental Models

To account for the processes of inference and implicit logic, Philip Johnson-Laird (1983) proposed the idea of mental models. Developed out of our experiences, mental models represent the structural analogues or propositional representations we have of the world and how it operates. We carry these representations and relational networks with us into new situations, using these models as a basis for our reasoning about the world. According to Johnson-Laird, "Mental models play a central and unifying role in representing objects, states of affairs, sequences of events, the way the world is, and the social and psychological actions of daily life. They enable individuals to make inferences and predictions, to understand phenomena, to decide what action to take and to control its execution" (p. 397). We can think of mental models as representing the tacit maps we construct in our minds about the way things work or relate (Haimes, 1996). They are our analogs of the world, providing the general framework or architecture for our understanding.[4]

Both mental models and beliefs represent core values and understandings. However, the two differ in that beliefs need not be based on experience, and they are not necessarily foundational for our reasoning, inference, or action. In fact, we can hold beliefs in complete isolation or even in opposition to our actions, representing only ideals or values that we strive to apply when appropriate. For example, take the ideal that all children can learn. This is a value that is easy and popular to espouse. However, unless this concept causes a fundamental change in the way we see children, that is, a change in our mental model, the belief alone is unlikely to result in a change in our action.

Uncovering teachers' mental models of thinking, rather than just their beliefs, provides a basis for understanding the types of thinking that they most value and view as salient. It is through this lens that teachers view the curriculum and make sense of their instruction. In addition, teachers' mental models of thinking provide the foundation for making decisions about how, when, and where to promote students' thinking as well as providing the criteria for assessing thinking. I contend that a rich mental model of thinking, although not a sufficient condition, is a prerequisite for developing the kind of thoughtful instruction that can nurture students' intellectual character. Such a mental model need not be complete, however. It is quite likely and perhaps even preferable that one's mental model of thinking be constantly under revision and adaptation.

To uncover teachers' mental models of thinking, I used a process originally developed by George Kelly (1955) for revealing individuals' relational thinking about other people. As a part of this process (explained more fully in the Appendix), I asked teachers to create a list of thinking actions or activities. Basically, the task was to answer the question: When you tell someone you are thinking, what is it that you are doing? "Creating a mental picture," "generating options," or "evaluating information" are examples of possible responses. Each teacher then sorted these thinking actions, which resulted in the formation of a set of overarching categories, such as "creative thinking" or "front-end strategies." The teacher then ranked, on a scale from one to seven, how each of the thinking actions fit within each of the overarching categories. I analyzed teachers' responses using cluster analysis, and each teacher interpreted the clusters by giving them names and identifying their relationships.

I present each teacher's mental model of thinking in the form of a diagrammatic figure at the close of a brief sketch of their practice. Each of these figures consists of a series of circles and ellipses representing the major categories of thinking identified by the teacher. These major categories appear in bold lettering inside the circles. Within these major categories, individual teachers also may have identified subcategories of thinking. The labels for these subcategories appear in roman type. A final feature included in some of the diagrams is individual thinking actions identified by the teacher but not directly linked by the teacher to a larger cluster of thinking actions. These lone thinking activities can be found set outside any ellipse or circle, sometimes with a descriptive heading. These headings are in roman type to indicate that the action represents a minor category for the teacher. I offer these diagrammatic models without elaborate interpretation to encourage you to make your own connections between the examples of practice you have read previously, the teacher's red threads presented in the sketch, and the teacher's thinking about thinking. I pose some questions to facilitate this connection making and encourage an exploration of teachers' similarities and differences. At the end of the chapter, I offer concluding commentary about how mental models might affect teaching practice.

SKETCHES OF THE TEACHERS

In another venue designed to achieve other ends, I might have presented each of the teachers I studied in the form of a literary portrait. Such a portrait would have provided a rich and contextualized picture of each teacher as an individual. Instead, I chose to focus attention on common elements of practice seen across the teachers. To do that, I pulled liberally from my observations and in the process sacrificed contextualization for exemplification. You have seen, rather than a portrait, only a series of glimpses of each teacher. As a result, you've received quite an imperfect picture of these remarkable teachers. In this section, I attempt to remedy this somewhat, not by presenting a portrait but by providing a final sketch of each teacher that should be useful in filling in some of the gaps.

Even though I handpicked the teachers in my study for having thoughtful classrooms and expressing an interest in promoting student thinking, they are very much individuals, as you no doubt have seen in the examples of practice already shared. Naturally then, the teachers differ somewhat in the instructional values they hold most passionately and in their thinking about thinking. The following sketches seek to present these differences in values and beliefs not in terms of teachers' weaknesses but in terms of teachers' passions and the red threads that direct their teaching.[5] Each of these teachers displays practices and qualities well worth emulating. The differences I have detected do not call into question their expertise as teachers but merely help us understand how certain factors may influence efforts to teach for intellectual character. As a part of each of these sketches, I present information on each teacher's mental model of thinking, discussing what it implies about the teacher's understanding and knowledge of thinking.

John Threlkeld

Even though the building John Threlkeld teaches in is only four years old, his classroom has a very lived-in look. With all the wooden blocks, iron puzzles, games, toys, paper models, blueprints, and construction materials, you might mistake it for a design laboratory or a shop room. Stepping in, you might change your assessment and think you are in a technology lab, once you see all the flickering computer monitors and projection equipment. But ultimately the familiar algebraic scribbles on the white board, the eight-foot-long slide rule hanging from the ceiling, and the posters displaying various proofs of the Pythagorean theorem would convince you that you were in a math classroom—quite a unique one.

John's room is a playground of sorts, both physically and mentally: students are invited to play mathematical games, manipulate puzzles, and create physical models, but they also are invited, coerced, cajoled, and ultimately forced to play with ideas as part of a learning community. In talking about his teaching, the importance of play and ideas emerge as central themes for John:

> My goal is for [my students] to understand that math is something they can really love doing. I think I want them to feel the same way I do; I want them to feel my passion for it, I guess. . . . I use the word *play* a lot. Playing with ideas, that's what this is all about. If you look at thinking as a chore, then that's what it is; it's a chore. If you're looking at it as a challenge, it's just something sort of fun to do and see what you come up with. That's when things become productive. . . . It's that wondering and thinking and asking questions they learn from. . . . Sometimes, they've just got to take an idea and say, "How can I use that idea here?"—when they've never seen it before. How do you use the things we've talked about for four days and use experiences that have gone on in class? I think so much of math and the way I teach is that kids gain experience and exposure to ideas.

Teaching an honors section of eighth-grade algebra at a private school, John has some advantages when it comes to getting students excited about ideas and engaged in thinking. Nonetheless, he does this amazingly quickly with students he has never taught and who, in other circumstances, might be more concerned with grades than ideas. Recall the discussion John's class had the first week of school regarding the different meanings of the expressions x^2, $(x)^2$, $-x^2$, and $-(x)^2$. Although this is the kind of arithmetic convention most textbooks would handle perfunctorily by providing a set of rules, John makes it an opportunity to develop mathematical ideas, explore one's thinking, and learn how to work as a community. In a fifty-minute period the first week of school, John manages to stress the importance of understanding and thinking in mathematics. But he does more than that: he begins to weave a red thread of mathematics as a community endeavor in which everyone must play a part. He engages the class in arguments, forces them to take sides and defend positions, and includes himself when talking about the collective meaning making that goes on. John expresses the importance of this communal dialogue: "I think for students to be successful in my class, they've got to listen to me, but perhaps equally important, they've got to listen to each other. They've got to hear the questions that others ask. . . . The learning takes place from the questions that come up, and I may completely change what I was planning to do midstream if the right questions come up. And kids need to be aware of that and be ready to respond to it."

John's two red threads, "mathematics is a community endeavor" and "our classroom is a playground of ideas," are also expressed in his views about thinking in general. In his description of a good thinker, John rounds out what it means to play with ideas and be part of a community, identifying the need for broad and adventurous thinking, being skeptical of ideas, and being generous in communicating one's position:

> The first thing I would say about good thinkers is that they're not shy. By that I mean that they won't stick to the straight and narrow. They won't stick to what they know. They use what they know to try things out: "What about this?" or "What about that?" I guess I think risk taking is a big piece of it for me. Not sitting back and waiting, not being afraid to say, "Here's my idea." . . . A big characteristic of a thinker is that not only do they think but they make other people think. They challenge you and say, "Well, I don't know about that" or "What do you think about this?" I think good thinkers are unselfish. It's not about them; it's about the idea."

John's mental model of thinking (see Figure 8.1) reveals thirty-two thinking items grouped in six major categories.[6] You can see how the detail and organization of John's mental model reveals a rich conception of thinking that stresses openness in thinking, understanding, and organization. John's model also reveals somewhat of a linear process that is particularly suited to problem-solving tasks. What sense of John as a learner and a teacher do you get from his model of thinking? What connections do you see between his thinking about thinking and his teaching?

Chris Elnicki

Walking into Chris Elnicki's classroom, you leave the generic and institutional blandness of a large suburban public school behind, and you encounter an intense visual delight. The foldable walls are plastered with posters, cartoons, historical photographs, maps, and student work, conveying a sense of energy and activity. Everywhere you look are quotes about freedom, the Bill of Rights, and learning. Stretching

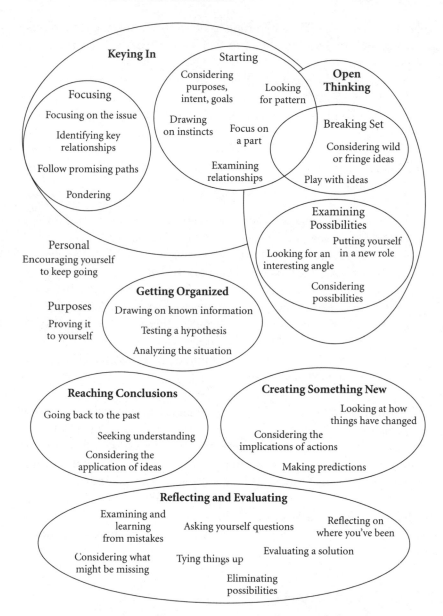

Keying In

Starting

Considering purposes, intent, goals

Looking for pattern

Open Thinking

Focusing

Focusing on the issue

Identifying key relationships

Follow promising paths

Pondering

Drawing on instincts

Focus on a part

Examining relationships

Breaking Set

Considering wild or fringe ideas

Play with ideas

Examining Possibilities

Putting yourself in a new role

Looking for an interesting angle

Considering possibilities

Personal

Encouraging yourself to keep going

Purposes

Proving it to yourself

Getting Organized

Drawing on known information

Testing a hypothesis

Analyzing the situation

Reaching Conclusions

Going back to the past

Seeking understanding

Considering the application of ideas

Creating Something New

Looking at how things have changed

Considering the implications of actions

Making predictions

Reflecting and Evaluating

Examining and learning from mistakes

Asking yourself questions

Reflecting on where you've been

Considering what might be missing

Tying things up

Evaluating a solution

Eliminating possibilities

Figure 8.1. John Threlkeld's Mental Model of Thinking.

across the room's two small windows is a banner that reads: "A ship in port is safe, but that is not what ships are built for." In the center of the room, a large U.S. flag hangs from the ceiling, proudly proclaiming "American Studies."

Chris's classroom provides not only visual but emotional engagement. Chris keeps his students on their toes with his quick wit and sense of humor, carefully honed over fourteen years as a teacher to the sensibilities of middle school students. His good-natured ribbing, teasing, and jocular manner help break the ice and keep his eighth graders from taking themselves too seriously. Chris also encourages humor in his students, asking them to draw their own political cartoons later in the year. For Chris, humor is a creative process that requires looking at situations from unique and unusual perspectives.

Chris's teaching emphasizes creating meaning, both individually and collectively. You can see this as students present their opinions and ideas during their discussion on the meaning of the American Dream. In this discussion, Chris pushes students to make their points clear and to provide evidence. He also challenges them to consider other perspectives and points of view alongside their own. Although he focuses on identifying themes and big ideas, Chris presents these as transitory and changing rather than fixed. As a result, students come away from the discussion with a better recognition that meaning is something that people create for themselves rather than something that another person can give them.

This red thread of "meaning is something you create" is captured in Chris's goals for his teaching:

> I guess it goes back to what historians really do as well as increasing students' ability to access information. They need to know how to analyze information, determine what it is they need, and then determine the durability of what they use and create. And put it in some kind of context. That's a major life skill or goal that I think gets practiced and valued a lot in my class. . . . So that's a big piece. . . . Also, it's important for students to understand how their own thinking and perceptions are formed. I want students to approach other people with a fairness that goes beyond the immediate and to see past stereotypes. To do that requires being able to understand a little bit how your own perceptions are formed and to be able to question those a little bit.

For Chris, meaning making is an intense, creative, and multifaceted endeavor, calling on a variety of different types of thinking. Chris sees this process grounded in curiosity and "a desire to know." However, this knowing isn't simply a matter of finding answers. It is an open-ended process of "approaching things from different angles and taking different roles with an idea or with a concept, being able to minimize things and maximize things or mix them up or rearrange them to see what else comes out." Meaning making also involves perspective taking, "going beyond their own point of view." Finally, Chris identifies a metacognitive or introspective quality as part of making meaning: "understanding where your own perceptions come from and how you can have a role in determining those. [This leads] to a person who deals with other people in a fair way because they understand how some aspects of their own minds work, their own background, and how they see the world."

As you can see, Chris's red thread of "meaning is something you create" is rich in thinking. In fact, it is dependent on thinking, calling on curiosity, inquisitiveness, broad and adventurous thinking, open-mindedness, perspective taking, metacognition, healthy skepticism, and a guiding search for understanding. Not surprisingly, Chris's view of thinking encompasses these same dimensions in an interconnected way: "I think passion is important to great thinking. And that goes back to desire. And that gets determination going. . . You know, all these things are linked up together."

How do the themes of Chris's instruction connect to his mental model of thinking (see Figure 8.2)? In what ways do you see his thinking about thinking connecting to his teaching of history? Do you see differences in Chris and John's conceptions of thinking that reflect their subject matter backgrounds?

Susan McCray

From the linoleum floors to the wooden chalkboard tray, from the twelve-foot ceilings to the coat hooks, Susan McCray's seventh- and eighth-grade humanities classroom instantly takes me back to my elementary school years. For me, everything about the room and the building itself is emblematic of the word *school*. However, the teaching that goes on inside this classroom is a far cry from anything I experienced as a student. Noted as being progressive, the school has a feeling of informality about it. Students call teachers by their first names; there is no dress code; and no bells signal the beginning and

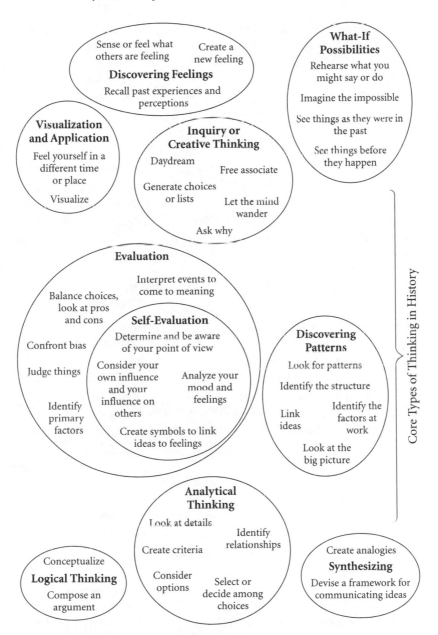

Figure 8.2. Chris Elnicki's Mental Model of Thinking.

end of classes. The progressive nature of this public school is also seen in such practices as project-based learning, social activism, extended field trips, multiage groupings, thematic instruction, block scheduling, and portfolio assessment. Within this setting, students and teachers carry on an ongoing friendly and even familial banter. And as in many families with adolescents, there is a constant testing of limits, negotiating demands, cajoling, and laughter among the teachers and the diverse group of students attending the school.

Susan's entire seven-year teaching career has been spent in progressive public schools such as this one, and she is very comfortable with its practices and the diversity of students she teaches. As a humanities teacher, Susan wants to help her students get inside ideas and understand the importance of perspective and point of view in history:

> One of the things I want kids to be able to do is really sort of get inside of ideas . . . coming at it from all different sides and all different angles and all different understandings: the different perspectives, the different points of view, the different shapes and forms that that idea or information can take. So that's first or second, and then it's to really understand it in depth and be able to play with it. Once you've identified it and got it safe in its form from all these things, then being able to play with it, craft it, mold it, reshape it, build it into something else, make connections between it and other things, other parts of your experience.

For Susan, this red thread of "getting inside of ideas" is closely connected to and dependent on two of her other goals: (1) for students to push and challenge themselves to take risks in their learning and (2) for students to engage in an ongoing self-reflective dialogue to understand their own understanding, what Susan refers to as "being aware of your journey":

> Another thing that's important to me is that someone is willing to take a risk, someone who's willing to put themselves out there and their ideas and their work, because it does many things: one, it's how someone grows. You've got to be willing to express yourself, I think, and learn about what you're thinking and what you're doing in your own self. And then it inspires others to do it in kind. And that's, as we all

know, that at this age group it's one of the hardest things. . . . The reason it's connected with the self-reflective piece is if you're doing those things [pushing yourself], you're able to sort of assess: Where am I at? What are my strengths? What are my weaknesses? Where do I want to go from here? And then you do the hard thinking.

These red threads— "getting inside ideas," "mapping your journey," and "going beyond"—are seen in the various structures, such as the reading response journal, that Susan puts in place to guide and direct students' work throughout the year. The assessment system that Susan uses also communicates her red threads. She assesses students' work on a four-point scale, defining a four as "going beyond, boldly." According to Susan, the idea is that students "take the work and do something else with it that is beyond the assignment, that's their own." This isn't just work that will get them an A grade; it is "that next level of thinking." Portfolios are also a part of the assessment system, providing another vehicle for students to reflect and map their journey as learners. In talking about self-assessment and reflection, Susan states, "I think a lot of that comes through in the portfolio process. It's reflected there, and that's a place where I can focus on and sort of highlight it for them, [that] this is something that is important to us."

Susan's red threads are also evident in her thinking about thinking (Figure 8.3). For her, a big part of thinking is playing with ideas to create something new that can be communicated to others: "It's being able to hold a lot of ideas simultaneously and being able to fairly abruptly prioritize them, categorize them, find the connections between them, find the points of tension between them. Do all that in the head and then put it back out there in a way that is palatable for others." For Susan, doing this kind of work requires paying attention to perspectives and to your own thinking, taking risks, and asking questions of yourself and others. This process is very much a community endeavor in Susan's eyes. Thinking is not something done completely solo or only for one's own benefit: "A thinker is someone who's willing to say, 'This isn't mine. This is to throw around. It came at me and what does it mean?' It's the finding out. You know, what's the point of this? . . . [You] take an idea and help it grow, help it to move to its next level."

How do these themes of reflection, risk taking, and understanding emerge in Susan's mental model of thinking? Do you see her

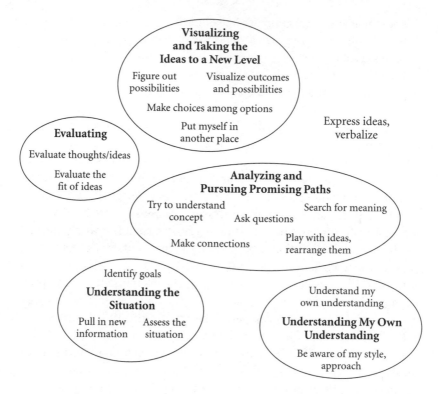

Figure 8.3. Susan McCray's Mental Model of Thinking.

individuality as a teacher emerge in her mental model? What similarities and differences do you notice between Susan's conception of thinking and that of John and Chris?

Doug Tucker

Three years ago, Doug Tucker decided to leave the corporate world and become a teacher. When he went looking for a job, he didn't have to look any further than his neighborhood public middle school, and Doug lets his students know that he is more than willing to exploit his community connections to make sure students stay on track. He tells his students he will talk to their parents in the grocery store or wherever he might see them. Jokingly, he even holds out the ultimate threat, "Don't forget, I know where you live. I'll go to your house if I need to."

As a new teacher, Doug has been exposed to and trained in a lot of the messages of mathematics education reform. He is an enthusiastic advocate of technology; his background is in computer science. Doug also embraces the view that mathematics is about problem solving, application, and thinking. As Doug says, "You can train anyone to get through algebra, geometry, trig, calculus, show them all the formulas and all the steps. But then when they get into the real world and they're presented with a problem, they don't have any clue how to solve it, because they don't know how to think."

Because of his own experience as a student in the district, Doug knows the challenges students face in developing the ability to think when constantly confronted with a heavily knowledge-based curriculum. He also knows how important thinking is to his students' future success. Consequently, Doug wants to teach in a way that will give students more long-term power, ownership, and meaning. The kind of intellectual empowerment Doug is after is built on their having the determination and will to keep going when faced with a difficult problem, having confidence that they will eventually succeed, and knowing how to access and use all the resources at their disposal. "For me, it's not so much teaching them how to solve that equation and leave x all by itself, although I do that. What's more important to me is that if they see a problem and they have an unknown, that they know how to find the unknown, whether they have to go and get a book out and read it or they have to pull out a calculator to punch in some numbers. [It's] that they know that there are resources. They don't have to just be stuck because they don't know the answer to the problem."

For Doug and his students, this message of self-sufficiency and determination represents the major red thread of his instruction. He has a name for it: "teaching you how to fish," based on the old adage about giving a man a fish versus teaching a man how to fish. Doug introduces this red thread early in the year in the context of a problem-solving warm-up. The warm-up is usually a nonroutine type of problem or a brainteaser. Every day, he presents a new problem. But last Friday's problem—I have as many brothers as sisters, but each of my sisters has only half as many sisters as brothers—went unsolved, and today Doug returns to it. "Who has a solution from Friday's warm-up? Who thought about it?" About three-quarters of the hands go up, and one student offers a solution: four boys and three girls. Doug works through the proposed solution as he has all the past proposals, and the class sees that this solution does work. Doug asks again,

"Honestly, who thought about it over the weekend?" A few hands go down, but still half the class has responded. Doug uses this as an opportunity to launch into his homily:

DOUG: You'll get things like that all year long: warm-ups, brainteasers. Some of them will be easy for you. Some of them will be hard. Keep in mind, I will rarely if ever give you the answer. Because—you'll hear this a lot—if you give a person a fish, they eat for one day. But if you teach a person to fish, they'll eat for a lifetime. Who knows what that means? . . . Jason.

JASON: If you give 'em the answer today, they'll just have it for today. But if you teaching 'em how to work it out, they'll always have it.

DOUG: Right, if I give you the answer, you'll stop thinking about the problem. I don't want you to stop thinking about the problem. . . . So you're going to think. You're going to learn how to think.

Asking students to do this kind of thinking and providing them the opportunity to do so is new for a lot of students, but Doug feels it has its rewards. As students gain experience, they not only gain confidence and skill but become motivated by the experience of solving problems, and they develop greater curiosity and passion. As Doug says, "I think you get a high off of being able to solve a problem." Although the progress is sometimes slow, Doug mentions that students often come up to him at the end of the year and comment: "'You're not like the other teachers. You let us talk. You listen to us.' Comments like that. And I know for some of the kids it's literal. The teachers don't let them talk. They open their mouths: 'Be quiet.' For other kids, what they're saying really is, 'You're allowing me to explore. You're not just giving me the answers.' And they sort of like that. They're not just sponges absorbing everything. They're creating their own answers."

Doug sees thinking, like mathematics, as largely a process of problem solving. As opposed to simply knowing the answers or being aware of the correct procedures, thinking involves "working through it" and "[using] their resources." Doug uses the analogy of fixing things around the house to describe this process. First, you need to just get in there and try something, not be afraid of making the situation worse, at least initially. It is then important to learn from your mistakes, be willing to seek help and ask questions, and stick with the problem until it is fixed. Ultimately, being successful requires more

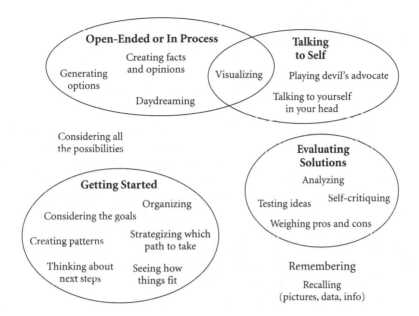

Figure 8.4. Doug Tucker's Mental Model of Thinking.

than a set of skills or background knowledge. For Doug, success in both problem solving and thinking depends on determination, some degree of passion and interest, taking risks, and using one's resources.

How is Doug's problem-solving focus embedded in his mental model of thinking (see Figure 8.4)? Doug's red thread focuses primarily on independence rather than on an aspect of thinking. Does this fit with his conception of thinking?

Heather Woodcock

Although the desks, storage cubbies, and chalkboard definitely mark this as a classroom, the porch off the back door, the large bank of double-hung windows, the separate sitting area with a sofa and comfortable chair, and the small anteroom with its own sofa and large desk give Heather Woodcock's room a homey and relaxed feel. Indeed, Heather wants her classroom to serve as a home of sorts for the nineteen seventh-grade students who are just entering a middle school setting in which most of their courses will be within a departmentalized structure. Although she has been a teacher for only six years, Heather has remarkable presence, poise, and confidence that makes for smooth transitions and strong student engagement. Her calm and approachable manner helps students, who sometimes feel a lot of pressure to excel in this private school setting, remain calm themselves. At the same time, Heather's high expectations and thoughtfulness help students begin to approach the discipline of history with a new rigor. Heather's chief goal is for students to take responsibility for their own learning. For her, this means that students begin to see that intellectual authority doesn't rest with a single source, such as the teacher or a book, but that they have to evaluate ideas and theories and make sense of them on an individual level. "I think one of the big goals for me is that students take responsibility for their own learning, that they don't depend on me or other kids to give them the answers, that they're willing and capable to do the work themselves and to make of the work what they make it. And I don't mean just getting the work done, I'm assuming that. . . . [It's that] they get it done with some kind of a sense of purpose in mind."

For Heather, "doing the work" is about doing the work of making sense of, evaluating, and generally coming to understand ideas. This requires students to examine issues, problems, and ideas at various levels and make connections for themselves. Heather sees this kind of understanding as a process of building one's own theories and explanations. She explains what this kind of theory building means for her and her students: "I think that a theory implies that you're making your own connections. And that you're imagining. I think a theory has a lot to do with imagining something because it's not necessarily the truth. It's an idea. It's a possibility. And so a theory then suggests to me that a child has taken an idea or an event and imagined what might have happened, what might have been the cause for those events. . . . That's a risk. They're almost becoming historians." Through this process of students' constructing meaning and developing their own theories, Heather feels that students come to own their learning.

Closely connected to this red thread of "taking responsibility for your learning" and the idea of ownership is something Heather calls conscious learning. According to Heather, "*Conscious learning* is having a sense of where you started and where you're ending up. And that could be where people start at the beginning of the year and end up at the end of the year or where people start at the beginning of [one day's] class and end up." Heather explains how this consciousness helps make the learning personal and meaningful: it's important "for them to think about what they're learning, why they're learning it, and why it matters. It needs to be conscious, not just to go through the motions of school. . . . It's important for them and for me to stop and say, 'Why did we learn about verbs this morning?'" Achieving this level of consciousness about one's learning requires taking time to reflect. Heather ensures that students reflect on their learning by keeping journals. She asks them to write about "what they've learned during the week. Why? How they learned what they learned, how they know that they've learned something, and why they think they learned it." At the beginning of the year, Heather requires this writing but gradually wants students to internalize these kinds of questions for themselves.

In thinking about thinking, Heather identifies these same qualities of making connections, building one's own theories, and pushing one's thinking as key components of the thinking process. In describing a student whom she considers a good thinker, Heather also identifies the need for time, depth, communication, and questioning: "He took his time with everything, and he dissected things really well. And he was very good at showing me and other people how he was thinking about things. And he was very good at asking the right questions to get him to a better understanding. And he was not afraid of saying, 'I don't get it.' He was not afraid of looking foolish in front of the other kids." Although Heather isn't sure how important communication is to thinking in general, she sees it as an important quality to nurture in the classroom. She wants students to think about developing understanding independently but also as part of a community.

Do you see Heather's emphasis on understanding and connection making in her mental model of thinking (Figure 8.5)? How is her conception of thinking similar to Susan's, another humanities teacher? What aspects of her teaching do you see as most related to her thinking about thinking? Looking over all of the mental models presented, how do they individually and jointly inform your understanding of the teachers and their practice?

Karen White

A Contrasting Case

Until now, I have mentioned Karen White only briefly in this book because her teaching reveals little about the effective teaching of intellectual character.[7] However, her case reveals a great deal about how a teacher's beliefs, values, and knowledge about thinking affect instruction. Because Karen explicitly cares about the teaching of thinking and

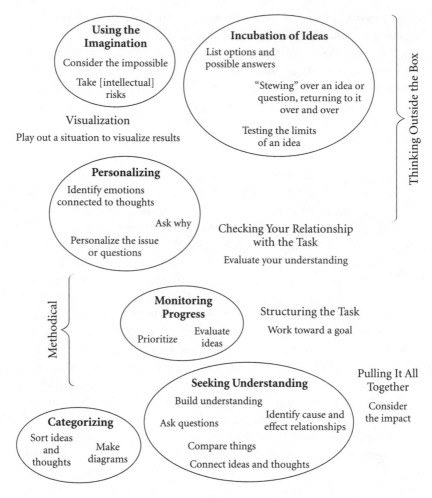

Figure 8.5. Heather Woodcock's Mental Model of Thinking.

has a strong desire to promote students' thinking, her practice presents an excellent contrasting case when it comes to trying to understand where teaching for intellectual character begins. Here is a teacher who says that she values getting students thinking and that she actively seeks to promote thinking. Why isn't her classroom a more thoughtful place? Furthermore, because Karen is an experienced, award-winning, National Board certified teacher, the reasons for the gap between her stated and realized agenda of thinking is not likely due to poor subject-matter knowledge or a lack of instructional skills.

In this sketch, you can see how Karen's red threads actually eclipse her desire to promote thinking. Her efforts are further hampered by a somewhat narrow conception of thinking. Understanding what lies behind Karen's instruction helps us not only to understand her as an individual teacher but also to understand how one's values and beliefs about teaching operate when they are in conflict.

When Karen moved this year from her middle school classroom to one in a newly built high school within the same district, she carried with her a poster that had hung in her suburban classroom for most of her seventeen years as a math teacher. In black and white, the poster proclaims four things to students: (1) "You are welcome here," (2) "I love teaching," (3) "This is a mistake-making place," and (4) "There is a teacher in every student." These statements deliver a message of support and caring that dominates Karen's classroom, wherever it may be. It is also a message that Karen lives each day as she greets her students at the door, offers after-school help sessions, provides students with her home phone number, attends students' extracurricular events, and encourages students to write messages to her in their math journals.

Perhaps most pervasively, Karen's caring is conveyed in her consistent good humor and positive attitude—something that puzzles, inspires, and at times even annoys her students and colleagues. As Karen says, "My students will write me, like in April, they'll say, 'Mrs. White seems to be never in a bad mood.' You know, it drives them nuts." Karen sees this quality of consistent happiness as one of her defining attributes not only as a person but also as a teacher and a thinker, "It's ingrained in me. I really do think it's part of my nature. . . . I always know things are going to be happy, and that is really a part of my thinking. I don't know where that impacts, whether it's the emotion or whatever, but there's a confidence there that the world's not going to come to an end, you know. . . . That's got to be something that gives me an advantage to my thinking."

Karen's deeply felt caring for students is coupled with a firm commitment to helping the thirty-two ninth graders in her first-year algebra class be successful. For Karen, student success means achieving a level of confidence and fluency through hard work and personal effort, what she terms "earned success." This is an incremental process of completing the work and building a repertoire of skills and knowledge through experience. Karen makes the connection between fluency and confidence: "The more that they do the math and it's similar math that they've done, then they're more patient with themselves. They have more confidence, and they'll stick with the struggle a little bit longer and do something a little bit more difficult. If they know that they can solve one-step equations, they'll stick with ones with fractions or bigger numbers or something like that longer than if they've never had any experiences or success with linear equations. So it's just a matter of a little bit of rhythm that comes with patience and familiarity."

You can see Karen's emphasis on caring, success, and incremental development of fluency as she helps students prepare to take a chapter quiz at the end of the first quarter. Karen begins the class as she does every day by welcoming the students and telling them she is glad to see them. Turning to the whiteboard, where the day's objective and schedule are written, Karen explains the goals and flow of the day's instruction. "I want to set us up for a successful quiz. You know me by now, and you know that I'm not going to pass it out until everyone feels they can be successful on it. I'm setting you up for success on the quiz today." Running through the rest of the schedule, Karen explains, "After the quiz, you'll write in your journals so [that] I can get an indication of how you feel you did on it. And my final goal today is to get to a review game at the end of the period to give away some kind of sweet reward."

As on any other day, Karen then checks for homework effort: "I appreciate your honesty. May I see the hands of people who did not do page 92?" After writing on the board the names of students without homework, Karen adds, "For those of you who did do your homework, thank you for earning five points in the grade book." The homework check then moves along quickly with Karen making corrections and giving explanations when students give wrong answers to the mostly skill- and knowledge-based questions. Frequently, Karen "checks for understanding" by asking students who did not do their homework if they understand the solutions. Throughout, quite a few students take notes that they will be allowed to use during the quiz.

Following the homework discussion, Karen writes a series of problems on the board and carefully guides students through each one as a final preparation for the quiz. She presents an example of each type of problem appearing on the quiz and reminds students once again that they can take notes. Karen concludes the review, "Thanks for that review. It was good participation. Anyone not thinking they're going to be able to give it a good try?" As she passes out the eleven-problem quiz, Karen adds, "OK, hope there's lots of confidence."

Throughout this review and the course, Karen tries to convey to students, some of whom are repeating the course, that they are ultimately in charge of and responsible for their success. In the review, this means doing the preparatory homework, taking the needed notes, and asking questions when you don't understand. She frequently invites students to participate in these actions but applies no pressure, other than that of grades. In the course as a whole, responsibility means doing the work and showing effort consistently. Although the answers do not have to be correct, homework is to be completed each day; a student who skips one problem receives no credit. This daily effort is so important that students who get all A's on their tests and quizzes but do not do homework will only just pass the course.

To help students know exactly where they stand in the class and make decisions accordingly, Karen posts grades weekly beside the front door. Although this overriding emphasis on grades, points, and doing well academically seems to be the dominant motivator in the class, Karen doesn't see it that way. She feels that some students will be motivated by grades, others by understanding, and still others by rewards—such as a soda pop for a perfect quiz score. Karen feels that she can't change what motivates students, but she can tap into it, whatever it happens to be.

Karen's red threads of "earn your success" and "build confidence one step at a time" extend to her thinking about thinking. For her, good thinking comes first and foremost from a place of confidence and a relaxed and easygoing attitude, what she calls flexibility or not getting uptight in a situation. This approach to situations provides time for thinking and helps to avoid impulsivity. Thinking also requires applying effort and having strategies to try when solving novel problems. This access to a repertoire of different strategies characterizes the process of thinking for Karen: "A thinker may not have the facts all lined up ready to grab in their mind, but they can go through the process in a comfortable way." Finally, she feels that a lot of thinking and being comfortable is about making connections on a personal level as well as with other ideas. She sees this as a metacognitive process involving identifying your feelings, reactions, and responses to situations, such as what occurred when students wrote about the quiz.

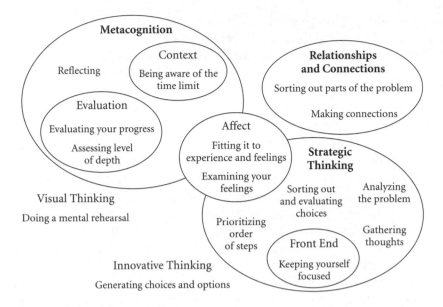

Figure 8.6. Karen White's Mental Model of Thinking.

These ideas are visible in Karen's mental model of thinking (Figure 8.6): she generated fifteen thinking actions that she placed in three major clusters. The importance of affective issues and problem-solving strategies and techniques can be seen in both the metacognition and strategic thinking clusters. Karen's model tends to be focused primarily on problem solving, which is typical of the math teachers I studied. However, in contrast to John, the problem-solving tools and processes she describes are less comprehensive and less open-ended in nature, which seems to fit better with school-generated problems than real-life problems.

WHERE IT BEGINS

As these six sketches demonstrate, the red threads of a teacher's practice may emphasize thinking centrally or only peripherally. For example, several of the teachers have red threads that focus on ideas, constructing meaning, and building understanding. Such practices are hard to accomplish without employing thinking practices such as perspective taking, making connections, evaluating ideas, and constructing theories of explanation. On the other hand, Karen and Doug have red threads that were more connected to building confidence and independence in students. These goals aren't incompatible with thinking and are certainly important in their own right. However, teachers' goals often represent end states they are after more than benchmarks along the way. Consequently, teachers are more likely to work backward from their goals to address prerequisite needs than to work forward to extend a goal they feel has been met. This means that teachers who are focused on getting inside ideas or playing with ideas are probably more likely to attend to building students' confidence than teachers focused on building confidence are to play with ideas.

Something else that emerges from this look into foundations is that the teachers with the more thinking-centered red threads also have a richer knowledge and conception of thinking. For instance, Karen, whose red threads focused on social and motivational issues, generated fifteen thinking items grouped in three major categories, and Doug had three major categories out of a list of eighteen thinking items. Heather and Susan generated more elaborate mental models with five overarching categories from lists of twenty-two and eighteen items respectively. Similarly, Chris and John each generated more than thirty items grouped into at least six clusters.

In the concluding chapters, I further explore the importance of teachers' thinking about thinking and their instructional goals. I also provide some suggestions for how you can uncover your mental model of thinking and discern your own red threads. As the cases of these teachers demonstrate, teaching for intellectual character begins with these foundational elements.

⟿ **Key Ideas for Developing Intellectual Character**
BEYOND TECHNIQUE: WHERE TEACHING FOR INTELLECTUAL CHARACTER BEGINS

- *The Red Thread.* The red thread is a metaphor for the central goals and guiding purposes that connect, bind, and unite our practice, giving it its cohesiveness. The red thread captures the implicit curriculum of our classroom, our underlying message. These most deeply held instructional values and goals take precedence over other agendas and exert a great deal of influence on our teaching. When we have a red thread that doesn't connect well to nurturing thinking and intellectual character, we will find it hard to make that goal a lived priority in our classrooms. At the same time, knowledge of our red thread gives us power to shape it in the direction we want it to go.

- *Mental Models.* We all have an internalized mental model or internal map of what thinking is, what kinds of thinking are most important, how we use our thinking abilities, and when certain types of thinking are useful. Uncovering our mental map of thinking can help us enhance our conception of thinking by broadening our scope, increasing our awareness, and enhancing our inclination and motivation. It also helps us to spot and exploit occasions for thinking when they appear in the classroom. Having a rich mental model of thinking helps us to help our students develop their thinking.

CHAPTER NINE

Three Lessons

What to Keep in Mind About Teaching for Intellectual Character

*S*tand and Deliver, Music of the Heart, Dangerous Minds, Mr. Holland's Opus, Dead Poets Society—all these films present portraits of excellence in teaching. In these Hollywood portrayals, we characteristically see the teacher presented as an iconoclast, battling against the odds so that his or her students succeed in ways never before imagined. Although these stories celebrate what is possible for teachers to achieve, they seldom provide a direction for others to follow. Instead, these cinematic classroom tales reduce good teaching to the force of personality accompanied by an unlimited level of commitment and boundless energy. If one is not a charismatic Jaime Escalante or a tough but caring LouAnne Johnson, it seems the world of the classroom is likely to be a scary and difficult place. As inspirational and uplifting as these films are, in the end the message for teachers and others in the audience is often very slim.

Case-study research of teachers runs this same risk of enshrining the teacher and marginalizing the practice. To make each teacher's practice understandable, I have presented information about the teacher's beliefs and values along with his or her thinking about thinking. To make each teacher's practice real and contextualized, I have tried to create pictures of practice that reveal the uniqueness of each classroom and instructional setting while still highlighting practices that can be adapted to other contexts. In doing so, it is possible that for some readers the specific has overwhelmed the general. Perhaps you have come to identify with one teacher over another or to see the practices of these teachers as inspirational but not directly linked to your own situation because you do not teach the same grade or subject. In this chapter, I attempt to step back from the particulars of the individual cases and identify the broader lessons that we can take away from this set of teachers.

The lessons I present here have their basis in issues and ideas raised in previous chapters and do not represent a separate set of new findings. Rather, these issues are currents that have risen to the surface, and many readers will have felt their presence much earlier. However, these are the kinds of big-picture issues that bear repeating and warrant their own discussion. The three currents are:

- For teachers to effectively cultivate students' disposition toward thinking, they must themselves be dispositionally oriented toward thinking.
- Teaching for intellectual character often involves breaking the rules of so-called effective teaching.
- Teaching for the development of intellectual character depends on the natural synergy present in a curriculum focused on developing students' disciplinary understanding.

Following my discussion of each of these three lessons, I examine some of the implications they have for schools, teachers, and those who work with them.

LESSON ONE: THE IMPORTANCE OF TEACHERS' DISPOSITIONS

In the United States, we put an abiding faith in programs, curriculums, and increasingly in state- and district-mandated standards. There is a widely held perception that education can be micromanaged from the outside by legislating specific instructional approaches, imposing testing, and dictating how time is spent in schools.[1] The idea persists in many administrators' and policymakers' minds that with the right programs, materials, and mandates we can easily shape the learning that goes on in classrooms. Although this top-down approach might be used to some effect when one is only after the basics, if one is after something more, something like the development of intellectual character, such an approach is likely to be woefully ineffective.

In order for teachers to develop students' ability in, inclination toward, and awareness of thinking, teachers must possess these qualities themselves. Teachers must be sensitive to opportunities for thinking that arise in the present curriculum or that spontaneously arise in class, and they must be aware of the specific types of thinking that best fit a particular situation. To take advantage of these opportunities, teachers must be inclined to value that thinking and recognize the potential benefits that occur as a result of using class time to explore the opportunity. This inclination has to be strong to triumph over the many competing demands teachers face for the use of class time. Finally, to scaffold students' performance within such thinking opportunities and to model effective approaches, teachers themselves must possess strong abilities in the types of thinking that a particular occasion calls for. These qualities cannot be easily replaced by well-designed curricular materials or other external influences. Although adopting certain curricular materials might increase thinking opportunities, such efforts only address the development of ability and do little to cultivate students' awareness and inclination.

You can see how a teacher's own intellectual character and disposition toward thinking affect what goes on in the classroom in the cases we have examined. This influence is especially vivid in the practice of John Threlkeld and Karen White. Although both are experienced teachers and each is effective in his or her own way, differences in their ability, inclination, and awareness with respect to thinking affect the implicit and explicit curriculum they deliver to their students.[2]

John Threlkeld

A Disposition Toward Thinking Realized

John demonstrates a rich understanding of thinking in general as well as within the discipline of mathematics. This is evident in his mental model of thinking (see Figure 8.1), the extensive list of thinking items he generated in the mental-model exercise, and his use of thinking-based language (see Table 6.2). John's red threads of "playing with ideas" and "mathematics as a community endeavor" indicate a strong inclination toward thinking. John's awareness of thinking occasions allows him to spot potential thinking opportunities in the curriculum. However, these opportunities become a reality for students only when John's awareness is combined with his ability and inclination. Thus, the evidence for John's awareness, to be found in the opportunities he creates for students' thinking, are actually a manifestation of his disposition toward thinking—the coming together of awareness, general and situation-specific inclination, and ability—at work.[3]

John's strong ability, inclination, and awareness help him create a classroom that is very thoughtful and rich in thinking opportunities for students.[4] We see this in John's ability to create opportunities for students to explore big ideas in mathematics, such as the origin of mathematical conventions versus mathematical truths, the meaning of variability in algebra, or the presence of the distributive property in much of the mental math we do. His disposition is also apparent in his recognition of the thinking behind students' questions and his understanding of where that thinking might take the class. John's consistent modeling of curiosity, skepticism, and being strategic are a further indication of his disposition toward thinking.

Karen White
A Disposition Toward Thinking Frustrated

Karen's practice is particularly informative for understanding how a teacher's inclination toward, ability in, and awareness of thinking influence what happens in the classroom. Karen represents a very interesting case precisely because she cares about and is interested in promoting students' thinking, but she has a classroom that tends to be textbook-driven and to focus on mastering basic skills and procedures. Because her practice is so informative when it comes to understanding the obstacles we face when we try to teach for intellectual character, I've devoted more space here to trying to understand and illuminate what is going on than I did with John. I will take additional space to ground my observations and assertions about Karen. Although readers have had many glimpses into John's practice, I have said relatively little about Karen's teaching.

Although Karen demonstrates many strengths as a teacher with regard to her ability to create a safe and comfortable environment and to develop students' confidence, the overall level of thoughtfulness in her classroom tends to be low.[5] The thinking opportunities that exist are present mostly in the independent problems of the week that

Karen designs and assigns regularly to her students, such as figuring out how long it would take to say your name a billion times. However, these weekly projects also tend to be highly structured and focused on the application of mathematical procedures without really pushing students' thinking. The openness that does exist in these problems is often in the presentation of the work and to some extent in the methods used. In examining Karen's practice, you can see how her inclinations as a teacher and her understanding of thinking shape and influence the environment she strives to create for her students.

KAREN'S INCLINATION. Although Karen values promoting students' thinking as a goal of her instruction, her inclination toward this goal is eclipsed by the other values and beliefs she holds. As Thomas Green (1971, p. 41) points out, "Nobody holds a belief in total independence of all other beliefs. Beliefs always occur in sets or groups. They take their place in belief systems, never in isolation." For Karen, the overriding goal is to promote student confidence and support students' success, with success being defined in terms of grades and mastery of mathematical procedures. Within this belief system, it is hard to identify a strong role for thinking or to see how thinking can best serve Karen's main instructional objectives. Consequently, Karen's most strongly held beliefs incline her to employ practices, techniques, and routines that support her main goals but actually undermine the development of students' thinking. For example, the dominant emphasis on grades and keeping score supports Karen's emphasis on monitoring work and expending effort, but such practices tend to undermine students' orientation toward learning.[6] In the long run, students come to relate to the content superficially, as work to be done rather than as ideas to think about and explore.

KAREN'S ABILITY. Karen's understanding of thinking further complicates her efforts to promote thinking. This understanding has been influenced by her training in cognitive coaching, a teacher and school enhancement program developed by Art Costa and Robert Garmston (1994). Although Costa and Garmston describe five passions—efficacy, flexibility, craftsmanship, consciousness, and interdependence—as basic human forces that "drive, influence, motivate, and inspire our intellectual capacities" (p. 196), Karen sees these five forces as constituting thinking itself. Thus, rather than looking to create these conditions as the basis from which good thinking can spring, Karen sees the development of these particular passions as synonymous with good thinking.

The development of thinking abilities further breaks down as Karen reduces each of these passions to more basic elements. For example, Karen equates craftsmanship with having skill, though Costa and Garmston actually define it as a yearning for clarity, elegance, and precision. Similarly, Karen reduces efficacy to a feeling of self-confidence, though Costa and Garmston define it as a quest for life-long learning and mastery. Karen defines flexibility as an ability not to get emotionally overwhelmed by circumstances and demands, though officially in cognitive coaching it is defined as the human endeavor to change and expand.

We can also see this more stripped-down view of thinking in Karen's mental model of thinking presented in Figure 8.6. Karen generated only half as many explanations of thinking as did John and had a more basic mental model in terms of the presence of organizing categories. A further indication of Karen's understanding of thinking can be found in the language of thinking she uses in class, which tends to be somewhat constrained (see Table 6.3). In the final analysis, Karen's efforts to develop students' thinking are a reflection of and are consistent with her own understanding of thinking. Karen does in fact spend a great deal of time developing skill, confidence, and calm in her students, which for her are all-important dimensions of thinking.

KAREN'S AWARENESS. Karen appears to be less aware of thinking occasions than other teachers in the study. However, it is difficult to judge to what extent this might be a reflection of her inclination and ability as opposed to awareness alone. For instance, the math journals that she has her students keep provide an opportunity for students to be reflective and analyze their thinking. However, Karen generally has students write about their feelings or report on classroom activities in the journals, and in her responses to these journals she focuses mostly on acknowledging students rather than pushing or commenting on their thinking. These actions might reflect a weak understanding of the nature of reflection, which implicates ability; a lack of sensitivity to the opportunity present, which implicates awareness; or a manifestation of her desire to draw out students' emotions, which would implicate inclination. After discussing these journals and their purpose with Karen, I believe that she does feel like she is engaging students in metacognition and that the journals represent a serious attempt to promote students' thinking. Thus, it appears that Karen's understanding of what it means to reflect and be metacognitive is the major factor shaping her actions in this instance. Therefore, it is actually ability rather than awareness that lies at the root of Karen's failure to use the journals to better advantage.

Another example of a missed thinking opportunity lies in the way Karen dealt with a classroom controversy about interpreting graphs. Discussing the results of a survey on Japanese students, Karen invited her students to share their reactions. However, she never provided any basis for evaluating opinions or drawing accurate interpretations. As a result, students offered stereotypes and overgeneralizations that she never challenged. At one point, a student did challenge another student's assertions, but a more popular and outspoken classmate shut down the challenger. During this episode, Karen herself showed a tendency to biased thinking in the interpretation of data, indicating that her ability in this area might not be sufficient to spot the thinking opportunity. In addition, Karen seems to value students' sharing ideas as inherently positive, and she is inclined to accept and acknowledge what she sees as students' "taking a risk" by speaking out in class without pushing them to provide appropriate evidence and support for their positions.

KAREN'S DISPOSITION TOWARD THINKING. As these examples show, ability, inclination, and awareness are not independent but act in concert. Our ability and inclination are likely to influence our awareness. Without the requisite ability, we simply don't know what to look for in a given situation. Without the supporting inclination, our attention is likely to be diverted elsewhere. When these two weaknesses are combined, it can be especially difficult to spot the thinking opportunities that present in a situation. But without awareness, we don't know where to look or what types of markers or indicators we should be on the lookout for.

It is important to recognize that Karen is by no means a weak or a poor teacher by the standards of the profession. She is a National Board Certified teacher, has received numerous awards for her caring and dedication as an educator, and has been recognized as an effective trainer of new teachers. Throughout my observations, I was consistently impressed with Karen's management abilities and her preparedness as a teacher. But her case demonstrates that teaching for intellectual character is a mission that receives little attention in schools and in the professional development of teachers. Karen's case also demonstrates that teachers interpret rather than merely implement all programs, and perhaps in particular thinking-based programs.

Implications

A teacher's dispositional profile need not represent his or her destiny as a teacher of thinking. Just as we believe it is possible to influence students' intellectual character, we must believe that it is possible for teachers to develop their intellectual character as well. However, it is important to note that teachers seldom make attempts at such development. Although research on teachers' knowledge of subject matter has shaped the content-area training that many preservice teachers receive, teachers' preparation seldom addresses issues of thinking. Similarly, in-service training of teachers in thinking-skills programs or thinking-oriented curriculum seldom seeks to develop teachers' understanding of what it means to think. The focus is almost always on implementing the program rather than interpreting it.

If we take seriously the fact that to promote students' thinking dispositions teachers themselves must possess thinking dispositions, then we need to design encounters for teachers in which they can develop their thinking abilities, increase their inclination toward thinking, and become more aware of thinking opportunities in the curriculum. Many math and science professional development programs have recognized that teachers must first have a more meaningful experience with mathematics themselves to provide such experiences for students.[7] In the same way, thinking-based programs might look at ways to immerse teachers in thinking rather than merely train them in activities, or they might at least look for ways to enhance teachers' understanding of thinking alongside their implementation of new practices and activities. This might mean that teachers form study or support groups to talk about issues of thinking and intellectual character as they go about their instructional efforts.

I feel the need to offer a caveat here, however. In the thoughtful classrooms I studied, the teachers' views of thinking are tightly woven with their views of the subject matter. In addition, these teachers have a deep interest in their disciplines and a desire to help students understand and enjoy them in the same way the teachers do. The practice of these teachers suggests that teaching for intellectual character may in part depend on teachers' enthusiasm about and involvement in the big ideas of the discipline. It is difficult to see how teachers who lack such interests might meaningfully tack on thinking routines, create thinking opportunities, or use thinking language in a way that has the same power as when those practices emerge from a more authentic engagement with the discipline. Thus, motivation and inclination toward thinking, even more than ability and awareness, seem a necessary precondition for optimal success.

LESSON TWO: BREAKING THE RULES OF SO-CALLED EFFECTIVE TEACHING

Several popular books for teachers present a vision of effective teaching that is clear-cut, black and white, and completely unambiguous. These materials draw on the process-product research of the 1970s and define effectiveness as doing the right thing, doing what is obvious rather than what everyone else is doing, and establishing a climate of work that will help all students succeed (Wong & Wong, 1997, p. 163). According to these authors, effective teachers have positive expectations, are excellent classroom managers, and know how to design lessons for mastery. Likewise, the road to being an effective teacher is equally clear. One need only establish and consistently enforce routines and procedures that limit student disruptions and focus students on their work while maintaining a friendly and helpful attitude.[8]

Unfortunately, the student and teacher success these materials advocate is never fully explored and certainly never challenged. Instead, it is taken as a given in the proponents' view that student success means doing well in the school environment, which in turn tends to be defined as scoring well on standardized tests and getting good grades. Teacher success is defined as having students who are successful at these endeavors while also having a smoothly run (read: quiet) class.[9] These themes of discipline and work are at the center of the advice such authors provide. In these materials, the authors never question these basic assumptions about success, knowledge, and work, and they even go so far as to warn teachers about questioning what they are asked to teach or deliver to students.

Redefining Good

Of course, words like *success, effective,* and *good* are not only open to interpretation, their societal and institutional meanings are quite variable over time and across circumstances. For instance, within educational research, what it means to be a good or effective teacher has been continually evolving. In his essay "The Good Teacher," Christopher Clark (1995) explores how our definition of what makes a good teacher has changed over the past three decades. Although process-product research has focused on grades and scores as measures of success and effectiveness, subsequent research agendas have defined good teachers as those who are effective decision makers or who possess a certain body of knowledge. Other educators, such as Neil Postman and Charles Weingartner (1969) and Parker Palmer (1998), have extended the definition of good teaching even further by rejecting the objectivity of grades and scores and advocating instead for the importance of developing interpersonal connections and enhancing students' sense of empowerment. In my study of teaching, I have defined effective, good, and successful teaching as that which produces thoughtful environments and promotes students' thinking and development of intellectual character.[10]

When we no longer define student success as merely getting good scores and good grades and when we begin to view good teaching as more than having a well-behaved classroom, then we must challenge many of the so-called effective practices born from the process-product paradigm. Confronting these practices is particularly important because many of these techniques have become so ingrained in teachers' practices that they are now truisms of teaching. For example, the American Federation of Teachers advocates that new teachers be inducted into school districts through systematic training in these practices. The long-running success of Harry and Rosemary Wong's (1997) book on how to be an effective teacher is further testament to the appeal of these clear-cut techniques. However, in the most thoughtful classrooms I observed, teachers break from many of these so-called effective practices, particularly at the beginning of the year, while maintaining good classroom control and engaging students more consistently in thinking. In contrast, in rooms where these supposedly tried-and-true methods are most employed, the thinking opportunities are often less rich.

New Rules of Practice

Consider this well-respected truism presented by Wong and Wong (1997, pp. 141, 143): "Effective teachers introduce rules, procedures, and routines on the very first day of school and continue to teach them the first week of school. During the first week of school, rules procedures, and routines take precedence over lessons. The ineffective teacher is too eager to present lessons. . . . The effective teacher invests time in teaching discipline and procedures, knowing that this will be repaid multifold in the effective use of class time." This sounds like solid advice. It certainly makes sense to get started on the right foot, share what you expect of students, and establish ground rules earlier rather than later. However, if followed rigidly, this approach misses the point that it is also crucial to establish norms of learning and inter-action during the first days of school. Such norms communicate to students what you and the course are about and convey important messages about class expectations. When teachers spend the first weeks of school delaying lessons, one of the implicit messages they convey is that learning is less important than order, which may well be true to some people's minds.

In contrast to this traditional approach of starting with the rules, teachers in the thoughtful classrooms I studied began the year by jumping into a big subject-matter problem. This initial activity ex-posed students to the kinds of issues they would be expected to con-front in the course and introduced students to thinking, as opposed to management, routines that they would use throughout the year. Chris Elnicki engaged students in interpreting historical photographs. John Threlkeld began a weeklong investigation into the origin and pur-pose of order of operations rules. In neither class did discipline or class-room management suffer. Both teachers established and maintained rules of classroom interaction and order while communicating to stu-dents both the value of class time for learning and an expectation of students' thinking and engagement.

Both John and Chris recognize, at least implicitly, that middle school students have well-established scripts, that is, internalized expectations about how things work, for behavior in classrooms and are apt to operate within those scripts, provided teachers respond to any missteps or challenges accordingly. These scripts also are rein-forced by the school, the community, and the grade-level team of teachers in assemblies and in written form in student handbooks. Although these teachers rely on the existing management scripts that students hold to maintain classroom order, they also want to inter-rupt and challenge the traditional learning scripts students have devel-oped that impede learning. Specifically, they want to show students exactly what the course will demand of them in terms of thinking and begin to enculturate them in new norms of thinking and ways of interacting with curricular content.

In contrast, teachers such as Karen and Doug who followed the received wisdom and delayed lessons until after the first week of school did not seem to gain by doing so. Rather than inspire students about learning or develop a culture of thinking, such instruction appeared to deflate students' interest in the course and in some cases to frustrate them. The slow start also seemed to indicate that the pace of the class itself would be slow, laborious, and work-oriented. This was further compounded by the fact that students were often asked to take pretests that seemed to serve no real purpose in their learning. Consequently, students' introductory experiences in these classrooms tended to reinforce the mundane and control-oriented nature of school.

As a new teacher at a school with a history of discipline problems, Doug Tucker does spend a lot of time at the beginning of the year going over rules and expectations, as well as establishing management routines that contribute to a smoothly running class. However, Doug includes thinking-rich learning routines in his introductory activities as well. His daily warm-up problems are one example: these introduce students to mathematics as problem solving. Through discussing these problems, Doug also establishes norms for discussing ideas within a group and for not relying on the teacher for answers. Although Doug gives a pretest at the beginning of the year, he finds it less useful than he had thought he would and expresses reservations about having spent the time to do it.

Striking a Balance

Classrooms need to be orderly and well disciplined to be productive. I'm not advocating lax discipline or suggesting that students don't need disciplinary guidance. In Susan's room, many of the great thinking opportunities she develops for students suffer because of discipline problems and a work-avoidant attitude that students bring with them to class. Susan has management routines but acknowledges that she struggles with achieving the appropriate balance among enforcement of rules, encouragement of self-efficacy, promotion of students' interests, and development of an atmosphere of mutual respect. At times, these can seem like competing goals, and Susan struggles to find the balance among management, work, and learning routines that will work on any given day with a particular class.[11]

My point is actually the same one that the Wongs emphasize in their book: "What happens on the first days of school will be an accurate indicator of your success for the rest of the school year" (1997, p. 3). If teachers judge success by classroom order and by students' working quietly and independently, then it makes sense for them to emphasize rules and consequences early on. However, if they judge success by intellectual character, then it may make more sense to focus on thinking-rich learning routines at the beginning of the year to establish a culture of thinking. The former procedure conveys an implicit message that school is about completing work—often nonsensical and meaningless to the student—quickly, quietly, and efficiently and that learning happens in externally structured and controlled environments. The latter position conveys to students that learning and school are about thinking and engaging with curricular content as part of a community.

Implications

How we define good teaching and the goals of that teaching is not a trivial matter. We need to be clear about the kinds of outcomes we desire for ourselves and our students before we can work toward them. Perhaps more importantly, we need to constantly challenge the practices, routines, guidelines, and methods of teaching by uncovering the assumptions that lie behind them. This means becoming aware of the foundations and philosophical underpinnings of both accepted and new practices. What vision of good teaching do they advocate?

We also need to find a way to help teachers, particularly new teachers, balance the need to establish a productive atmosphere for learning and the building of a culture of thinking that will support learning. The experienced teachers I observed, with the exception of Karen, have already figured out how to strike this balance. However, the newer teachers sometimes struggle to bring order and a thinking atmosphere together. This is not an easy task. It requires a good deal of self-confidence and consistency. It also requires having a large repertoire of routines for housekeeping, management, discourse, learning, and thinking at one's disposal. When we focus preservice teacher training and new teacher induction only on housekeeping and management routines, we do new teachers a disservice. We give the false impression that once control is in place, learning will follow. Instead, we need to make sure that teachers are aware of how all of the routines they employ work together to help establish a learning environment, that without strong thinking and learning routines classrooms can be orderly but lifeless places.

LESSON THREE: THINKING AND UNDERSTANDING ARE A POWERFUL MIX

Some thinking-skills programs and proponents advocate an infusion approach to the teaching of thinking. Such an approach seeks to develop students' thinking skills within the context of meaningful subject-specific content rather than through discrete and often artificial thinking exercises found in more traditional thinking-skills curricula. For example, rather than teaching students how to apply pro and con reasoning within an abstract situation, a program might engage students in evaluating options as part of a larger and purposeful problem-solving task. *The Voyage of the Mimi* developed at Bank Street College of Education and *The Adventures of Jasper Woodbury* from the Cognition and Technology Center at Vanderbilt University are examples of math-and-science-oriented simulations that provide such contexts. Similar opportunities can be found in the Mini Society economics simulation of The Kauffman Center for Entrepreneurial Studies and in the Junior Great Books program of The Great Books Foundation.

As good as these programs are at engaging students in thinking, teachers don't need a special thinking-skills or thinking-infused program to enculturate students into the process of thinking. The best and perhaps ultimate thinking-infused program is a curriculum focused on understanding. When teachers take understanding seriously as a goal, thinking automatically becomes the primary tool for achieving that goal.

Defining Understanding

When I speak of understanding, I'm referring to what Jerome Bruner (1973) has described as the ability to go beyond the information given, to use our skills and knowledge in novel circumstances and in the creation of new ideas. David Perkins often speaks of understanding in terms of "knowing one's way around" a particular topic.[12] This metaphor for understanding suggests that every topic has multiple sides for us to navigate and that we need always to be on the lookout for new perspectives and opportunities to explore. Understanding a particular topic then leads not just to familiarity but also to a state of enablement. In contrast, we can possess knowledge and skills in isolation and without the accompanying understanding that would permit us to use them flexibly and adaptively in new situations.

Understanding is often viewed as richly integrated and connected knowledge.[13] This means that we do not possess a set of skills or collection of facts in isolation; rather, our knowledge is woven together in a way that connects one idea to another. This web of connections and relations is often the vehicle for putting ideas to work and seeing the applicability of our skills in new contexts. In contrast, when knowledge isn't well integrated, it can be difficult to access and use. Furthermore, we must challenge our own naive conceptions and replace them with more sophisticated and nuanced perspectives. Unfortunately, replacing old concepts with new ones is difficult. As a result, our minds include the old ideas and the new ideas side by side, and we may still use the older, intuitive conceptions rather than the newer, more reliable conceptions in our daily activities.

An Agenda of Understanding

To accomplish this kind of understanding—an understanding that stresses exploring a topic from many angles, building connections, challenging long-held assumptions, looking for applications, and producing what is for the learner a novel outcome—we must engage in thinking. In the most thoughtful classrooms I studied, this agenda of understanding is what carried the day for the teachers. However, the teachers know that they can accomplish such an agenda only by pushing students' thinking and putting students in situations where they have to confront their own and others' ideas. In these classrooms, thinking and engagement with ideas go hand in hand. In contrast, when the principal objective of the classroom is not rich understanding but the acquisition of knowledge and skills, there are fewer opportunities for thinking and fewer reasons to engage in thinking.

In the end, it seems unreasonable to assume that classrooms can have either understanding apart from thinking or thinking divorced from a mission of understanding if the aim is to develop students' intellectual character. One agenda serves and complements the other. Nonetheless, in too many schools, a passing familiarity with skills and ideas is all that teachers and administrators seek. In such settings, teachers often confuse understanding with mastery—students' ability to replicate the skills and knowledge presented when they are called on to do so. Those who view understanding in this way naturally value thinking less than memorization. Furthermore, such settings are often antagonistic to some of the very practices that promote thinking. For example, in settings where they seek mastery of facts and procedures, teachers tend to view confusion and ambiguity, factors that some teachers use to prompt thinking, as undesirable and dangerous. Within a mastery agenda, good instruction equals presenting facts and procedures in a way that facilitates easy memorization and replication. Thus, an agenda that focuses more on mastery than understanding can actually squeeze out opportunities to engage students in thinking.

The converse tends not to be true, however. An agenda of thinking and understanding actually serves the goals of retention and application of knowledge and procedures quite well. When material is understood, more connections exist to facilitate its recall. In addition, understanding and thinking specifically attend to issues of application in new situations. Furthermore, it is the ability to think through new situations, not merely the possession of a set of skills, that is empowering. In all the thoughtful classrooms I observed, the teachers know this and are not worried that their students will lack skills or knowledge if they teach for understanding.

Implications

To promote thinking, we need something worth thinking about. Memorization and skill practice aren't going to do the trick; only a larger goal of developing understanding will suffice. But that is easier said than done. With curricula packed full of objectives and programs that have been adopted by panels, it isn't always clear where to find an agenda of understanding. One place to begin is by identifying the larger picture behind the skills, knowledge, and facts. Why are these things important? What do they help students to understand? How can we link them to a larger idea or purpose? If we can find these bigger ideas, they may point us toward what it is we really want students to understand. Keeping firmly in mind a sense of where we want students to go, we can turn our attention to issues of thinking and dispositions. What kinds of thinking are required to build a solid understanding of these ideas? What thinking dispositions can we nurture within this context?

In previous chapters, I've written about guiding questions as tools for laying out an agenda of understanding and for focusing opportunities on big ideas. Such questions were a cornerstone in Heather Woodcock's classroom. In trying to formulate guiding questions, it is often helpful to think in terms of central themes or overarching goals that run through a course. What is it that guides the work we will be asking students to do? When all is said and done, what do we want students to take away? What do they leave our classrooms having a better grasp of? In all the various units we teach, to what core issues, ideas, or puzzles do we keep coming back? If we could interview our students one on one at the end of the year as a way of assessing what they have learned, what three or four questions would we most like to hear them talk about? If we tend to generate a lot of questions beginning with "what," we should try to move our thinking more along the lines of "how" or "why" questions. These types of questions tend to be more effective at inviting exploration.

A final implication of the important connection between thinking and understanding is that we don't necessarily need to adopt new programs to get students thinking. No thinking-skills programs are in use in any of the classrooms I observed, yet these are among the most thoughtful classrooms I have ever experienced. Although some programs can be useful enhancements and offer helpful suggestions for teachers, what carries the day in terms of developing intellectual character is consistency and a steady immersion in the process of thinking. To the extent that thinking-skills programs stand outside the bulk of students' day-to-day activity, they are not likely to be very effective. To the extent that teachers regularly engage students in thinking as a part of their ongoing class work, such programs are not likely to be needed.

IN CLOSING

The three lessons I have presented here take a broad view. Collectively, they outline some of the basic conditions needed in teaching for intellectual character. These lessons are foundational issues that all teachers need to address and understand. As such, they are worthy of our attention both on a community-wide scale as well as an individual basis. We need to consider how our training and development of teachers may in some ways impede rather than support efforts to teach for intellectual character. We need to be willing to challenge and rethink some of the received wisdom we pass on to new teachers. We need to explore ways to break through the barriers that may be hindering our progress as orchestrators of learning environments. Although some of these barriers are constraints imposed from the outside, we need to recognize that many obstacles are of our own making. At the very least, we control the way we respond to the constraints imposed by others. Finally, we need to be clear about what we are teaching for. How do we measure successful teaching?

In almost every school or district I have visited, I have managed to find teachers doing wonderful and amazing things. While many of their colleagues bemoan what they can't do or the policies hindering their teaching, these creative teachers manage to look beyond the constraints to see what is possible. These individuals are not Pollyannas, always looking on the bright side of things; it is that they focus on and invest energy in what they can do and what they can control. These individuals constantly develop their own dispositions toward thinking and demonstrate, through their approach to the obstacles they face, that just as good thinking is partly a matter of awareness, inclination, and motivation, so is good teaching. These teachers tend to know what they are teaching for and are willing to challenge assumptions of conventional effective teaching models. Finally, these individuals see that pursuing an agenda of understanding and thinking is likely to serve many of the other goals and objectives that are thrown their way; they recognize that such an agenda prepares students well for whatever eventuality or test they may face in the future.

—∿∿— **Key Ideas for Developing Intellectual Character**
THREE LESSONS TO KEEP IN MIND

- *Teachers' Dispositions Matter.* To promote thinking in students, teachers need to be students of thinking themselves. Teachers do not have to be great thinkers or brilliant intellectuals, but they do need to constantly strive to develop their understanding of thinking, their awareness of thinking opportunities, and their inclination and motivation toward thinking. If teachers do not know what good and productive thinking looks like within the domain of their teaching, they will have trouble fostering it in their students. If teachers cannot recognize occasions for thinking, they will have trouble making the best of thinking opportunities as they arise. If teachers are not primarily inclined and motivated toward promoting thinking, they may find themselves trying to manage competing agendas.

- *Challenge the Rules of So-Called Effective Teaching.* Models of what constitutes good and effective teaching are not fixed. They are always evolving. Consequently, the practices associated with effective teaching are not neutral but convey certain assumptions about the expected outcomes of teaching. Practices deemed effective by some standards may be ineffective or even counterproductive in teaching for intellectual character. Practices that focus on developing an attitude of school as work to be conducted in an orderly fashion do little to develop a culture of thinking or establish an agenda of understanding. Nowhere is the conflict so evident as between what new teachers are told about how to begin the school year and the first-days practices of most of the teachers presented here.

- *Thinking and Understanding Are a Powerful Mix.* One cannot have understanding without thinking. Likewise, one cannot have thinking without some substance to wrap it around. When students are involved in an active search for understanding, they are likely to run across numerous opportunities for thinking. Within these contexts, their

(continued)

THREE LESSONS TO KEEP IN MIND
(*continued*)

thinking abilities, inclination, motivation, and awareness
have a chance to develop. Identifying the big ideas of the
curriculum and framing them in terms of guiding questions or generative topics is often the first step in establishing an agenda of understanding.

CHAPTER TEN

Some Practical Advice

How to Get Started Teaching
for Intellectual Character

⟶∿∿⟵ I began this book by making the point that new methods and constant tinkering toward better ways to teach can take us only so far when it comes to educating our children. What we really need to do is to reexamine our purposes and rethink the goals we believe education can and should achieve. If we truly want smarter children, we need to know what smart looks like and stop confusing it with speed and knowledge. We also need to recognize that much of the substance of schooling is fleeting. After the final test has been taken, when students have long since left our doorways and the chalkboard has been erased for the last time, what will stay with our students isn't the laundry list of names, dates, computations, and procedures we have covered. What endures are the dispositions and habits of character we have been able to nurture. What stays with us, what sticks from our education, are the patterns of behavior and thinking that have been engrained and enculturated over time. These are the residuals of education. These are the foundations of intellectual character.

In putting forth the development of students' intellectual character as an appropriate ideal of education, I've endeavored to provide a picture of what this ideal looks like in the hands of skilled teachers.

I've sought to offer glimpses into classrooms in which students' intellectual character is an ongoing concern and in which its development is supported. In this process, I've tried to identify many effective practices and to show the diverse forms those practices may take. At the same time, I've attempted to get behind these practices to examine why they work and what makes them effective vehicles for developing intellectual character. These practices and the theories that ground them are certainly something to grab hold of and make your own, but how do you actually begin this process? Once you've embraced the ideal of teaching for intellectual character, how do you get started making it a priority in your classroom or at your school? I take up these questions in this final chapter by offering some practical advice.

This advice, though grounded in my observing thoughtful classrooms, comes not so much from my research as from my experience in working with teachers of every stripe, grade level, and subject area around these concerns. Through this work, I have learned some of the obstacles teachers often face as they strive to begin and some approaches they have found useful. As you read through the recommendations that follow, consider each of them individually as a potentially useful aid rather than as a collectively prescribed step-by-step course of action. Just as each of the teachers portrayed in this book has his or her unique approach, strength, focus, and personality, so too will you have your own unique approach as you strive to teach for intellectual character.

START WITH YOURSELF

Teaching is a uniquely individual endeavor. We bring who we are into the classroom and breathe life into our subject matter through our individual experiences and background. As Parker Palmer (1998, p. 2) writes, "Teaching, like any truly human activity, emerges from one's inwardness, for better or worse . . . knowing myself is as crucial to good teaching as knowing my students and my subject." When it comes to teaching for intellectual character, it is especially important to begin with ourselves. No technique, method, or practice can hide our values, beliefs, and passions about thinking. By first knowing ourselves as thinkers and learners, we can gain the kind of self-knowledge that we can build and capitalize on in our teaching.

In this section, I lay out three questions that can help in this regard:

- What is thinking?
- When is it useful?
- Toward what kinds of thinking am I most inclined?

I also sketch a process for exploring these questions that is likely to be illuminating and useful. However, other approaches are possible. For instance, you might be more comfortable with a less formal process, or you might want to reframe the questions as an interview you conduct between yourself and a trusted colleague.

Uncover Your Mental Model of Thinking

Your mental model of thinking, that is, your understanding of what constitutes good, productive, and worthwhile thinking, constitutes the foundation for many of your decisions about what, when, and how to address issues of thinking in your teaching. This mental model is a part—along with your awareness, motivation, and inclination—of your intellectual character. Uncovering your mental model of thinking and examining your own dispositions as a thinker can be a useful place to begin the process of teaching for intellectual character. This exercise raises your awareness of thinking in general and your own thinking in particular. In addition, working through the three questions helps clarify some of your values and beliefs about thinking. Don't think of this as a formal evaluation of your thinking; it certainly isn't that. It's a technique for beginning to expand and develop your understanding of thinking and to increase your awareness of it.

What Is Thinking?[1]

To begin, simply list all of the different possible meanings of the word *think*. These aren't synonyms so much as they are descriptions of what it is you might be doing when you tell someone else, "I'm thinking." For instance, you might write down "creating a mental picture in my mind" or "generating alternative options." Give yourself fifteen to twenty minutes to develop your list. If you get stuck, start thinking about the types of thinking you do in various situations. After this initial time is up, put the list someplace where you will see it often, perhaps on your desk or bureau. Over the next week, read through the list and keep adding new ideas as they come to mind.

At the end of the week, sit down and review your list. Look over what you have written and think about connections and similarities between items on the list. On another sheet of paper, place the items together in groups. What thinking actions seem to go together or to represent a general type? It's fine to put a thinking action in more than one group or to have some major overarching groups and some smaller groups. You can quickly look at the examples in Chapter Eight, but try not to let those examples influence you. Some people find it helpful to write each of the thinking actions on a strip of paper or sticky note so that they can move the individual items around easily. Don't worry about doing it correctly or having the right answer. The point here is to uncover how you think about thinking at the moment. This isn't a static picture, as it will continue to grow and develop over time. Once you've put your thinking actions into groups, give each group a label. What general type of thinking does each group represent? What ties them together? Do they share a common purpose or function?

Develop Your Awareness and Inclination

Using your mental-model list of thinking actions and categories, turn your attention to considering thinking occasions and your own thinking inclinations. In this exercise, you'll be asking yourself two questions:

- When is a particular type of thinking important?
- Toward what kinds of thinking am I most inclined?

These questions will help you develop your awareness of opportunities for thinking and to target areas of thinking in which to strengthen your inclination.

WHEN IS IT USEFUL?[2] For each of the groups you identified using your mental-model list, ask yourself: When is it difficult to engage in this type of thinking? For instance, one of John Threlkeld's categories was "keying in." Therefore, John would ask himself: When is it difficult for me to engage in the process of keying in? The list of thinking actions within this group might be useful to consider as part of this process, so make sure you have it before you. One of John's thinking actions was "identifying key relationships." He might want to think about occasions when it is particularly challenging to identify key relationships. Such an instance might be when a lot of new information is coming at him very quickly, as in a lecture. As you make your list, you are trying to identify occasions broadly, but you might find it useful to think of occasions that relate specifically to your teaching as well. These might be occasions that come up when you consider things from a student's perspective.

In trying to generate your list of occasions, work at whatever level feels right to you. For instance, you may find it hard to focus on the overarching categories you have identified because they are too broad. In that case, you may want to identify a smaller subgroup or focus on some of the individual thinking actions themselves. However, if you find yourself focusing on the thinking actions, you may want to pick and choose only a couple of key actions from each of your categories to keep the task from becoming unwieldy. Make a list of as many of these thinking occasions as you can generate for each of your categories.

Next, ask yourself: When is it particularly important or worthwhile to engage in this type of thinking? What you want to do here is to identify high-leverage occasions. These are the types of occasions you want to become more aware of and sensitive to so that you can more easily spot them. In John's example of "keying in," it might be important for him to key in when he is starting something new, such as trying to solve a new problem or trying to understand something new. In some cases, items in your list of important instances will be the same as in your list of occasions when engaging in this type of thinking is hard. In other instances, the two might not relate at all.

TOWARD WHAT KINDS OF THINKING AM I MOST INCLINED? Look back over your list of thinking actions and the categories you derived from them. Mark the four or five items that you feel are most valuable, not only for a teacher but for someone operating in the world generally. In making this determination, you may find it helpful to ask yourself a few questions: If I could work to develop only four or five different kinds of thinking moves in my students, what would I choose to focus on? What kinds of thinking do I find most useful in my own life? Which give me the greatest benefit as I go about solving problems, making decisions, and understanding my daily life? Which thinking actions do I most admire when I see them in someone else? Mark these types of thinking with a *V* for value.

Next, identify the types of thinking and thinking actions toward which you find yourself readily inclined. These aren't necessarily the types of thinking you do most often but rather those types of thinking and ways of operating that you feel characterize your general approach to things. For instance, you might find it easy and natural to look at things from various perspectives, and you find yourself readily doing this in a variety of circumstances. You feel that this type of thinking is useful and readily spot occasions to engage in it. That is, you are both aware of and inclined toward this type of thinking. Mark these items with an *I* for inclined.

Now, identify a small set of thinking actions, perhaps one or two at which you would like to work to improve. One way to do this is to see if there are thinking actions on your list that you have marked *V* (for valued) but not *I* (for being inclined toward). Another way is to think of those actions that you know you struggle with from time to time. Mark these items with a *W* for work.

Work at Developing Your Awareness

For each of the thinking actions you marked *W,* start a new list on which you will identify occasions for that type of thinking. Over the next week, find a time each day to sit down for a few minutes and think over the day. Add to your list any occasions you have come across when you could have or did engage in your targeted type of thinking. Next, add any instances in which you observed others engaging in your thinking target. Write yourself a brief note regarding what struck you about each of these occasions and the thinking performance or lack thereof. For instance, you may have been struck by how other demands for your attention squeezed out the opportunity to think. Or you may have been struck by how useful it was when a colleague actually did engage in the type of thinking you've targeted.

Working through these exercises should give you a place to start on both a personal and a pedagogical level. You've uncovered your conception of thinking through the mental-models exercise, expanded your awareness of thinking occasions, thought about your own inclinations, and identified areas of thinking of which you would like to become more aware. Revisit these exercises from time to time, as your thinking about thinking will change.

ENLIST OTHERS IN THE PROCESS

Although development and change are uniquely individual endeavors, engaging the help of others in these processes can often be helpful. Exactly when to do this is not always clear, however. For some people, it is important to build a foundation of personal understanding individually, then pull in colleagues as a means of deepening the work. For others, having a network of support and encouragement from the outset is important. In either case, a group of colleagues can act to prompt inquiry, encourage reflection, push thinking, and hold each other accountable for taking action. Such a network also helps create momentum and a sense of buying into the undertaking. Having colleagues who are interested in and see the importance of teaching for intellectual character even though they are still exploring what it means for themselves can be a tremendous support.

Study Groups

One form a support network might take is a study group focusing on exploring what it means to teach for intellectual character. To be successful and manageable, such a group is usually small, between four and six people, and is made up of individuals who have chosen to be there. The group might have a facilitator, but having an official leader or expert isn't necessary. The idea is to learn from one another in a process of ongoing dialogue and exploration. To focus this learning, the group can select questions to guide the members' work together. Some possible questions related to intellectual character include the following:

- What thinking dispositions are most important for our students and why? How can we better promote these? How will we know when we have been successful?

- When we say that a student is smart, a good reader, or a good student of history, what do we mean by that? What does that look like in terms of the work and thinking we expect?

- What kind of environment do we have at our school and in our classrooms: work-oriented, learning-oriented, or work-avoidant?[3] How do we know? Is it the kind of environment we want? How can we change or reinforce it?

- What are the routines that dominate our school and classrooms? How are they shaping the way students think and learn? How can we learn more about effective thinking routines? (You can adapt this set of questions to focus on any of the cultural forces discussed in Chapter Seven.)

- What is our school's real red thread (as opposed to our mission statement)? How is it related to the individual red threads of the teachers? How are these being communicated to students? If we want to change or modify these, how can we go about it?

These questions present just a few starting points for study groups. To work, the questions need to capture the interests and needs of the group. However, in forming your group's guiding questions, keep in mind a couple of things. Notice that the questions presented here are grouped into clusters. The first question in each cluster often deals with evidence and information. This helps everyone in the group get oriented and clarify meanings. These kinds of questions also help ground the discussion in what actually occurs rather than in desired or dreamed-of outcomes. The next question in the cluster is often a question beginning with "how." These questions may get at actual methods that the group will explore and try out, focus on additional data gathering, or both. Having these different types of questions is important. If we jump right into how to do something, we may fail to take into full account the circumstances to which we will be applying those methods. If we look only at what is, we fail to take actions that can move us in a more fruitful direction. If we don't look at the results of our actions, we won't know what effect those actions are having.

Throughout the study group process itself, it is often helpful to read materials, such as this book and other associated articles and books, to gain new information. It is also helpful to look at and discuss actual data: student work, a videotape of a class session, or a set of reflections that students have written. Having this data helps to ground the discussion in reality. From time to time, the group might want to engage in an experiment. For instance, perhaps each member tries a new thinking routine, and the group discusses what happened. So a study group need not be just a book group. It is important to strike a balance between gaining new information, taking action, and evaluating action.

Find a Buddy

Support need not take only the form of a study group. Having a single buddy, a trusted colleague with whom one can discuss and share, can be helpful. This person can act as a sounding board, restating what he or she hears you saying and asking questions that help you clarify your ideas. The buddy also can supply you with feedback on your teaching. It is sometimes very difficult to get a good sense of your own classroom. You may be too close to things or have been doing things for so long that they become invisible to you. Other times, you might have too much on your mind while teaching to fully decipher what is going on. A second pair of eyes in the room to catch the routines you may not even be aware of, to notice your thinking language and interactions, to assess the attitudes about learning and thinking that you are communicating can be very useful.

Finding such a buddy isn't always easy. Some teachers are lucky enough to have developed close mentoring relationships with a fellow teacher at the same grade level or in the same subject area that they can readily turn to for this kind of advice. For others, it will require a search. If this is the case for you, I've found that sometimes the best buddy is someone not so close to your teaching area but for whom you have a lot of respect as a teacher. It can often be easier and less threatening to listen to clarification questions and suggestions from someone outside our field. A high school teacher and a kindergarten teacher can learn a lot from each other, as can a Spanish teacher and a math teacher. Stepping outside our familiar circumstances can give us new eyes for appreciating and making sense of our teaching practice.

LOOK AT YOUR TEACHING PRACTICE

As you've read through this book, particularly the examples of classroom practice, you've probably done some reflecting on your own practice or that of other teachers you know or work alongside. As the first-days practices of these teachers were introduced, you probably thought about how you begin the school year and why you do it that way. When the idea of thinking routines was introduced, you most likely considered the types of routines you use and evaluated to what extent they promote thinking. You've probably also thought about the teachers who have been presented. Who are you most like? Whose goals and values seem to resonate most with your own? This kind of ongoing reflection and connection making is important. In advancing your own process of teaching for intellectual character, it may be helpful to extend and formalize these reflections further. Two specific suggestions are to identify the red thread of your teaching and to carefully examine the cultural forces at work in your classroom.

Identify Your Red Thread

The red thread, a metaphor presented in Chapter Eight, is that theme, passion, or guiding force that connects and holds together your teaching practice. It is the core of your teaching, the ideas and values that surface over and over again. Every teacher has a red thread, whether he or she knows it or not. Your students generally know what your red thread is: it is what makes you unique as a teacher and gives your class its distinctive flavor and personality. Identifying your red thread is a way of taking more control of your teaching by making the implicit explicit. It's hard to control, modify, or change things that we aren't fully aware of in our teaching. However, when we raise things to the surface, we can do something about them if we choose. In teaching for intellectual character, you want a red thread (or threads) consistent with that mission.

In trying to identify your red thread, you need to look closely at your teaching to examine what you say and do, as well as what your values and beliefs are. I often tell teachers that I can identify their red threads quickly by just asking their class one question: What is it that your teacher says over and over again? Our speech reveals us. What we harp on and bring up repeatedly is what we care about, at least at some level. In Doug Tucker's classroom, he would repeatedly say, "I'm teaching you to fish." This saying reflects the weight he gives to developing student independence and control over mathematics. John Threlkeld frequently talked about playing with ideas or said, "Great question." These phrases communicate the importance he places on working with and exploring ideas from a variety of angles.

In workshops I conduct, when I tell teachers that what they say over and over again reveals their red thread, I'm often greeted by nervous giggles. In one session, a teacher in the front of the audience put her head down and started laughing and shaking her head in an embarrassed but lighthearted way. I asked her why she was laughing and shaking her head. She said, "Because what I'm always saying is,

'Where's your pencil?'" We all laughed, and then I asked her, "Is it pencils you really care about?" She responded that it wasn't the pencils, though that was a real frustration, so much as students not being prepared. She further revealed that she really valued students' taking control of their own learning and being responsible. For her, seeing students who did not have pencils even though they knew they would be asked to write was just a symptom of their not taking responsibility for learning.

Next, take a look at what these sayings reveal about your values. Are your values well represented in what you are saying? If not, how can you change or append what you say to better capture what it is you truly care about? For example, as the workshop attendee and I talked back and forth, we generated an alternative phrase she might use that better reflected her true values: "What's your responsibility as a learner?" She decided to try and use this phrase instead of "Where's your pencil?" to better engage students with issues of responsibility. This new phrasing did not accomplish magic, but it did help change her tone in the class and focus her students more on the real issue at hand. It's important that this rewording not sound artificial or contrived. You need to find the right fit between your values, your words, and your students' ears, just as John did by saying "playing with ideas" or Doug by saying "teaching you to fish." Finding your red thread should inform and help you to be more of who you are.

Examine the Cultural Forces at Work in Your Classroom

In Chapter Seven, I presented a collection of cultural forces at work in all classrooms and educational environments. These forces include:

- The expectations that are conveyed
- The routines and structures in place
- The way that language is used
- The opportunities created
- The modeling done by the teacher
- The attitudes of teachers and students
- The interactions and relationships among everyone in the class
- The presence of artifacts of thinking within the physical environment of the classroom

Examining these cultural forces as they are at work in your classroom or school can be a useful first step in leveraging them to support students' intellectual character. Often, we have a tendency to jump in and try new things without first understanding and building upon what is already in place. However, when we fail to understand what exists, our attempts at change may feel like mere stick-on patches that don't fully integrate with the rest of the fabric of the classroom.

I've identified eight cultural forces, which is a lot to examine and reflect on. To start, I suggest that you choose one or two forces that particularly engage you. You can turn your attention to the others later. Begin your examination with some reflections on the cultural force. How would you characterize it in your classroom? If others were to focus on your use of language or your modeling, what might they notice? What specific examples of routines, modeling, interactions, and so on readily come to mind?

The next step in your examination is to begin collecting some data to get specific about what is going on. If you think you provide a lot of rich thinking opportunities for your students, what's the evidence? Write down some examples of those opportunities and the specific thinking they were able to produce. That means not just locating the paper you graded with an A but finding an example of students looking at things from different perspectives, making connections, or taking ideas in a new direction. You may be able to do much of this yourself. However, in some cases, you may find it useful to have someone help you. For instance, it is hard to be aware of the language we use on a regular basis. You might want to have a colleague come in and keep track of your thinking language, or you may want to set up a video camera to record yourself teaching a class. These techniques can also be useful for attending to interactions, modeling, and attitudes. All of these forces are so engrained and spontaneous in our teaching that we often have trouble noticing them. Once you have a better sense of how the cultural forces are operating in your classroom, you'll be ready to work on modifying them in the direction you want to go.

TAKE IT TO THE CLASSROOM

The preceding advice may all seem a bit slow paced and methodical for some. I know that once I get intrigued by new ideas and practices, I'm often eager to put them to work. Some teaching practices readily lend themselves to such an approach. For instance, some of the routines presented in Chapter Five can be readily applied. Other practices need more advance thought and ongoing consideration. Planning activities for the first day of school or developing guiding questions are examples. There are also differences in how people like to go about learning new things. Some people find it easier to learn from action followed by reflection than the other way around. Whatever the case, you will need action as well as reflection. To create a classroom that supports the development of students' intellectual character, you need to get your feet wet and try things out, to begin the process of adopting and adapting practices. This section offers general advice to guide that action in the classroom as well as specific steps you might take.

Communicate Your Goals

Although we often communicate our true values implicitly through our daily words and deeds, it is still important to make our values explicit, to tell our students and their parents what we as teachers are all about. This means talking about thinking and the kinds of thinking you expect from and hope to develop in students. This needn't simply be a lecture, however. You can show kids what you expect through a particular lesson. This is what Chris Elnicki does with his students the first day of school by engaging them in historical interpretation.

Another approach is to involve students in a group brainstorm that explores good thinking. You might begin such a session like this:

> In this class, I'm interested in helping you to develop your thinking, to become better thinkers. I'm working at trying to understand just what that will mean for us as a class, and I want to involve you in that process. In small groups, I'd like for you to generate a list of what you consider good thinking to be about. What does good thinking look like? What does it involve? What kinds of things do you need to be doing to be a good thinker both in this class and in the world? We'll then work from your lists to come up with a core set of thinking qualities and actions that can guide our work together in this class.

Such an approach gets students to consider the whole issue of thinking and its purposes more carefully. At the same time, it involves them directly in setting goals.

Both of the approaches mentioned here, the thinking lesson and brainstorming, can be easily adopted for use with parents. This will help give parents a better understanding of and actual feel for what it is you are after and why. We often tell parents what our classes will cover, the topics and units, without really telling them what our classes are about. What are the core values and goals that connect what we do in the classroom? Activities such as these can ground your thinking and your goals for thinking in a concrete way.

Attend to the Quartet

In Part One of this book, I made the point that we have a stilted view of what intelligence is and what it means to be smart. Part of that distortion comes from our single-minded focus on abilities. The view of intellectual character moves beyond ability to consider intelligent action and the inclination, awareness, and motivation that are needed to close the gap between ability and action. In beginning to teach for intellectual character, beware of the danger of falling back into an abilities-based view. Our efforts to promote students' dispositions toward thinking should not just focus on developing thinking skills.

As teachers, we tend to be more comfortable teaching skills than developing attitudes. That means that as you teach for intellectual character, you need to take special steps to attend to the dispositional quartet as a whole. Here are some questions, which you can ask yourself from time to time, that might help direct your attention more to inclination, awareness, and motivation.

1. Inclination
   - Have I communicated why certain types of thinking are important and useful?
   - Have I given students an opportunity to experience that usefulness?
   - Am I modeling on a regular basis the power and utility of the thinking I want my students to develop?
   - As a class, do we ever take a look at the thinking behind events, decisions, inventions, or ideas to see where thinking leads?

2. Awareness

- What am I doing to raise students' awareness of occasions for engaging certain types of thinking?
- Am I deliberately pointing them out?
- Am I giving students opportunities to spot occasions on their own without my prompting?
- What have I done to raise students' awareness of thinking traps and to help them identify the things that sometimes stand in the way of good thinking?
- How am I using thinking language to help cue students' thinking?
- How can I see if students are becoming more aware of thinking occasions?

3. Motivation

- What am I doing to motivate students' thinking in the moment?
- Are there reasons for students to use their thinking skills in my class?
- Have I communicated clear expectations for thinking as part of the work I ask students to do?
- When was the last time I saw students experiencing a cognitive emotion in my class?
- How did I capitalize on that experience?
- How can I increase the odds that students will experience these emotions?

Attending to the quartet, particularly given that we are more comfortable with skills, takes special effort. As the questions in this list suggest, part of this attention involves increasing our own awareness of the opportunities that exist for sending students messages about awareness, inclination, and motivation. Notice that the list of questions does not include anything along the lines of, Have you taught a lesson on awareness of thinking? Attending to dispositional development seldom takes such forms, though a targeted lesson or focused discussion can be helpful occasionally. What tends to be more useful is paying ongoing attention to the quartet by exploiting the small opportunities that occur as we go about teaching.

Attend to the Cultural Forces

The examination of cultural forces discussed earlier provides a knowledge base from which you can change those forces in the direction you need them to go. Remember that cultural forces already exist, so they don't need to be created, only recreated. However, this examination and movement can occur somewhat simultaneously if you like. By beginning to attend to a specific cultural force, such as the use of language, you often simultaneously become more aware of how it is operating. In whatever way you start, the cultural forces aren't something you can just put in place and forget about. You can't spend a week working on your relationships and interactions and then check it off your to-do list. Attending to the cultural forces takes ongoing work. Every so often, you may find it useful to conduct a cultural forces audit. This could be setting aside a time to reflect specifically on how one or more of the forces is playing out in your classroom. Another form this audit might take is to ask students for their observations. For example, you might ask students any of the following:

- In this class, I try to use language to help guide and direct your thinking. What kinds of thinking words do you hear me using?

- I've tried to establish certain routines or ways of doing things that will help us think and learn more effectively in this class. Can you think of any routines, procedures, or ways of approaching things that characterize how we go about thinking and learning in this class? These might not have specific names, so you can just describe the process.

- How does it feel to be in this class? What are some of the emotions you experience as you participate in and do the work of this class?

Additional forms the audit can take are similar to the suggestions given in the section on examining your practice. These include videotaping your class or having a colleague come in to observe. Whatever form you choose, the goal is the same: to raise your awareness of how the cultural forces are playing out in your room so that you can more readily attend to them. This is much more a process of ongoing refinement and constant improvement than fixing things once and for all.

GIVE IT TIME

Teaching for intellectual character is an ideal to be strived for rather than a standard to be achieved.[4] Understanding this distinction between ideals and standards has implications for teaching. Ideals represent the larger goals and purposes that guide and direct our actions. They are what we are teaching for. Standards, on the other hand, represent explicit specifications of behavior or performance. They are hurdles to pass over. If you try to apply a standards approach to the teaching of intellectual character, you are likely to be frustrated, disappointed, or worse.

Like all ideals, intellectual character is something to be worked toward rather than a destination at which to arrive. Change and improvement aren't going to happen quickly, even through a carefully concentrated effort. Developing intellectual character is not something you will ever be done with. "Intellectual character? We did that last semester. I've got the results of the final exam right here. We'll do a review at the end of the year." Furthermore, ideals don't have clear benchmarks by which we can chart progress. Working your way through each disposition is not likely to have lasting effects. Similarly, you can't approach the dispositional quartet piecemeal: "OK, class, we've just finished awareness, next up is motivation." This lack of clear markers is likely to be frustrating for some, particularly in this era when everything gets measured and marked. However, the question to ask ourselves is not, What level have the students achieved? but Where do I see development? To be successful, teaching for the ideal of intellectual character must be recognized as an ongoing concern in which one expects to see glimmers of progress and hope alongside occasional setbacks and disappointing performances. Enculturation into new ways of thinking takes time. Consequently, take a long-term view as you enter into this process and do not expect to see quick and quantifiable results.

IN CLOSING

Under the best of circumstances, teaching can be a difficult endeavor. When we accept the challenge to develop students' intellectual character as a part of our overall mission of teaching, the complexity of the undertaking grows exponentially. And yet this undertaking is not an insurmountable task. As we have seen in the stories and practices of the teachers explored here, it is possible to create thoughtful classrooms in a variety of different environments. But this task is not one that we can accomplish merely by adding a line to the school's mission statement: "Our goal is to develop every students' intellectual character and disposition toward good and effective thinking." As these teacher portraits demonstrate, the development of students' intellectual character ultimately depends on teachers' conviction, dedication, and belief in the importance of thinking to students' current understanding, future enjoyment, and long-term success both in the subject area and in life. It is only when teachers possess thinking-rich red threads to tie together their practice and breathe life into them through their own disposition toward thinking that the development of students' intellectual character becomes a natural, energizing, and meaningful endeavor for students and teachers alike. May your and your students' efforts in this terrain be long and fruitful as you seek to raise education to new heights.

Key Ideas for Developing Intellectual Character
PRACTICAL ADVICE ON GETTING STARTED

- *Uncover Your Mental Model of Thinking.* What do you think constitutes thinking? What major categories of thinking are important from your perspective?

- *Examine Your Awareness and Inclination.* When are different types of thinking useful? Toward what kinds of thinking are you most inclined?

- *Increase Your Awareness.* Becoming more aware of thinking opportunities will help you exploit thinking opportunities as they arise in the classroom.

- *Form a Study Group.* Work with others to explore what teaching for intellectual character means for you at your school. Focus study groups on understanding, reflection, data collection, and action.

- *Find a Buddy.* It can be hard to look at your own teaching or evaluate progress. A buddy can offer support and observe you in your classroom.

- *Identify Your Red Thread.* What is the driving force in your classroom? What connects and motivates your teaching? Your red threads will eclipse other agendas in your classroom.

- *Examine the Cultural Forces at Work in Your Classroom.* These forces are at work in all educational settings. Look at how they operate in your setting and what messages they are sending students about the role of thinking.

- *Take Action.* Reflection and developing understanding must be complemented by action. What will you actually do in your teaching?

- *Communicate Your Goals.* Let students, parents, administrators, and colleagues know what your class will be about. What are you trying to accomplish versus just covering?

- *Attend to the Dispositional Quartet.* Make sure your efforts aren't just focused on developing ability. It is important to work to enhance inclination, motivation, and awareness as well.

(continued)

PRACTICAL ADVICE ON GETTING STARTED
(*continued*)

- *Attend to the Cultural Forces.* Individual forces provide avenues for your attention. As you work to enhance one area, your awareness of how it is operating also increases. The forces demand ongoing attention.

- *Give It Time.* Intellectual character is an ideal to strive for in your teaching rather than an objective to achieve. Keep your sights focused on development rather than achievement.

——— Appendix

METHODOLOGICAL NOTES

Although the rich pictures of practice and accompanying commentary found in this book are sufficient for most, those readers inquisitive about the nature of the research process itself have further questions: What data did I collect over the course of my study? How did I go about collecting those data? How did I analyze the data to derive my findings, and how do I know my interpretation is right? This methodological appendix addresses these questions.

This book is based on the collective case study, using ethnographic methods, of six teachers. Specifically, the study had four components: teacher selection, classroom observations, teacher interviews and videotaping, and the use of a repertory grid methodology. All of these methods are interpretive in nature, including the repertory grid, even though it relies in part on statistical analysis. I chose these interpretive methods to produce rich and contextualized portraits of each teacher's practice, even though in this book I chose to present only pieces of the teacher's practice. My intent was to understand what makes an effective teacher of thinking and not to evaluate teacher effectiveness. Nor was my intent to understand these classroom environments holistically as communities. Therefore, my study tried neither to evaluate the effectiveness of instruction nor get the students' perspectives on the classroom. Rather, I relied at the outset on selecting classrooms that provided the best opportunity for my learning about the teacher and effective practice.

During the 1998–99 school year, I spent four to five weeks in each of the teachers' classrooms. To help me capture the nuances of instruction and the environmental richness, I videotaped and took field notes of each observation. Following my observations, I wrote narrative summaries both to capture my own feelings about what I had seen and to begin to identify themes and issues for further exploration. These periods of observations were intertwined with a series of interviews with each teacher, through which I explored the individual's goals and thinking about thinking. At some of these interview sessions, we would watch and discuss segments from the classroom videotapes. These discussions helped me to get the teacher's perspective on his or her teaching and to check my own developing understanding and interpretation.

TEACHER SELECTION

To find out about the development of intellectual character and the cultivation of thinking dispositions, we must go among the teachers whose classrooms "have it." We must seek out those classrooms where thinking is valued and regularly demonstrated to find cases that will be instrumental in understanding how intellectual character is cultivated in classroom settings.[1] My search for thinking classrooms began in the spring of 1998 by asking people who knew schools, teachers, and individual classrooms—fellow researchers, teachers, professors working in schools, curriculum coordinators, teacher leaders, state department liaisons, staff developers, school superintendents—for names of teachers whom I might want to visit. Specifically, I asked them for the names of "good teachers who really care about getting students to think." In some instances, I explained more about the types of classrooms I was looking for or spoke with people who already understood my interests. In many cases, my requests were passed along to others and reinterpreted along the way.

I restricted my search of classrooms to middle school math and social studies classes. Because I was interested in how classroom environments are shaped and routines established, I wanted to observe all of the instruction in my selected classrooms during the first weeks of school. This kind of intense observation would not have been possible in multiple elementary classrooms where teachers see one set of students throughout the entire day. Therefore, in order to study more classrooms, I chose to exclude elementary teachers. At the same time, my prior work in the MacArthur Patterns of Thinking Project indicated that the middle school years were a time when thinking patterns were ripe for development, making this age an interesting one for study (Perkins, Tishman, Ritchhart, Donis, & Andrade, 2000). I chose to focus on mathematics and social studies classrooms to explore the types of thinking nurtured in two very different subject areas; this allowed me to learn from different examples in each discipline.

The community nomination process yielded forty-five teachers. Of these, I contacted twenty-eight and eventually identified fourteen for interviews and observations.[2] The main criteria guiding my selection of teachers were (1) an expressed interest in promoting student thinking and (2) the presence of a thoughtful classroom environment.

Though all of the teachers I interviewed knew that my study focused on understanding how teachers nurture student thinking, several never expressed an explicit interest in promoting thinking when I asked them to talk about their classroom, instructional focus, or goals for students. More than a few teachers talked about the importance of meeting district standards, inspiring students, or helping students develop understanding, but they never mentioned the role of thinking in achieving these aims. In contrast, many others explicitly mentioned the importance of helping students to be metacognitive, to think like mathematicians or historians, to learn to reason well, or to be able to communicate their thinking. Because I was interested in understanding teachers' agendas regarding thinking and the factors shaping those agendas, I eliminated from consideration teachers who did not express an explicit interest in promoting student thinking.

To assess the level of classroom thoughtfulness, I observed each teacher's classroom, applying criteria for classroom thoughtfulness developed by Joseph Onosko and Fred Newman (1994) (see the exhibit, "Criteria for Classroom Thoughtfulness," at the end of this Appendix).[3] Of course, a single lesson is sparse information on which to base such an assessment, and I found it necessary to draw on additional information from classroom bulletin boards and displays as well as examples of available student work and projects to make my assessments.[4]

Based on my observations and interviews, eight teachers met my criteria. I then added one more quality: diversity of school setting, makeup, and population. The presence of diversity in the sample allowed me to look for similarities and differences across cases to explore questions of how intellectual character can develop in a variety of classroom environments. Table A.1 presents a collective profile of the six teachers I studied. This profile highlights some of the major background variables of the teachers and their classrooms, allowing you to see both what the teachers have in common and how they are different.

CLASSROOM OBSERVATIONS

Classroom observations took place during the 1998–99 school year in three separate waves: two weeks at the beginning of the school year, one week in mid-October or November, and one week in the winter term. I made approximately twenty visits to each classroom over the course of the study. I negotiated with each teacher the specific class period that I would observe. In the classroom, I was a nonparticipant observer, sitting in the back of the room and videotaping the proceedings while simultaneously taking field notes. For the most part, I used a wide-angle shot to capture the action of the class and minimize my need to attend to the camera. I used a remote microphone in the videotaping, allowing me to fully capture the teacher's speech even at a great distance and low volume, such as when a teacher was whispering to a student out in the hallway. The remote microphone allowed me to remain in the back of the room and still not miss the instructional action, thus minimizing my obtrusiveness in the classroom. The drawback to the remote microphone was that students' voices in whole-class discussions were sometimes difficult to hear. However, I had the option of disconnecting the remote microphone and switching to the general microphone at any time.

Analysis of the observational process was an ongoing and recursive process focusing on two things: (1) understanding what was happening during the first weeks of school and identifying what messages teachers were sending either implicitly or explicitly about teaching and learning in this class and (2) identifying and understanding the opportunities for thinking that existed and that teachers created. During the first wave of observations, I began the process of sense making immediately following each classroom observation by using my field notes to write a narrative summary. These summaries recorded my initial understanding of events and the early emergence of themes, issues, and questions for further exploration. To further immerse myself in the data and develop my observational and analytic skills during

Teacher	Gender	Years of Experience	College Major	School Type	School Configuration	Class Title*	Grade	Class Structure	Percentage (%) of Students of Color	Class Size	Special Features
Doug Tucker	M	3	Computer science	Urban public	6–8	8th grade math	8	Alternate day blocks 95 min.	~75	22	Technology Academy magnet program open to top 25% of district students; Course: Pre-algebra
John Threlkeld	M	19	Math	Urban private	K–9	Algebra	8	Daily class periods 50 min.	~6	17	A high but not accelerated section
Karen White	F	17	Math education	Suburban public	9–12	Integrated algebra 1	9/10 mixed	Daily class periods 48 min.	~8	26	Karen's first year at newly opened school, using new math series, last required math course
Susan McCray	F	7	American studies	Urban public	K–8	Humanities	7/8 mixed	Integrated daily block 105 min.	~39	18	Due to multiage grouping, the history program alternates yearly; school chosen by parents
Heather Woodcock	F	6	English	Urban private	K–9	Central subject**	7	Semi-self-contained class 160 min.	~10	19	Core subject teacher (English, S.S., homeroom), one group of students for approximately three hours a day
Chris Elnicki	M	12	History	Suburban public	7–8	American studies	8	Daily class periods 50 min.	~12	34	School has quadrupled in size over last five years; most families new to school and the area

Table A.1. Profile of Teachers.

Notes:

*For humanities or central subject teachers, I observed both language and history instruction but focused on the teaching of history in the interviews.

**Central subject is the core of students' instructional time at this school and combines homeroom, social studies, language arts, and social development the initial phase of the study, I watched the videotapes on the day of taping and created video logs (Pirie, 1997). These part-description, part-verbatim documents included my initial codings of key events, opportunities for thinking, and teaching strategies.

During the remaining observation phases, I abridged these labor-intensive practices. Following my observations, I would review my field notes and write observer comments (Bogdan & Biklen, 1982) in the margins, writing longer analytic memos as themes began to emerge. In my observer comments, I also identified classroom moments to review on the videotape. Having made an interpretation or identified a puzzling event in a classroom episode, I would then tag these portions of videotape for review with the teacher. In this way, I checked my interpretations of what was happening with the teacher's perception (Maxwell, 1996).

Once the data collection period was over, I engaged in another round of data analysis. Using my familiarity with both the teacher interviews and classroom observations, I identified key themes and metaphors (Miles & Huberman, 1994) to capture each teacher's practice. I used these themes and metaphors as the basis for writing a descriptive profile of each teacher, a type of condensed case study or portrait that captured the teachers' red threads. This process helped me to focus on the teachers individually and keep their instructional intent and personal stories close to the surface in my writing. Once I had written the chapters, each teacher reviewed and commented on them, suggesting corrections and clarifications when appropriate.

Returning to my field notes, I identified and listed all classroom episodes that were rich in thinking or seemed to stand out as efforts to promote students' thinking. I coded this list of episodes by the type of thinking involved and by whether development of awareness, inclination, motivation, or ability was involved. I then grouped the episodes based on their similarity. For example, one group included the development of routines; another group included instances of cuing students' thinking; yet another included teacher modeling of thinking. I used this initial list of groupings and codes to code the other sets of field notes, staying attentive to the need for new codes for other types of classroom episodes. Thus, the practices I report come from the teachers' practice and not from an a priori set of practices for which I merely sought examples. This is not to say I had no assumptions guiding my analysis. For example, I suspected that beginning-of-the-year practices and language would be important, but the notion of thinking routines emerged after looking at the data.

For reporting on the general patterns and features of practice, I sought exemplars of practice. I reviewed all coded episodes of a particular practice, for example, modeling, and identified the strongest. I reviewed these exemplary episodes on videotape and transcribed them for use in reporting. For the sake of variety, I also tried to include examples from both math and humanities classes and from different teachers.

TEACHER INTERVIEWS

In addition to the initial screening interview, each teacher participated in a series of six interviews conducted over the course of the study. Three interviews were conducted during the first wave of observations, two in the second wave, and one during the last wave. These interviews served three purposes: (1) to elicit teachers' instructional values and goals, (2) to explore teachers' thinking about thinking, using a repertory grid methodology, and (3) to review classroom videotapes and gain teachers' perspective on and interpretation of their actions. A single interview would often engage more than one of these purposes. For example, in one interview, I might explore the teacher's goals and values for the classroom and then end by generating a list of types of thinking that would be used later in the repertory grid process. Most interviews were about one hour in length, though interviews focusing on discussing the videotapes often lasted for an hour and a half.

I audiotaped each interview and took written notes. Because my focus was on what was said rather than how and because I was not doing a linguistic or voice-based analysis, I edited out of the transcripts the naturally occurring *um*s and *er*s of standard conversation. However, in my field notes, I did try to take into account how teachers responded to my questions as well as what they said. If the teacher became tentative, withdrawn, animated, or puzzled, I made note of this.

Analysis of the interview data was a multilayered process of identifying what dispositional attributes teachers valued as well as identifying the teachers' red threads. For coding purposes, I defined a *disposition* as any type of overarching trait or state that could be used to describe a person. Key conversational markers of dispositional constructs were *to* and *to be*. For example, the comments "I want students to be curious" and "I want them to look for bias" express general traits, not specific abilities, that teachers desire. In contrast, skill and knowledge constructs are often marked by language such as *to know how to.* "I want students to know how to identify bias in the texts they read" is skill-oriented, whereas "I want students to be aware of bias" is dispositional. Of course, these linguistic markers serve as only general heuristics for coding and are not hard and fast rules. Ultimately, the decision whether or not to code something as a disposition required asking whether the teacher was describing an overarching trait that he or she wanted students constantly to express and bring to situations or whether the teacher was identifying a skill that he or she wanted students to have at their disposal. I identified the teachers' red threads by connecting the interview transcripts with classroom observations in order to discover crosscutting themes.

THE REPERTORY GRID METHODOLOGY

The repertory grid technique was developed by George Kelly (1955) as an interpretive methodology for understanding an individual's personal construct system: his or her implicit theories, categories, or frameworks for organizing information about people and relationships.[5] Due to its effectiveness at capturing implicit thinking, the methodology increasingly is being used to understand teachers' beliefs (Calderhead, 1996; Middleton, 1995; Munby, 1984; Thompson, 1992).

The basic repertory grid technique involves engaging individuals in generating a list of elements from the domain being investigated. Because I was interested in teachers' implicit models of thinking, the domain I investigated was "different types of thinking." "Creating a mental picture" and "generating alternatives" would be examples of elements from this domain. Participants then sort and classify these elements to generate a set of constructs or attributes that meaningfully apply to these elements. These constructs are broad conceptual categories, for example, "front-end strategies" and "being curious." The list of constructs each individual generates represents his or her repertory of constructs. Now, imagine a matrix in which each row represents a different element generated and each column a different construct, and you see why it is called a repertory grid. Participants fill in the grid by rating the fit of each element on each construct. A variety of methods exist for eliciting elements, constructs, and ratings.[6] Below, I describe the process I used with the teachers in my study and show how the interview technique unfolded over time.

In the first interview, I asked each teacher to generate a list of different types of thinking. The question I posed was, "What are you doing when you tell someone you are thinking?" I also provided two examples as prompts: "create a mental picture" and "consider the consequences of actions." Once the teacher was clear about the task, I recorded as the teacher thought out loud. If the teacher became stuck in generating types of school or discipline-specific thinking, I would ask: "What about thinking in other situations, like at home or every day?" Another prompt I used was: "We often say we are thinking when we are trying to solve a problem or make a decision. What type of thinking are you doing there?" Once the teacher stopped generating items for the list, we stopped the process. I then left the list with the teacher and asked him or her to continue to add new items as they came to mind. The teacher returned the list to me at our next interview one week later.

Once I had all six teachers' lists, I combined them into a single list. After eliminating duplicates, I had a final list of seventy-nine items. I used this common list with each teacher to avoid an individual's impoverished list of elements leading to an impoverished list of constructs. I wrote each description of a type of thinking from this common list on a separate index card. In the fourth interview, I asked the teacher to use these cards to generate a list of constructs. Spreading the cards face down, the teacher selected three cards randomly. The teacher then identified two of the three cards as fitting or belonging together in some way. The similarity between these two cards was expressed as a common characteristic or attribute. This attribute constitutes a construct. As the teacher continued with this process of grouping cards, I recorded the constructs generated. The process continued until no new constructs were generated. I organized each teacher's constructs and elements into a grid. I asked the teacher to rate each element on a scale from one to seven based on how well it exemplified or fit within each construct.

Although the repertory grid is a qualitative methodology, individual grids (data are not aggregated) are analyzed using statistical methods.[7] My analysis of individual grids used cluster analysis to reveal the underlying structure of the data. Basically, cluster analysis takes the rows of elements and rearranges them so that the adjacent rows match up as closely as possible in terms of the numerical rankings each was given. Thus, once the list of elements is rearranged, any given element is viewed as being more similar to its neighbors than to elements spaced further apart. This analysis is done in a hierarchical manner so that the elements wind up grouped in clusters of similarity as opposed to just a linear arrangement of rows.

Figure A.1 shows John Threlkeld's dendogram. Each of the original seventy-nine thinking constructs appears in a list on the left-hand side. The number beside each item indicates the position of that item on the original list of thinking constructs. These numbers correspond to the individual branches of the tree diagram shown on the right-hand side. In this diagram resulting from the analysis of John's ratings, items appearing near each other are more related than are items further away from each other on the diagram. For example, John saw items numbered one and two as being more closely related to each other conceptually than either is to item number three. The strength of any particular association between pairs of items is indicated by the length of the individual branches connecting those items. For instance, John associates items twenty-four and twenty-seven more closely to each other than he associated the pair of items sixty-three and seventy-one. Looking at the diagram from right to left, you can identify the major clusters. A cluster is a group of branches that are all associated and therefore grouped together. The first cluster in the diagram is composed of items one, two, seventeen, seventy-eight, and twenty-nine. Looking at the diagram, you can see that item twelve appears to be in a different cluster. It is not immediately connecting to this first cluster. Clusters are also identified by a common geometric symbol immediately to the left of the numbers in the dendogram.

In my final interview, I asked each teacher to review the dendogram produced from my analysis of his or her grid and interpret the meaning of this structure (Munby, 1984). This involved examining each cluster to see if it hung together. I asked each teacher, "Do you agree with the arrangement derived from the analysis, or are there elements that you feel don't belong in this grouping?" If the teacher spotted a problem, I circled that element and placed a question mark beside it, indicating that the teacher might want to move it to another group later in the process. Next, I asked the teacher to generate a name for each cluster: "What general type of thinking does this cluster describe? What do they all have in common?" This process often

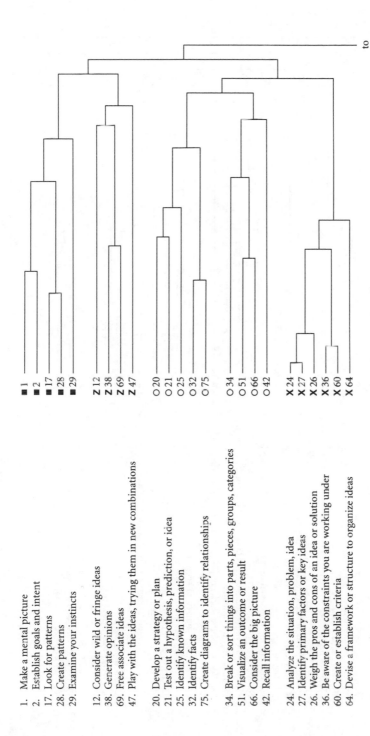

■ 1. Make a mental picture
■ 2. Establish goals and intent
■ 17. Look for patterns
■ 28. Create patterns
■ 29. Examine your instincts

Z 12. Consider wild or fringe ideas
Z 38. Generate opinions
Z 69. Free associate ideas
Z 47. Play with the ideas, trying them in new combinations

O 20. Develop a strategy or plan
O 21. Test out a hypothesis, prediction, or idea
O 25. Identify known information
O 32. Identify facts
O 75. Create diagrams to identify relationships

O 34. Break or sort things into parts, pieces, groups, categories
O 51. Visualize an outcome or result
O 66. Consider the big picture
O 42. Recall information

X 24. Analyze the situation, problem, idea
X 27. Identify primary factors or key ideas
X 26. Weigh the pros and cons of an idea or solution
X 36. Be aware of the constraints you are working under
X 60. Create or establish criteria
X 64. Devise a framework or structure to organize ideas

to A

Figure A.1. Dendogram Generated from Cluster Analysis of John Threlkeld's Repertory Grid Data.

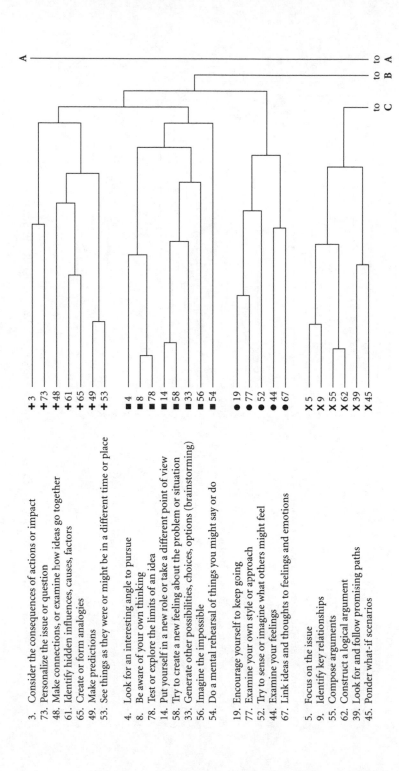

A   to to
           A

to
B

to
C

+ 3. Consider the consequences of actions or impact
+ 73. Personalize the issue or question
+ 48. Make connections, or examine how ideas go together
+ 61. Identify hidden influences, causes, factors
+ 65. Create or form analogies
+ 49. Make predictions
+ 53. See things as they were or might be in a different time or place

■ 4. Look for an interesting angle to pursue
■ 8. Be aware of your own thinking
■ 78. Test or explore the limits of an idea
■ 14. Put yourself in a new role or take a different point of view
■ 58. Try to create a new feeling about the problem or situation
■ 33. Generate other possibilities, choices, options (brainstorming)
■ 56. Imagine the impossible
■ 54. Do a mental rehearsal of things you might say or do

● 19. Encourage yourself to keep going
● 77. Examine your own style or approach
● 52. Try to sense or imagine what others might feel
● 44. Examine your feelings
● 67. Link ideas and thoughts to feelings and emotions

X 5. Focus on the issue
X 9. Identify key relationships
X 55. Compose arguments
X 62. Construct a logical argument
X 39. Look for and follow promising paths
X 45. Ponder what-if scenarios

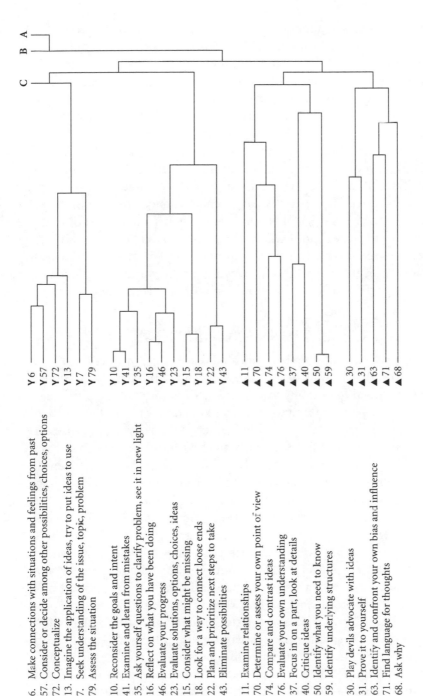

6. Make connections with situations and feelings from past
57. Consider or decide among other possibilities, choices, options
72. Conceptualize
13. Imagine the application of ideas, try to put ideas to use
7. Seek understanding of the issue, topic, problem
79. Assess the situation

10. Reconsider the goals and intent
41. Examine and learn from mistakes
35. Ask yourself questions to clarify problem, see it in new light
16. Reflect on what you have been doing
46. Evaluate your progress
23. Evaluate solutions, options, choices, ideas
15. Consider what might be missing
18. Look for a way to connect loose ends
22. Plan and prioritize next steps to take
43. Eliminate possibilities

11. Examine relationships
70. Determine or assess your own point of view
74. Compare and contrast ideas
76. Evaluate your own understanding
37. Focus in on a part, look at details
40. Critique ideas
50. Identify what you need to know
59. Identify underlying structures

30. Play devils advocate with ideas
31. Prove it to yourself
63. Identify and confront your own bias and influence
71. Find language for thoughts
68. Ask why

Figure A.1. Dendogram Generated from Cluster Analysis of John Threlkeld's Repertory Grid Data (*continued*)

involved playing around with words and trying out labels. I recorded the teacher's ideas during this phase. When the teacher became stuck, we moved on to other clusters and then returned, or I might ask the teacher to just talk out loud about the problematic cluster and then feed back what I heard him or her saying. In addition to generating labels, the teacher also identified relationships between the clusters. This technique of returning the cluster analysis to the teacher for interpretation has three advantages: (1) it engages participants in the research process, (2) it allows for disagreement with the computed clusters, and (3) it avoids the imposition of an outside interpretation.

To produce the actual display of each teacher's mental model, I used the teacher's original list of thinking items and the list of over-arching categories and relationships that he or she identified in the interpretive process. This display provided the most accurate representation of the mental model because it used information derived only from the teacher and expressed it in that person's own words.

REFLECTIONS AND CRITIQUE

In the preface to this book, I indicated that my perspectives and passions would be fully evident in this story of the teachers. I also stated that I planned to examine teachers' practices through the particular lens and theoretical framework of thinking dispositions. Rather than seeking the truth of each teacher's practice, I have used the cases of these six teachers instrumentally to shed light on the issues surrounding the development of intellectual character. As a consequence, I often have left things out of my accounts of teachers' practice, and in doing so, I may have presented the teachers too ideally.

In my observations, I did in fact see practices that were not always admirable. I saw teachers get mad and frustrated. I saw good teachers miss occasions for thinking or teachers so eager to express their ideas that they trampled over students' contributions. Although I generally left classrooms with a sense of hope and awe at the teaching I observed, there were other occasions when I wished things had gone better for both the teachers and the students. This was particularly the case on those occasions when classroom discipline was a problem. In my reporting, I have left out these instances, not to idealize these classrooms or these teachers but because the incidents were often isolated and didn't reflect the totality of my experience in the teachers' classrooms. Such incidents also provided little insight into how teachers went about either developing or impairing students' thinking. However, when practices inhibiting students' thinking dominated in a classroom and seemed to have a noticeable effect on what students were learning, I did explore, analyze, and try to report on them to the extent that it seemed useful to do so.

In addition to focusing my theoretical lens on intellectual character development, I entered into this work with a bent toward inquiry-based teaching and a belief in the power of active learning processes. As a teacher, I've always felt that when students can be led to construct meaning on their own, the learning is more powerful and lasting. This predisposition may have led me to view Karen White's classroom more skeptically than others would have. Of the teachers with whom I worked, Karen was the most unlike me as a teacher and an individual. Because of this, I engaged several other researchers and colleagues in examining and reacting to her practice in order to check my perceptions and analysis and to be sure that I wasn't missing the thinking that was or was not going on in her classroom. My interviews with Karen were also much longer and more detailed than those with other teachers as I sought to understand her perspective and the basis for her actions. In addition, I spent more time analyzing and trying to understand Karen's practice than I did any other teacher's.

In the end, Karen's practice provided me with invaluable insights for which I am most thankful. I feel the perspective I gained from her helped to make this a more interesting and informative study. I developed a deep appreciation for her perspective on teaching and the values she holds and attends to faithfully. Although I may not be comfortable with her style of teaching for myself or advocate it to others, I can nonetheless recognize what she offers her students in terms of care and support. For that, her students should be most appreciative.

In addition to being constructivist in nature, I also admit to not having any great fondness for textbooks and to being skeptical about their usefulness to exemplary teachers. This attitude affected my selection of teachers for the study to some extent. I was less sure of what I would gain from observing those teachers who based their instruction on textbooks. Although some of the teachers I observed in my screening were using excellent reform-oriented curricular programs, I worried about my ability to separate the teacher from the textbook to uncover the teacher's beliefs, values, and practices as distinct from those of the text. I was instinctively more comfortable when the teacher used the text as a resource and not the main instructional instrument. However, all of the math teachers in the study did use a text to some extent. Still, it is important to acknowledge that some instructional materials might actually be effective at establishing learning routines, focusing on understanding, and helping to foster a culture of thinking and that I have not adequately explored such circumstances to see if this is or is not the case.

—∿∿— **Key Ideas for Developing Intellectual Character**

CRITERIA FOR CLASSROOM THOUGHTFULNESS

Rate classes from 1–5: 1 = very inaccurate description; 5 = very accurate.

1. In this class, there was sustained examination of a few topics rather than a superficial coverage of many.

2. In this class, the lesson displayed substantive coherence and continuity.

3. In this class, students were given an appropriate amount of time to think, that is, to prepare responses to questions.

4. In this class, the teacher carefully considered explanations and reasons for conclusions.

5. In this class, the teacher asked challenging questions and/or structured challenging tasks (given the ability level and preparation of the students).

6. In this class, the teacher pressed individual students to justify or to clarify their assertions in a Socratic method.

7. In this class, the teacher tried to get students to generate original and unconventional ideas, explanations, or solutions to problems.

8. In this class, the teacher was a model of thoughtfulness. (Indicators are [1] the teacher showed appreciation for students' ideas and appreciation for alternative approaches or answers if based on sound reasoning; [2] the teacher explained how he or she thought through a problem; [3] the teacher acknowledged the difficulty of gaining a definitive understanding of the topic.)

9. In this class, students assumed the roles of questioner and critic.

10. In this class, students offered explanations and reasons for their conclusions.

11. In this class, students generated original and unconventional ideas, explanations, hypotheses, or solutions to problems.

12. In this class, student contributions were articulate, germane to the topic, and connected to prior discussion.

Source: Adapted from Onosko and Newman (1994).

Preface

1. For a critique of schools' preoccupation with knowledge and skill acquisition, see, for example, Brown (1993), Bruner (1996), Gardner (1991), Henry (1963), and Kohn (1999).

2. The term *intellectual character* first arose in my consciousness while reading a book in which author Stephen Covey (1989) discusses character in terms of habits. This reading coincided with my own work on thinking dispositions and habits of mind, and the connections between character and intellect was formed. Around the same time, I heard the term *intellectual character* from Shari Tishman as a way of bringing moral and ethical considerations into the realm of critical thinking. I believe her use of the term is the first I saw in print (Tishman, 1995). However, I note that others have used the term as well (Strong, 1990). I want to acknowledge all of these sources as contributing to the formulation of intellectual character presented here.

Chapter One

1. Of course, the textbook I refer to here doesn't actually exist. However, the de facto textbook on teaching for many is *The First Days of School: How to Be an Effective Teacher* (Wong & Wong, 1997). These authors are among the leading proponents of teachers using the strategies identified through the process-product research of the 1970s. These strategies often emphasize classroom management as the most important goal of the first days of school. Although I do not know whether Karen has read or is familiar with

this particular book, she had been recently trained in the specific techniques and strategies derived from process-product research on effective classroom management. As a result of this training, Karen leads a district induction program for new teachers in which she trains and familiarizes others in these techniques.

2. This is my estimate based on information from the 1998 State and Local Government Employment and Payroll Estimates (U.S. Census Bureau, 2001) and from data from *The Digest of Educational Statistics: 1997* (National Center for Educational Statistics, 1997).

Chapter Two

1. For studies on how the general populace conceives of intelligence, see, for example, Siegler and Richards (1982); and Sternberg, Conway, Ketron, and Bernstein (1981).

2. On intelligence as overarching mental abilities, see, for example, Guilford (1982) and Thurstone (1938); as general neural efficiency, see Jensen (1988) and Spearman (1973); as sets of cognitive processes, see Campione and Brown (1978) and Sternberg (1985). Many theories of intelligence are somewhat eclectic in nature, emphasizing a certain set of abilities while acknowledging and taking others into account. For example, David Perkins (1995) places his emphasis on "mindware" or the mental strategies accompanying the reflective dimension of intelligence while acknowledging the contribution of neural efficiency and general experience.

3. Although it is predominant, an abilities focus on intelligence is not universal. Several recent theories of intelligence focus on the mental mechanisms and contexts that underlie intelligent behavior and avoid focusing exclusively on the set of skills or abilities one possesses. PASS theory (Das & Jarman, 1991) and Sternberg's triarchic theory of intelligence (1985) are two notable examples. For a review of other alternative theories, see Rowe (1991). In addition, recent advances in neuroscience are changing views of intelligence by expanding Western culture's understanding of how emotions shape thinking and influence behavior.

4. Statistically, when one speaks of one particular measurable entity as being a good predictor of other outcomes, one is referring to the fact that the two measures seem to be well correlated with one another in the population being examined. Consequently, the predictive nature of the measure is for group performance and outcomes rather than for that of individuals. Furthermore, this predictive quality doesn't say anything about how the two

variables are actually related or linked. Thus, one can never say that one variable is the cause of the other.

5. Most proposals for new conceptions of intelligence call into question the usefulness of IQ as a predictor. See, for example, Felsman and Vaillan (1987), Gardner (1983), Goleman (1995), Gould (1981), and Sternberg (1996).

6. The degree to which IQ tests are coachable and reflective of middle-class experiences with language and culture has been an issue as long as the tests have been around. See, for example, Gould (1981) and McClelland (1973).

7. This argument is developed more fully in Hutchins (1996).

8. In print, Tishman (1995) has used the term *intellectual character* to mean a blending of ethics and higher-order thinking. However, in our conversations, she has indicated that it might also be used to describe the set of dispositions toward thinking that an individual possesses. The term also appears in others' writings, for example, in an unpublished manuscript by educator Michael Strong (1990) that I came across early in my research.

9. The literature on this construct and the various words used to describe it is reviewed extensively in Ritchhart (1997).

10. The phrase *habits of mind* appears increasingly in curricular frameworks and assessment materials. On the use of habits of mind in curricular frameworks, see, for example, American Association for the Advancement of Science (AAAS) (1989), Massachusetts Department of Education (1995), and Goldenberg (1996). These documents tend to present habits of mind as process skills that students should be able to call on and use in a variety of situations. For example, Cuoco, Goldenberg, and Matk (1994, p. 378) state that "we are after mental habits that allow students to develop a repertoire of general heuristics and approaches that can be applied in many different situations." Similarly, Project 2061 (AAAS, 1989, p. 133) states that "taken together, these values, attitudes and skills [in disciplinary thinking] can be thought of as habits of mind." The project's list of skills includes both basic skills computation and "critical-response skills" (p. 139).

    On the use of habits of mind in assessment materials, see Baron (1987) and Jorgensen (1994). For a discussion of habits of mind as general abilities that facilitate learning, see Marzano (1992) and Meier (1995). For examples of the use of the term *habits of mind* that is most compatible with the idea of thinking dispositions being developed here, see Barell (1991) and Kallick (1989).

11. On the connection between thinking dispositions and such psychological constructs as the "need for cognitive closure," "need for cognition," and

"mindfulness," see Perkins, Tishman, Ritchhart, Donis, and Andrade (2000). Readers interested in exploring dispositional aspects of personality should see, for example, Hogan (1983), Kagan (1989), and McCrae and Costa (1987).

12. Throughout this discussion, I have portrayed thinking dispositions as good and positive forces. However, dispositions can certainly be negative, debilitating, or inhibiting forces. The disposition to jump to conclusions and seek early closure is a common example. At the same time, it is possible to over-apply or carry a positive disposition to an extreme. For example, constantly considering alternative options, choices, and perspectives could lead one never to make a decision; skepticism can turn into cynicism; and perseverance can lead to perseveration. Clearly, these types of thinking are no longer productive. By implication if not definition, those who concern themselves with thinking dispositions and intellectual character are concerned with the positive and productive ends of thinking, just as those concerned with the development of moral character are concerned with promoting the positive rather than negative sides of morality as they see it. This is, of course, not to imply that one can only attend to the positive while ignoring the negative. In cultivating intellectual character, we must give attention to developing positive dispositions while combating and reining in negative dispositions.

13. This definition of *good thinking* has found a broad consensus in the critical-thinking community. See, for example, Baron (1985); Ennis (1987); and Perkins, Jay, and Tishman (1993).

14. Other philosophers discuss dispositionally related constructs but have not sought to develop comprehensive lists of dispositions. See, for example, Norris (1995), Scheffler (1991), and Siegel (1988).

15. Ennis has proposed a number of different lists, with numbers of thinking dispositions varying from three to fourteen. I use the list presented here because it is the most current in print. In creating his list of dispositions, Ennis has sought to address criticism about lack of content in the critical-thinking movement, counter public perception that critical thinkers are just skeptics, and ensure that critical thinkers are listened to. See, for example, Ennis (1987, 1991).

16. Marzano (1992) cites the work of David Perkins and Theresa Amabile for the four habits supporting creative thinking, the work of Ann Brown and John Flavell for the five mental habits related to self-regulated thinking and learning, and the work of Robert Ennis and Richard Paul for six critical-thinking habits.

17. For a discussion of how these habits of mind were developed, how they are used in the school, and how they affect students' learning, see Meier (1995).

18. The question of which dispositions are most productive and crucial to the promotion of good thinking is necessarily laden with value. As such, the lists of dispositions discussed in this chapter represent not only the points of view of their respective authors but a cultural point of view as well. They are all representative of a Western tradition and approach to intelligence and thinking. Consequently, there is an implicit valuing of investigation, challenging of ideas, and novelty. However, the values and intellectual traditions of other cultures are likely to have a slightly different focus. For example, whereas Westerners often focus on testing the limits of an idea in developing understanding, other cultures may stress the importance of recognizing the history and lineage of ideas and expressing appropriate appreciation and reverence for that history. See, for example, Horton (1973).

Chapter Three

1. Some personality psychologists reject this characterization of dispositions as offering explanatory power. They see dispositions only in descriptive terms and use *dispositions* as a label for grouping similar types of behaviors together. For more on this approach in personality measurement, see Buss and Craik (1983).

2. The theoretical underpinnings of this model will be discussed in the next section. Although these three constructs emerge in the writings of several individuals, I draw here principally on the work of the MacArthur Patterns of Thinking Project at Harvard Project Zero with which I worked. Principal investigators for the project were David Perkins and Shari Tishman.

3. Robert Ennis (1991) refers to dispositions in this way and proposes a model of critical thinking in which dispositions assume a general supporting role, acting as a kind of surround or boosting mechanism behind critical thinking.

4. Dewey's stipulated definition of habits, presented in Chapter Two, suggests that his view of habit is dispositional in nature. For simplicity and clarity, I use the word *disposition* rather than *habit*.

5. You may be more familiar with Buddhist or Eastern notions of mindfulness. The psychological theory of mindfulness that Langer proposes is complementary to this but does not emphasize issues of enlightenment or transcendence.

6. For a discussion of the role of culture in shaping cognitive development, see, for example, Henderson and Cunningham (1994), Rogoff (1990), and Vygotsky (1978).
7. Rexford Brown (1993) explores the implicit messages that schools send about thinking by the way they organize their day, curriculum, and instruction.
8. Explicit teaching is a prevalent component of most philosophically based thinking-skills programs as well as self-regulated learning and metacognitive strategy training. It is also a prevalent component in many character education programs. For discussion and examples of thinking-skills programs, see, for example, Ennis (1987) and Paul (1993). For discussion and examples of programs designed to foster self-regulated learning and metacognitive strategy training, see Meichenbaum (1984), Mulcahy (1991), and Palinscar and Brown (1984). For discussion and examples of character development programs, see Dougherty (1996).
9. This tendency to poor or routine ways of thinking has been well documented from numerous perspectives. For a discussion of mindlessness, see Langer (1989). For accounts of thinking shortfalls, see Perkins (1995). For a historical perspective, see Locke, (1881).
10. For a discussion of the problems of transfer of thinking skills, see, for example, Perkins (1992) and Perkins and Salomon (1988).

Chapter Four

1. The word *throughline* comes from Konstantin Stanislavski (1963, p. 145) and is used to describe "that inner line of effort that guides the actors from the beginning to the end of the play." Wiske (1998) describes throughlines as an instructional practice more fully.
2. Heather developed and refined these questions through her work with Lois Hetland and as a participant in a summer institute on learning to use the Teaching for Understanding framework, which specifically advocates posting the overarching course goals or guiding questions (Blythe, 1998).
3. Sara Lawrence-Lightfoot (1999) has written about the nature of respect in classroom settings, mentioning specifically the role that a mutual dialogue plays in creating respect. Doug's case is a good example of these principles and techniques.

Chapter Five

1. The research of Leinhardt and colleagues (1986, 1987) focuses on identifying differences in routines established by experienced and novice teachers.

What I refer to as housekeeping routines are dubbed management routines by Leinhardt and her team. What she calls support routines, I refer to as management routines; and what she names exchange routines, I call discourse routines. I have chosen my terms solely for the purpose of clarity and to help make a clearer distinction between the purposes of the various types of routines. Of course, it is the constructs rather than the labels that matter most. Readers might be aware of other terms used to describe routines, as these are not the only researchers to explore the topic. Routines have also been explored by researchers working within the process-product paradigm discussed in Chapter One. This line of research is concerned with identifying links between the early establishment of routines and effective classroom management.

2. Examples of conversation protocols can be found in Ritchhart and Blythe (2001).

3. The criteria for thinking routines grew out of discussions with my colleague Shari Tishman. I wish to thank her for deepening my understanding of the special qualities of thinking routines and what they offer students.

4. Gavriel Salomon and David Perkins have written about distributed intelligence. See, for example, Salomon (1993) and Perkins (1992).

Chapter Six

1. My understanding of Whorf and the ways in which his theories and ideas connect to education is based largely on the writings of Penny Lee (1997).

2. This is basically a sociocultural perspective on cognitive development that can be traced back to Vygotsky (1978). His original ideas have been expanded by others; see, for example, Rogoff (1990) and Wertsch (1995).

3. For more on how reciprocal teaching is used in settings similar to those being described, see Heller and Gordon (1992).

4. The three categories of thinking processes, products, and stances were identified by Tishman and Perkins (1997). I have added the fourth category of thinking states.

5. For a sample list of language of thinking words, see Tishman, Perkins, and Jay (1995).

6. These lists of thinking are drawn from my field notes and videotape logs. The issue of thinking language was one that I was aware of and sensitive to before undertaking my classroom observations. As a consequence, I specifically tried to capture in my field notes the thinking-based language that teachers used. In constructing the lists, I strove for an accurate representation of each teacher rather than trying to be completely

comprehensive. Thus, while I reviewed all of my notes and logs to complete these lists, I did not attempt the kind of fine grain analysis and review of the videotapes that would have made the lists comprehensive but quite long.

In constructing the lists that appear here, I eliminated duplicates within each list as well as common words such as, *think, idea,* and *thought.* I also eliminated variations of verb forms, such as *explain* and *explaining.* However, when words were used in both noun and verb form, such as *explain* and *explanation,* I included both. My first pass yielded between forty and fifty words for each teacher. Rather than eliminate words from one teacher's list or leave the lists uneven in length, perhaps suggesting that one teacher used more thinking words than another, I made a second pass through my notes to try to identify additional words for those teachers who had slightly shorter lists. Finally, I read through the lists for each teacher to get a feel for the representativeness of each list based on my familiarity with each classroom.

7. I assessed the level of thoughtfulness in each classroom using a scale developed by Onosko and Newman (1994) (see Appendix). This scale includes a set of twelve criteria and expands on the set of six common attributes of thoughtful classrooms discussed in Chapter Two. The scale was used mainly as a tool to focus classroom observations and to help guide the writing of individual cases. Although each teacher's classroom was rated on the twelve criteria (see Exhibit A.1) as a means of comparing one classroom to another, these ratings were done by only a single observer. Because rating a classroom, versus a single class period, is dependent on multiple viewings over an extended time, the use of multiple raters wasn't feasible. Consequently, the ratings must be interpreted as personal though informed judgments.

Chapter Seven

1. The idea of generative topics comes from the Teaching for Understanding framework, which specifically addresses the importance of focusing the curriculum on big ideas that are worth understanding. For a more thorough discussion of what makes a topic generative, see, for example, Ritchhart (1999).

2. Unfortunately, *scaffolding* is a word that has become overused and a bit meaningless in many educational circles. Although the word conveys a powerful image of a supporting structure that allows a work to reach

heights not otherwise possible, in practice the word has too often become synonymous with simply applying or imposing a structure on a task. However, there is quite a difference between providing the support structure that keeps a building up and providing the initial means by which to create a building that eventually will be self-supportive. The former implies dependence and instability, whereas the latter suggests independence and self-sustenance.

3. This is often referred to as working in the zone of proximal development, or ZPD. This term has its origin in the sociohistorical work of Lev Vygotsky. For an explanation and discussion of the zone of proximal development, see, for example, Rogoff (1995).

Chapter Eight

1. As James Calderhead (1996) points out in his review of the research on teachers' cognitions, that the line between values, beliefs, knowledge, and theories is not always clear. Calderhead separates the literature into two basic camps: (1) teachers' knowledge dealing with factual propositions and understanding and (2) beliefs, values, and implicit theories, which some scholars view as being more affective and evaluative in nature and consisting of untested assumptions and models based on experience. For a review of research on teachers' cognitions, see, for example, Shulman (1990) and Clark and Peterson (1986). For a discussion of the different types of knowledge important in teaching, see Shulman (1987).

2. In his review of the research, James Calderhead (1996) suggests that the effect of teachers' beliefs on their classroom practice is not clear. However, this conclusion may in part be due to the way much of the research on teachers' beliefs is conducted. Because it can be time-consuming and difficult to uncover teachers' beliefs, most of the research in this area has been case study research. However, such research does not easily transfer into quantitative measures of effect size that can be compared easily. Furthermore, because teachers hold a variety of beliefs that can sometimes be contradictory and that are applied situationally, it is quite likely that a superficial assessment of beliefs, for example by using only self-report measures, would not be good predictors of classroom behavior.

   Although more evidence is needed in order to make definitive statements, some evidence exists in the literature regarding effects between teachers' knowledge, theories, and beliefs and their practice. For example, Susan Stodolosky (1988) has shown how teachers' understanding of subject matter affects their instruction. Angela Anning (1988) has shown how teachers' theories about learning and learners affect their approach to structuring tasks and interacting with students. Various studies have shown that teachers' beliefs about the subject matter affect how they interpret curricula, standards, and curriculum reform efforts. See, for example, Haimes (1996); Richardson, Anders, Tidwell, and Lloyd (1991); and Cronin-Jones, (1991).

3. This focus on the naturally occurring words and constructs is sometimes referred to as uncovering emic concepts. In contrast, etic concepts are those that are imposed from the outside by the researcher. When I specifically asked teachers about their thinking about thinking, I was imposing an etic construct and forcing them to tell me about something I wanted to know and valued rather than something they might have viewed as most central (Maxwell, 1996).

4. The notion of mental models has been applied in a number of contexts to better understand the reasoning and decision making of individuals. Building on the foundational work of Johnson-Laird, Halford (1993) has sought to understand the role of mental models in students' misconceptions. Halford suggests that because our mental models are built up from our experiences, they typically are incomplete and approximate rather than true scientific theories. Furthermore, because these mental models "provide the workspace for inference and mental operations," (p. 23) understanding of students' mental models provides the basis for understanding students' reasoning and problem solving. At the same time, confronting and transforming these models is a necessary condition for conceptual change. See Strauss (1993) for a discussion of mental models and conceptual change in teachers. Working in the area of human relations, Senge (1994) uses the concept of mental models as a basis for understanding how individuals relate not only to ideas but also to each other. Mental models provide the lens through which one views the world and the basis on which inferences are made. By better understanding the mental models of one's associates, one can better predict behavior and reactions. Recognizing that inferences are made not from objective reality but from a reality filtered through one's mental model can enhance individual and group decision making.

5. Throughout these vignettes, I have tried to use teachers' own words to express their goals, values, and beliefs. In order to do this both honestly and effectively, I have removed the naturally occurring *um*s, *er*s, *you know*s, and so on from their speech. I have also eliminated the false starts and midsentence corrections that sometimes make written dialogue difficult to follow. At times, it was necessary to fill in missing words or to make

referents clear, and I have added these words in brackets. On other occasions, skipping a section of text made it easier to present a single idea more clearly, and I have indicated these jumps in dialogue with the use of ellipses.

6. The thinking items listed are in each teacher's own language. Likewise, teachers identified and named categories and relationships. To count as a main category, the category had to include at least two items and not be nested within or directly connected to another category.

7. Karen was recruited for the study because of her deep and abiding interest in the teaching of thinking. She was most enthusiastic about the study, and in my initial screening interviews she spoke repeatedly of the importance of reflection, metacognition, and thinking to her teaching. Although my initial observations indicated that her classroom might not be that thoughtful of an environment, I also recognized that Karen did not fit my preconceived notions of what thoughtful teaching should look like. Because of that discrepancy, I was anxious to observe Karen and get to know her teaching better. Initially, I felt that Karen potentially challenged my notions about what instruction for intellectual character might look like and offered new forms that effective instruction for thinking can take. However, I quickly realized that the strength of continuing to include her in my study lay in trying to understand what stands in the way of effective teaching of thinking even when the teacher embraces it as a goal.

Chapter Nine

1. For examples of this mentality, you probably need to look no further than your own municipality. Specific examples of teaching through legislation include the California legislature requiring the teaching of phonics. Texas and Florida have led the way in requiring students to pass tests for graduation, and most other U.S. states have now followed suit. In many instances, the test becomes the curriculum. For instance, for students to do well on the writing portion of the fourth-grade Colorado assessment, they must organize their writing in a prescribed manner. Consequently, writing instruction must focus on this specific organizational technique, though it is overly formal for the type of writing in which fourth graders are most likely to engage.

2. When I write about differences in teachers' ability, general inclination, and awareness toward thinking, I am writing about the differences that I observed rather than differences that formal assessments reveal. For example, a teacher's ability shows up in his or her mental model of

thinking. A teacher's inclination toward thinking shows up in that person's instructional throughlines, some of which are more thinking-rich than others. Finally, a teacher's awareness of thinking opportunities shows up in his or her ability to recognize, exploit, and scaffold occasions for thinking that come up in the classroom.

3. It is more difficult to isolate and assess awareness than either ability or inclination because awareness depends on spotting occasions without necessarily acting on them. To isolate and assess teachers' awareness alone, I might have asked them to watch a classroom episode on videotape and identify occasions for thinking.

4. The measure of thoughtfulness is the Onosko and Newman scale as presented in the Appendix. John's score on the scale, based on the totality of my observations, is 58 out of a possible 60.

5. Again, this assessment is based on the Onosko and Newman scale. Karen's score on the scale, based on the totality of my observations, is seventeen out of a possible sixty. Though this is well below my initial-screening cut-off score (see the Appendix), remember that the initial screening was based on only one observation, and the first priority for selection was a teacher's interest in and commitment toward promoting student thinking.

6. The research most relevant to this point comes from the field of achievement motivation on learners' orientations. A host of researchers have investigated learning versus performance orientations—though these constructs often go by other names, such as task versus ego or mastery versus grades. Studies have shown that a learning orientation tends to be inversely related to a grade orientation and that while students come to class predisposed to one orientation over another, over time the classroom situation tends to socialize them in the direction of the classroom. Furthermore, ego, grade, and performance orientations tend to be detrimental to students' achievement and engagement in the long run and lead to less intrinsic enjoyment of activities. See, for example, Beck, Rorrer-Woody, and Pierce (1991); and Meece, Blumenfeld, and Hoyle (1988).

7. Such content immersion is one of the key strategies for professional development advocated by the National Institute for Science Education. For an explanation of the role of immersion programs in developing teachers' knowledge base, awareness, and understanding of the learning process, see, for example, Loucks-Horsley, Hewson, Love, and Stiles (1998). Some examples of content immersion programs include: SummerMath, at Mount Holyoke College in South Hadley, MA; Teaching to the Big Ideas, at the Education Development Center, Inc. in Newton, MA; The Exploratorium

Teacher Institute, at The Exploratorium in San Francisco; and NASA Educational Workshops sponsored by NASA at its field centers.

8. These ideas are expounded in a variety of sources. I've merely cited one of the most popular (Wong & Wong, 1997).

9. Throughout *The First Days of School* (Wong & Wong, 1997), teacher testimonials and examples indicate that quiet and work-oriented students are the desired outcome of these practices. Teachers often mention that routines are so well established that students get right to work without any prompting from teachers. Several teachers even brag that their students are so self-sufficient that as teachers they could be gone for long periods of time and never be missed. In all of these examples, the authors imply that working alone and spending time on task are all that is required for learning.

10. Unfortunately, although the trend in educational research and philosophy has generally been to expand and challenge traditional notions of what it means for students to be successful, the current political and institutional trend has continued to focus on grades and scores. The current trend in educational reform actually contains little if any real reform in the way we view schools or treat students. Instead, educational reform has become synonymous with the catchwords *higher standards* and *accountability.* In the end, these standards often turn out to be just more of the same old emphasis on grades and scores; only this time, it is higher grades and higher scores. For a discussion of our continued preoccupation with grades and scores and its consequence for student learning, see, for example, Kohn (1999).

11. The dynamic in Susan's room might be described as work-avoidant. Rather than focusing on learning or completing work, students try to negotiate out of work. See, for example, Marshall (1987). One of the origins of this dynamic seems to be Susan's inconsistency in enforcing behavioral standards. However, the biggest factors seem to be that this work-avoidant orientation is part of the culture of the school, and the mixed-age group of seventh and eighth graders seems to perpetuate this attitude. Interestingly, the students are quite good at doing their homework. They simply do not like to work in class with their peers.

12. David Perkins frequently introduces his course "Cognition and the Art of Instruction," with this phrase. He teaches this course at the Harvard Graduate School of Education in Cambridge, MA.

13. See, for example, Brooks and Brooks (1993), Duckworth (1987), and Caine and Caine (1997).

Chapter Ten

1. The process I describe here is actually a modified version of how I assessed the mental models of the teachers I studied. That process is known as the repertory grid technique and is discussed further in the Appendix.
2. The questions offered in this exercise come from the Thinking Ideals program developed as part of the Innovating with Intelligence Project at Harvard Project Zero. This project is funded by Carpe Vitam International. I work on the project along with colleagues David Perkins, Shari Tishman, Patricia Palmer, Ylva Telegin, and Lotta Norell.
3. This classification of classroom environments as oriented either to work, work-avoidance, or learning has been developed by Hermine Marshall (1987, 1988). I presented these orientations in Chapter Four as part of a discussion of classroom agendas.
4. The distinction between standards and ideals receives little attention in educational circles these days. However, Arnstine (1995) provides an excellent discussion and explication of this distinction.

Appendix

1. Stake (1995) defines case studies as being either "intrinsic" or "instrumental." The intrinsic case is studied in order to better understand the case itself, whatever the case happens to be. The instrumental case is purposely selected for its potential to reveal a better understanding of a certain phenomenon in which the researcher is interested.
2. Reasons for not contacting teachers included incompatible school start dates, contacts with too many other more promising teachers from the same school, or late submission of nominations. Of the twenty-eight teachers I contacted, fourteen expressed interest in participating. I then observed and interviewed each of these teachers. After selection, I informed teachers of the demands the study would place on them and contacted their principals to obtain their permission for the study.
3. Onosko and Newman (1994) analyzed the extent to which secondary social studies teachers and departments challenged students to engage in higher-order thinking and to use their minds well. This was a four-year study conducted at the National Center on Effective Secondary Schools.
4. To test the reliability of my classroom ratings using the Onosko and Newman criteria (1994), I had a colleague join me for one of my classroom observations to do her own ratings using the criteria. Our scores never differed more than one point in any category, and our overall rankings were

within four points of each other. I had set a minimum acceptable score of forty-five for the initial screening, and both of us scored the teacher above this threshold.

5. This methodology goes by a variety of names: the Kelly rep test, Kelly's repertory grid technique, personal construct grids, personal construct methodology, repertory grids, RG technique, the repertory grid approach. This variety may be due to the fact that George Kelly described a basic clinical interviewing technique for identifying personal constructs rather than devising a formal testing procedure.

6. For examples of the basic repertory grid technique and ways in which it has been modified, see, for example, Easterby-Smith (1981), Fransella and Bannister (1977), and Ryle (1975).

7. The grid technique can be analyzed informally and without use of statistics if the grid is small, having only five or so elements and constructs. However, even in such an informal analysis, basic statistical ideas such as correlation and focusing (a basis for cluster analysis) come into play. See Easterby-Smith (1981).

━ᴡᴡ━ References

American Association for the Advancement of Science. (1989). *Project 2061: Science for all Americans.* Washington, DC: Author.

Anderson, R. C., Nguyen-Jahiel, K., McNurlen, B., Archodicou, A., Kim, S. Y., Reznitskaya, A., Tillmanns, M., & Gilbert, L. (2001). The snowball phenomenon: Spread of ways of talking and ways of thinking across groups of children. *Cognition and Instruction, 19*(1), 1–46.

Anning, A. (1988). Teachers' theories about children's learning. In J. Calderhead (Ed.), *Teachers' professional learning* (pp. 128–145). London: Falmer Press.

Aristotle. (1990). *Posterior Analytics Book I* (G.R.G. Mure, Trans.). In M. Adler et al. (Eds.), *Great books of the Western world* (2nd ed., Vol. 8, pp. 97-122). Chicago: Encyclopedia Britannica. (Reprinted from *The Works of Aristotle,* translated under the editorship of W. D. Ross, 1952, New York: Oxford University Press).

Arnstine, D. (1995). *Democracy and the arts of schooling.* Albany: State University of New York Press.

Astington, J. W., & Olson, D. R. (1990). Metacognitive and metalinguistic language: Learning to talk about thought. *Applied Psychology: An International Review, 39*(1), 77–87.

Bakhtin, M. M. (1981). *The dialogic imagination: Four essays by M. M. Bakhtin.* Austin: University of Texas Press.

Barell, J. (1991). *Teaching for thoughtfulness: Classroom strategies to enhance intellectual development.* New York: Longman.

Baron, J. (1985). *Rationality and intelligence.* Cambridge: Cambridge University Press.

Baron, J. B. (1987). Evaluating thinking skills in the classroom. In J. B. Baron & R. J. Sternberg (Eds.), *Teaching thinking skills: Theory and practice* (pp. 221–248). New York: Freeman.

Beck, H. P., Rorrer-Woody, S., & Pierce, L. G. (1991). The relations of learning and grade orientations to academic performance. *Teaching of Psychology, 18,* 35–37.

Billing, M. (1987). *Arguing and thinking: A rhetorical approach to social psychology.* Cambridge: Cambridge University Press.

Blythe, T. (1998). *The teaching for understanding guide.* San Francisco: Jossey-Bass.

Bogdan, R. C., & Biklen, S. K. (1982). *Qualitative research for education: An introduction to theory and methods.* Needham Heights, MA: Allyn & Bacon.

Brooks, J. G., & Brooks, M. G. (1993). *In search of understanding: The case for constructivist classrooms.* Alexandria, VA: Association for Supervision and Curriculum Development.

Brown, R. (1993). *Schools of thought.* San Francisco: Jossey-Bass.

Bruner, J. (1973). Going beyond the information given. In J. Anglin (Ed.), *Beyond the information given* (pp. 218–238). New York: Norton.

Bruner, J. (1996). *The culture of education.* Cambridge, MA: Harvard University Press.

Buss, D. M., & Craik, K. H. (1983). The act frequency approach to personality. *Psychological Review, 90,* 105–126.

Buzan, T. (1993). *The mind map book.* New York: Penguin Books.

Caine, R. N., & Caine, G. (1997). *Education on the edge of possibility.* Alexandria, VA: Association for Supervision and Curriculum Development.

Calderhead, J. (1996). Teachers: Beliefs and knowledge. In D. C. Berliner & R. C. Calfee (Eds.), *Handbook of educational psychology* (pp. 709–725). Old Tappan, NJ: Macmillan.

Campione, J. C., & Brown, A. L. (1978). Toward a theory of intelligence: Contributions from research with retarded children. *Intelligence, 2,* 279–304.

Carroll, J. B. (Ed.). (1956). *Language, thought, and reality: Selected writings of Benjamin Lee Whorf.* Cambridge, MA: MIT Press.

Clark, C. M. (1995). *Thoughtful teaching.* New York: Teachers College Press.

Clark, C. M., & Peterson, P. L. (1986). Teachers' thought processes. In M. Wittrock (Ed.), *Handbook of research on teaching* (3rd ed., pp. 255–296). Old Tappan, NJ: Macmillan.

Costa, A., & Garmston, R. (1994). *Cognitive coaching: A foundation for renaissance schools.* Norwood, MA: Christopher Gordon Publishers.

Costa, A., & Kallick, B. (2000). *Discovering and exploring habits of mind.* Alexandria, VA: Association for Supervision and Curriculum Development.

Covey, S. (1989). *The seven habits of highly effective people.* New York: Simon & Schuster.

Cronin-Jones, L. (1991). Science teacher beliefs and their influence on curriculum implementation: Two case studies. *Journal of Research in Science Teaching, 28,* 235–225.

Cuoco, A., Goldenberg, E. P., & Matk, J. (1994). Habits of mind: An organizing principle for the mathematics curriculum. *Journal of Mathematical Behavior, 15*(4), 375–402.

Das, J. P., & Jarman, R. F. (1991). Cognitive integration: Alternative model of intelligence. In II.A.H. Rowe (Ed.), *Intelligence: Reconceptualization and measurement* (pp. 163–182). Hillsdale, NJ: Erlbaum.

Dewey, J. (1922). *Human nature and conduct.* New York: Modern Library.

Dewey, J. (1933). *How we think: A restatement of the relation of reflective thinking to the educative process.* Boston: D. C. Heath.

Dougherty, K. (1996, Aug.). Building an ethical community: An interview with Michael Josephson. *Hemispheres,* pp. 21–26.

Duckworth, E. (1987). *The having of wonderful ideas.* New York: Teachers College Press.

Easterby-Smith, M. (1981). The design, analysis, and interpretation of repertory grids. In M.L.G. Shaw (Ed.), *Recent advances in personal construct technology.* Orlando, FL: Academic Press.

Eisner, E. W. (1994). *The educational imagination: On the design and evaluation of school programs* (3rd ed.). Old Tappan, NJ: Macmillan.

English, H. B., & English, A. C. (1958). *A comprehensive dictionary of psychological and psychoanalytical terms: A guide to usage.* New York: McKay.

Ennis, R. H. (1987). A taxonomy of critical thinking dispositions and abilities. In J. B. Baron & R. J. Sternberg (Eds.), *Teaching thinking skills: Theory and practice* (pp. 9–26). New York: Freeman.

Ennis, R. H. (1991). Critical thinking: A streamlined conception. *Teaching Philosophy, 14,* 5–25.

Facione, P. A., Facione, N. C., & Sanchez, C. A. (1992). *The California Critical Thinking Dispositions Inventory.* Millbrae, CA: California Academic Press.

Felsman, J. K., & Vaillan, G. E. (1987). Resilient children as adults: A forty-year study. In E. J. Anderson & B. J. Cohler (Eds.), *The invulnerable child*. New York: Guilford Press.

Fransella, F., & Bannister, D. (1977). *A manual for repertory grid technique*. New York: Academic Press.

Gardner, H. (1983). *Frames of mind*. New York: Basic Books.

Gardner, H. (1991). *The unschooled mind*. New York: Basic Books.

Goldenberg, E. P. (1996). *"Habits of mind" as an organizer for the curriculum*. Newton, MA: Educational Development Center.

Goleman, D. (1995). *Emotional intelligence*. New York: Bantam Books.

Gould, S. J. (1981). *The mismeasure of man*. New York: Norton.

Green, T. F. (1971). *The activities of teaching*. New York: McGraw-Hill.

Guilford, J. P. (1982). Cognitive psychology's ambiguities: Some suggested remedies. *Psychological Review, 89*, 48–59.

Haimes, D. H. (1996). The implementation of a "function" approach to introductory algebra: A case study of teacher cognitions, teacher actions, and the intended curriculum. *Journal for Research in Mathematics Education, 27*(5), 582–602.

Halford, G. S. (1993). *Children's understanding: The development of mental models*. Hillsdale, NJ: Erlbaum.

Heller, J. I., & Gordon, A. (1992). Lifelong learning: A unique school-university collaboration is preparing students for the future. *Educator, 6*(1), 4–19.

Henderson, R. W., & Cunningham, L. (1994). Creating interactive socio-cultural environments for self-regulated learning. In D. Schunk & B. Zimmerman (Eds.), *Self-regulation of learning and performance: Issues and educational applications*. Hillsdale, NJ: Erlbaum.

Henry, J. (1963). *Culture against man*. New York: Random House.

Herrnstein, R. J., & Murray, C. (1994). *The bell curve*. New York: Free Press.

Hogan, R. (1983). Socioanalytic theory of personality. In M. M. Page (Ed.), *1982 Nebraska Symposium on Motivation: Personality —current theory and research* (pp. 55–89). Lincoln: University of Nebraska Press.

Horton, R. (1973). *Modes of thought: Essays on thinking in Western and non-Western societies*. (R. Horton and R. Finnegan, Eds.). London: Faber.

Hutchins, E. (1996). *Cognition in the wild*. Cambridge, MA: MIT Press.

Irving, J. (1998). *Author reading and discussion of "A Widow for One Year."* The Brattle Theatre Author Series, Cambridge, MA.

Jensen, A. R. (1988). Psychometric g and mental processing speed on a semantic verification test. *Journals of Personality and Individual Differences, 9*(2), 243–255.

Johnson, T. H. (Ed.). (1979). *The poems of Emily Dickinson.* Cambridge, MA: Belknap Press of Harvard University Press.

Johnson-Laird, P. N. (1983). *Mental models.* Cambridge, MA: Harvard University Press.

Jorgensen, M. (1994). *Assessing habits of mind: Performance-based assessment in science and mathematics.* Columbus, OH: ERIC Clearinghouse for Science, Mathematics, and Environmental Education.

Kagan, J. (1989). *Unstable ideas: Temperament, cognition, and self.* Cambridge, MA: Harvard University Press.

Kallick, B. (1989). *Changing schools into communities for thinking.* Grand Forks: University of North Dakota Study Group on Evaluation.

Kelly, G. A. (1955). *The psychology of personal constructs.* New York: Norton.

Kohn, A. (1999). *The schools our children deserve.* Boston: Houghton Mifflin.

Lampert, M. (1985). How do teachers manage to teach? Perspectives on problems in practice. *Harvard Educational Review, 55,* 178–194.

Langer, E. (1989). *Mindfulness.* Reading, MA: Addison-Wesley.

Langer, E., Hatem, M., Joss, J., & Howell, M. (1989). The mindful consequences of teaching uncertainty for elementary school and college students. *Creativity Research Journal.*

Langer, E., & Piper, A. (1987). The prevention of mindlessness. *Journal of Personality and Social Psychology, 53,* 280–287.

Lawrence-Lightfoot, S. (1999). *Respect.* Reading, MA: Perseus.

Lee, P. (1997). Language in thinking and learning: Pedagogy and the new Whorfian framework. *Harvard Educational Review, 67*(3), 430–471.

Leinhardt, G., & Greeno, J. (1986). The cognitive skill of teaching. *Journal of Educational Psychology, 78*(2), 75–95.

Leinhardt, G., Weidman, C., & Hammond, K. M. (1987). Introduction and integration of classroom routines by expert teachers. *Curriculum Inquiry, 17*(2), 135–175.

Locke, J. (1881). *Locke's conduct of the understanding.* Oxford: Clarendon Press.

Loucks-Horsley, S., Hewson, P. W., Love, N., & Stiles, K. E. (1998). *Designing professional development for teachers of science and mathematics.* Thousand Oaks, CA: Corwin Press.

McClelland, C. M. (1973). Testing for competence rather than for "intelligence." *American Psychologist, 28,* 1–14.

McCrae, R. R., & Costa, P. J., Jr. (1987). Validation of the five-factor model of personality across instruments and observers. *Journal of Personality and Social Psychology, 52*(1), 81–90.

Magritte, R. (1928–1929). *The treachery of images.* Los Angeles: Los Angeles County Museum of Art.

Marshall, H. H. (1987). Building a learning orientation. *Theory into Practice, 26*(1), 8–14.

Marshall, H. H. (1988). In pursuit of learning-oriented classrooms. *Teaching and Teacher Education, 4*(2), 85–98.

Marzano, R. J., Brandt, R. S., Hughes, C. S., Jones, B. F., Presseisen, B. Z., Rankin, S. C., & Suhor, C. (1988). *Dimensions of thinking: A framework for curriculum and instruction.* Alexandria, VA: Association for Supervision and Curriculum Development.

Massachusetts Department of Education. (1995). *Mathematics curriculum framework.* Malden: Author.

Maxwell, J. A. (1996). *Qualitative research design: An interactive approach.* Thousand Oaks, CA: Sage.

Meece, J. L., Blumenfeld, P. C., & Hoyle, R. H. (1988). Students' goal orientations and cognitive engagement in classroom activities. *Journal of Educational Psychology, 80,* 514–523.

Meichenbaum, D. (1984). Teaching thinking: A cognitive-behavioral perspective. In J. Segal, S. Chipman, & R. Glaser (Eds.), *Thinking and learning skills* (Vol. 2). Hillsdale, NJ: Erlbaum.

Meier, D. (1995). *The power of their ideas: Lessons for America from a small school in Harlem.* Boston: Beacon Press.

Middleton, J. A. (1995). A study of intrinsic motivation in the mathematics classroom: A personal constructs approach. *Journal for Research in Mathematics Education, 26*(3), 254–279.

Miles, M. B., & Huberman, A. M. (1994). *Qualitative data analysis: An expanded sourcebook.* Thousand Oaks, CA: Sage.

Mulcahy, R. F. (1991). Developing autonomous learners. *Alberta Journal of Educational Research, 37*(4), 385–397.

Munby, H. (1984). A qualitative approach to the study of a teacher's beliefs. *Journal of Research in Science Teaching, 21*(1), 27–38.

National Center for Educational Statistics. (1997). *Digest of education statistics.* (DHEW publication No. EDD00004). Washington, DC: U.S. Government Printing Office.

Norris, S. P. (1995). The meaning of critical thinking test performance: The effects of abilities and dispositions on scores. In D. Fasko, Jr. (Ed.), *Critical thinking: Current research, theory, and practice.* Norwell, MA: Kluwer.

Onosko, J. J., & Newman, F. M. (1994). Creating more thoughtful learning environments. In J. N. Mangieri & C. C. Block (Eds.), *Creating powerful thinking in teachers and students: Diverse perspectives* (pp. 27–50). Austin, TX: Holt, Rinehart and Winston.

Palinscar, A. S., & Brown, A. L. (1984). Reciprocal teaching of comprehension-fostering and monitoring activities. *Cognition and Instruction, 1*(2), 117–175.

Palmer, P. (1998). *The courage to teach.* San Francisco: Jossey-Bass.

Paul, R. W. (1987). Dialogical thinking: Critical thought essential to the acquisition of rational knowledge and passions. In J. B. Baron & R. J. Sternberg (Eds.), *Teaching thinking skills: Theory and practice* (pp. 127–148). New York: Freeman.

Paul, R. W. (1991). Teaching critical thinking in the strong sense. In A. L. Costa (Ed.), *Developing minds: A resource book for teaching thinking.* Alexandria, VA: Association for Supervision and Curriculum Development.

Paul, R. W. (1993). *Critical thinking: What every person needs to know to survive in a rapidly changing world.* Santa Rosa, CA: Foundation for Critical Thinking.

Perkins, D. N. (1992). *Smart schools: From training memories to educating minds.* New York: Free Press.

Perkins, D. N. (1995). *Outsmarting IQ.* New York: Free Press.

Perkins, D. (1999). From idea to action. In L. Hetland & S. Veenema (Eds.), *The Project Zero classroom: Views on understanding.* Cambridge, MA: Project Zero, Harvard Graduate School of Education.

Perkins, D. N., Jay, E., & Tishman, S. (1993). New conceptions of thinking: From ontology to education. *Educational Psychologist, 28*(1), 67–85.

Perkins, D. N., & Salomon, G. (1987). Transfer and teaching thinking. In D. N. Perkins, J. Lochhead, & J. Bishop (Eds.), *Thinking: The second international conference.* Hillsdale, NJ: Erlbaum.

Perkins, D. N., & Salomon, G. (1988). Teaching for transfer. *Educational Leadership, 46*(1), 22–32.

Perkins, D. N., Tishman, S., Ritchhart, R., Donis, K., & Andrade, A. (2000). Intelligence in the wild: A dispositional view of intellectual traits. *Educational Psychology Review, 12*(3), 269–293.

Pirandello, L. (1952). In E. Bentley (Ed.), *Naked Masks, five plays.* New York: Dutton.

Pirie, S.E.B. (1996, October). *Classroom video-recording: When, why and how does it offer a valuable data source for qualitative research?* Paper presented at the Annual Meeting of the North American Chapter of the International Group for the Psychology of Mathematics Education, Panama City, FL.

Postman, N., & Weingartner, C. (1969). *Teaching as a subversive activity.* New York: Dell.

Richardson, V., Anders, P., Tidwell, D., & Lloyd, C. (1991). The relationship between teachers' beliefs and practices in reading comprehension instruction. *American Educational Research Journal, 28,* 559–586.

Ritchhart, R. (1997). *Thinking dispositions: Toward clarifying a construct.* Unpublished qualifying paper, Harvard University Graduate School of Education, Cambridge, MA.

Ritchhart, R. (1999). Generative topics: Building a curriculum around big ideas. *Teaching Children Mathematics, 5*(8), 462–468.

Ritchhart, R., & Blythe, T. (2001). *The power of the creative classroom* (Vol. 2). Burbank, CA: Disney Learning Partnership.

Ritchhart, R., & Perkins, D. N. (2000). Life in the mindful classroom: Nurturing the disposition of mindfulness. *Journal of Social Issues, 56*(1), 27–47.

Rogoff, B. (1990). *Apprenticeship in thinking.* New York: Oxford University Press.

Rogoff, B. (1995). Observing sociocultural activity on three planes: Participatory appropriation, guided participation, and apprenticeship. In J. V. Wertsch, P. D. Rio, & A. Alvarez (Eds.), *Sociocultural studies of mind.* Cambridge: Cambridge University Press.

Rowe, H.A.H. (Ed.). (1991). *Intelligence: Reconceptualization and measurement.* Hillsdale, NJ: Erlbaum.

Ryle, A. (1975). *Frames and cages: The repertory grid approach to human understanding.* London: Sussex University Press.

Ryle, G. (1949). *The concept of mind.* London: Hutchinson House.

Salomon, G. (Ed.). (1993). *Distributed cognitions.* New York: Cambridge University Press.

Salomon, G., & Perkins, D. N. (1989). Rocky roads to transfer: Rethinking mechanisms of a neglected phenomenon. *Educational Psychologist, 24*(2), 113–142.

Scheffler, I. (1991). *In praise of cognitive emotions.* New York: Routledge.

Semb, G. B., & Ellis, J. A. (1994). Knowledge taught in school: What is remembered? *Review of Educational Research, 64*(2), 254–279.

Senge, P. M. (1994). *The fifth discipline fieldbook: Strategies and tools for building a learning organization.* New York: Doubleday.

Shulman, L. S. (1987). Knowledge and teaching: Foundations of the new reform. *Harvard Educational Review, 57*(1), 1–22.

Shulman, L. S. (1990). *Paradigms and programs.* Old Tappan, NJ: Macmillan.

Siegel, H. (1988). *Educating reason: Rationality, critical thinking, and education.* New York: Routledge.

Siegel, H. (1997). *What (good) are thinking dispositions?* Unpublished manuscript.

Siegler, R. S., & Richards, D. D. (1982). The development of intelligence. In R. J. Sternberg (Ed.), *Handbook of human intelligence* (pp. 897–971). Cambridge: Cambridge University Press.

Spearman, C. (1973). *The nature of "intelligence" and the principles of cognition.* New York: Arno Press. (Original work published 1923)

Stake, R. E. (1995). *The art of case study research.* Thousand Oaks, CA: Sage.

Stanislavski, K. (1963). *An actor's handbook* (Elizabeth R. Hapgood, Trans.). New York: Theatre Arts Books.

Stanley, T. J. (2000). *The millionaire mind.* Kansas City: Andrews McMeel.

Sternberg, R. J. (1985). *Beyond IQ: A triarchic theory of human intelligence.* Cambridge: Cambridge University Press.

Sternberg, R. J. (1990). *Metaphors of mind: Conceptions of the nature of intelligence.* Cambridge: Cambridge University Press.

Sternberg, R. J. (1996). *Successful intelligence: How practical and creative intelligence determine success in life.* New York: Simon & Schuster.

Sternberg, R., Conway, B. E., Ketron, J. L., & Bernstein, M. (1981). People's conceptions of intelligence. *Journal of Personality and Social Psychology, 41*(1), 37–55.

Stodolosky, S. (1988). *The subject matters: Classroom activity in math and social studies.* Chicago: University of Chicago Press.

Strauss, S. (1993). Teachers' pedagogical content knowledge about children's minds and learning: Implications for teacher education. *Educational Psychologist, 28*(3), 279–290.

Strong, M. (1990). *Character and ability: A non-cognitive interpretation of genius.* Unpublished manuscript.

Thompson, A. G. (1992). Teachers' beliefs and conceptions: A synthesis of research. In D. A. Grouws (Ed.), *Handbook of research on mathematics teaching and learning* (pp. 127–146). Old Tappan, NJ: Macmillan.

Thurstone, L. L. (1938). *Primary mental abilities.* Chicago: University of Chicago Press.

Tishman, S. (1995, October). High-level thinking, ethics, and intellectual character. *Think,* pp. 9–13.

Tishman, S., MacGillvray, D., & Palmer, P. (1999). *Investigating the educational impact and potential of the Museum of Modern Art's Visual Thinking Curriculum: Final report to the Museum of Modern Art.* New York: Museum of Modern Art.

Tishman, S., & Perkins, D. N. (1997). The language of thinking. *Phi Delta Kappan, 78*(5), 368–374.

Tishman, S., Perkins, D. N., & Jay, E. (1995). *The thinking classroom: Learning and teaching in a culture of thinking.* Needham Heights, MA: Allyn & Bacon.

U.S. Census Bureau. (2001). *State and local government employment and payroll—March 1998* [On-line]. Available: http://www.census.gov/govs/www/apesstl98.html.

Vygotsky, L. S. (1978). *Mind in society.* Cambridge, MA: Harvard University Press.

Welty, E. (1979). *The eye of the story: Selected essays and reviews.* New York: Vintage Books.

Wertsch, J. V. (1995). The need for action in sociocultural research. In J. V. Wertsch, P. D. Rio, & A. Alvarez (Eds.), *Sociocultural studies of mind.* Cambridge: Cambridge University Press.

Whorf, B. L. (1956). Language, mind, and reality. In J. B. Carroll (Ed.), *Language, thought, and reality: Selected writings of Benjamin Lee Whorf* (pp. 246-270). Cambridge, MA: MIT Press.

Winne, P. H. (1995). Inherent details in self-regulated learning. *Educational Psychologist, 30*(4), 173–188.

Wiske, M. S. (Ed.). (1998). *Teaching for understanding: Linking research with practice.* San Francisco: Jossey-Bass.

Wong, H. K., & Wong, R. T. (1997). *The first days of school: How to be an effective teacher.* Mountain View, CA: Harry K. Wong Publications.

—~~— Index

Note: Note numbers in this index indicate chapter and endnote number (for example, 271n6.4 refers to page 271, endnote number 4 for Chapter Six). "P" indicates Preface; "A" indicates Appendix.

Culture, thinking routines as encultura-
tion force, 110–111, 113–114
Culture of moments, 162–163
Culture of thinking. *See* Thoughtful
classrooms
Cunningham, L., 270n3.6
Cuoco, A., 267n2.10
Curie, M., xv
Curiosity, as thinking disposition, 27, 28
Curriculum: at beginning of school
year, 61–69, 83; implicit, xxii–xxiii,
46; supporting development of
intellectual character, 46

D

Daily edit thinking routine, 94–97
Das, J. P., 266n2.3
Dewey, J., 18, 21; on dispositions and
reflective thinking, 38–39; term
habit used by, 19, 269n3.4
Dialogical thinking, 119–121, 143
Dialogue: for creating climate of
respect, 70–72, 270n4.3; dominated
by teacher, 115–116; laying foundation for, at beginning of school year,
69–75, 83; learning new patterns of
talking and thinking through, 121–
130, 143. *See also*
Discussions
Dickenson, E., xvi
Discourse routines, 88, 271n5.1
Discussions: leaderless, 123–125, 168;
public issue, 125–130, 138, 172. *See
also* Dialogue
Dispositional behavior: Covey's model
of, 39; Dewey's model of, and reflective thinking, 38–39, 269n3.4; elements of, 35–38, 242–244, 247;
example of, in museum, 34–35;
internal-external model of, 41–45;
mindfulness as, 40; self-regulated
learning as, 40; triadic model of,
40–41. *See also* Dispositions
Dispositions: as both descriptive and
explanatory, 33–34, 51, 269n3.1;
as component of intelligence, 18;

defined, xviii, 31, 255–256; development of, 44–45, 51; educational
perspective on, 23–26, 268n2.16; in
Ennis's model of critical thinking,
369n3.3; environments supporting
acquisition of, 45–48, 51; general
thoughts on, 21–23, 269n2.18; honoring students,' 164–165; integrated
list of, 26–30, 31; philosophical perspective on, 23, 24, 268nn2.14, 2.15;
positive and negative, 268n2.12;
toward thinking, 164–165, 210–217,
227; use of term, 19–21, 267nn2.10,
2.11. *See also* Dispositional behavior
Donis, K., 40, 251, 268n2.11
Dougherty, K., 270n3.8
Duckworth, E., 277n9.13

E

Easterby-Smith, M., 279nnA.6, A.7
Education: dispositions from perspective of, 23–26, 268n2.16; legislation
imposing requirements on, 210,
275n9.1
Eisner, E. W., xxii
Ellis, J. A., 9
Elnicki, Chris (pseudonym): arrange-
ments of classroom of, 59–60; big
subject-matter issue introduced
early by, 219; choice of evaluation
method permitted by, 157; dialogue
used by, to introduce teacher and
curriculum, 72–74; documents of
learning used by, 171; generative
topic of, 149–150; journal routine
of, 101–104; language in classroom
of, to learn thinking, 118–119, 120,
125–130, 138; mental model of
thinking of, 190, 191, 204; profile
of, 253; public issue discussion in
classroom of, 125–130, 138, 172; red
threads of, 189–190; sketch of, 187,
189–190; thinking modeled by, 161–
162; thinking routine of, for making
interpretations, 108–110
Emic concepts, 274n8.3